F. M. Dostoevsky:
His Image of Man

F. M. Dostoevsky:

His Image of Man

By Miriam T. Šajković

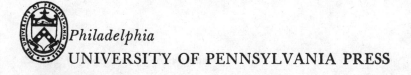

Philadelphia
UNIVERSITY OF PENNSYLVANIA PRESS

134646
PG 3328.26

7368
Printed in the United States of America

To My Mother and Father

Preface

THE PRESENT WORK is an initial attempt to introduce American educators to the thought of Fyodor M. Dostoevsky in the field of educational philosophy. The views of Dostoevsky on contemporary educational problems of his own time have been historically explored, and the central aspects of his philosophy have been studied in order to see what his contribution might be toward the formulation of a philosophy of education for today.

My interest in Dostoevsky originated many years ago when I began graduate study in the field of history and philosophy of education. The reading of Dostoevsky's works was a decisive "educational experience" of crucial significance for my own life. The questions raised by Dostoevsky provoked and inspired me to explore religion and philosophy; most important of all, Dostoevsky taught me to think. Since then I have kept in mind the possibility of undertaking a study of Dostoevsky for the purpose of introducing him to teachers here in America. I felt that he would have a great deal to contribute toward a new synthesis in educational philosophy.

The study of Dostoevsky's thought in this respect opens up for us the serious reconsideration of the areas of religion, metaphysics, and ethics for the education of man. Rather than continued emphasis upon pedagogical methodology in educational philosophy, Dostoevsky provokes the mind to reinstate serious study and reflection upon religion, metaphysics, and ethics for the formulation of a philosophy of education.

Dostoevsky is unquestionably one of the greatest minds of our contemporary culture and civilization. The German philosopher of history Oswald Spengler predicted a future millenium of Dostoevsky's Christianity, and Nicholas Berdyaev, an eminent philosopher of this century, has called Dostoevsky "Russia's greatest metaphysician." The Nobel prize winner Albert Camus has written that Dostoevsky has expressed our historical destiny in the most profound way, and that he dominates thought in our literature today. Camus goes so far as to say that our world will perish unless it admits that Dostoevsky is right.

Dostoevsky is the unrivaled and perspicacious seer of the human mind and heart; he emerges as a great friend and teacher of humanity. He has clearly read the signs of our times, for he lived through the agonizing doubts and despair of our present spiritual crisis. His sincerity, his spiritual heroism, and his moral courage have never been questioned, although, of course, one need not always agree with his conclusions. Dostoevsky combines a profound analytical mind with artistic genius. He is, as Boris Brasol, the translator of *The Diary of a Writer,* has written, "a noble and lofty *man,* a prudent teacher, an inspired prophet whose thought, like mountain peaks, were always pointed toward heaven, and who had measured the depths of man's quivering heart with all its struggles, sins and tempests; its riddles, pains and sorrows; its unseen tears and burning passions. For he did teach men to live and suffer."

I am greatly indebted to my teacher, Dr. James Mulhern, Professor of History of Education, The University of Pennsylvania, for his encouragement in the completion of this work, for his care in reading the manuscript and for his valuable critical suggestions. I also wish to acknowledge my gratitude to both Dr. Thomas Woody and Dr. Roderic D. Matthews of the University of Pennsylvania for their criticisms and suggestions. My sincere thanks is also due to my colleague and husband, Dr. Vladimir Šajković, Chairman of the Russian Department at Mount Holyoke College, for his time in many fruitful discussions on Dostoevsky's creative work and thought. To Miss Margaret Tongue, a young American poet now teaching at Vassar College, I extend my gratitude for her reading of the manuscript and for her valuable remarks.

Contents

F. M. Dostoevsky:
His Image of Man

What a piece of work is a man! How noble in
reason! How infinite in faculty! In form and
moving, how express and admirable! In action
how like an angel! In apprehension, how like
a god! The beauty of the world! The paragon
of animals! And yet, to me, what is this
quintessence of dust?

HAMLET

ACT II, SCENE 2 WILLIAM SHAKESPEARE

. . . As I lived through the cruel drama of my
epoch I began to love in Dostoevsky one who has
lived and expressed most profoundly our historical
destiny. For me, *Dostoevsky is first of all a
writer who, long before Nietzsche, knew how to
discern modern nihilism, to define it and predict
its monstrous consequences and to try to indicate
the road to salvation.* . . .

The man who wrote that "the problems of God
and immortality are the same as of socialism but
from a different angle" knew that hereafter our
civilization will demand salvation for all or for
none. . . . Dostoevsky's greatness, however, will not
cease growing, because our world will die unless
it admits that he is right.

"THE OTHER RUSSIA"

ALBERT CAMUS

NEW YORK *Herald Tribune,* DECEMBER 19, 1957

Chapter One

Nineteenth-Century
Russian Thought

BEFORE UNDERTAKING A STUDY, however brief, of Dostoevsky's philosophy, before discussing his comprehension of or commentaries upon educational problems, some historical background is necessary. This brief review of ideological developments in nineteenth-century Russian thought, and their relation to and implications for educational thought, it is hoped, will lend perspective to understanding the place and significance of Fyodor M. Dostoevsky.

In the study of the different ideological currents of nineteenth-century Russian intellectual history, the various ideologies on the nature and destiny of man lead to fundamental educational implications. Whatever man holds to be an ideal for himself and mankind is promoted in the historic life of a national people, and is implanted in the young, who are expected and encouraged to further the ideal in their way of life.

The nineteenth century in Russia and in Europe was a period of intellectual ferment. On the whole, it was an optimistic century which believed in the fundamental goodness of man, in man's autonomy through the methodological procedure of science, and in the rational powers of the human mind which would attain all the answers to the human situation. In the Russia of the nineteenth

15

century, several significant currents of thought criss-cross in the dynamic cultural life of this people. Let us first turn to the ideological position and the educational implications, practices and results of the official Tsarist government.

THE OFFICIAL REGIME

Under the reigns of Alexander I (1801–25), Nicholas I (1825–55), and Alexander II (1855–81), the official Tsarist government developed and carried into practice a national ideal of life and education which was in general consistent with its beliefs.[1]

Alexander I was a liberal, enlightened person with a politically astute mind. His civic, social, and educational ideas were humanitarian: he wanted the people to participate in affairs of state. He favored the constitutional idea of government, and, with this, the extension of formal education among the people.[2]

Alexander's vision was to establish an adequate and a permanent national system of education which would provide for all classes. Therefore, in 1802, he established the Ministry of Public Enlightenment which in effect centralized all educational institutions and cultural institutions, bringing them under state control.[3]

Alexander's chief adviser, Mikhail Speransky, saw, however, that in the field of education as well as in the political structure of the state, slow and cautious efforts had to be made. In the absence of a literate populace, how could Russia have a constitution; how could a national spirit be created without freedom of the press or without formal education? The political and educational problems clearly focused on the institution of serfdom. To spread education under the conditions of serfdom would be sheer folly, and to abolish serfdom without education was equally impossible. Thus, caution was exercised. First, ground had to be prepared for the limitation of serfdom. This problem became the main bone of contention throughout the nineteenth century in Russia. From above, however, the Tsars worked steadily toward the limitation and final abolition of serfdom.[4]

Many practical advances were undertaken and completed during Alexander's reign until the disruption of national affairs by the outbreak of the Napoleonic wars.[5] But the postwar period of reaction sought to stem the tide of secular liberal and democratic thought from the West. One way of accomplishing this, it was held, was to merge the religious and educational ministries, thus placing religious emphasis at the center of education. In 1817 the Ministry of Education did merge with the Ministry of Public Worship, in hopes of bringing about "Christian piety as the permanent basis of true enlightenment. . . ." [6] The aim was to enable the people to read the Bible for themselves, the translation of which had been made into the Russian language by Bishop Philaret. Opinions differ sharply as to the "advance" of such a merger. On the whole, the merger seems to have brought little progress.[7] This uniting of the two ministries did mean, however, that cultural education was replaced by a religious fundamentalism.[8]

Leonti Magnitsky, a conservative member of the official educational council of the Ministry of Education, stated the prevailing attitude which had crystallized as a result of the Napoleonic wars:

The whole mischief of Napoleon and his ideas which has been observed in our universities has been caused by the education, the books and the men we have imported from the German universities. There the infection of belief in the revolutionary principles which started in England and gained additional strength in prerevolutionary France has been erected into a . . . system.[9]

Admiral Shishkov, who became Minister of Education in 1824, summed up the official view which Nicholas I was to inherit:

Learning without faith and without morality does not constitute national happiness. Learning is as hurtful in a bad man as it is useful in a good man. . . . To teach the whole people, or a disproportionate number of them, to read and write would do more harm than good. To instruct a farmer's son in rhetoric would be to make of him a bad and worthless, if not a positively dangerous citizen. But instruction in the rules of conduct and in Christian virtues and good morals is necessary to everybody. . . .[10]

Upon the death of Alexander I, in 1825, Nicholas I became Tsar. Unfortunately for him and for his policies, his reign opened with a political uprising, the Decembrist revolt.[11] Nicholas quelled the rebellion, believing that he had saved his country from sedition. He dealt mercilessly with the revolutionaries, executing or exiling them. To Nicholas, this uprising revealed surprising disorder and abuse within the government, and he set out with intentions of a series of reforms. In his coronation address of July 13, 1826, Nicholas stated:

Not by impertinent, destructive dreams, but from above, are gradually perfected the statutes of the land, are corrected the faults, are rectified the abuses. In this order of gradual improvement, every modest desire for the better, every thought for the strengthening of the power of the law, for the spread of true enlightenment and of industry, in teaching us by the legal way, open for all—will always be received by us with grace: for we have not, cannot have any other desire but to see our country on the highest grade of happiness and glory, by Providence predestined.[12]

Nicholas first gave foremost attention to the question of popular education. Having in mind the eradication of further "sedition," he was intent upon directing the education of the people to form loyal, obedient subjects of the state among all classes. His leading principle was to give to each class its proper kind of education so as not to arouse "hopes and aspirations for rising from one class into a higher class." [13] The official regime's Committee on Education now stated that ". . . a public system of education should aim at securing for the children of each class such a training as could fit them to be useful and contented in that rank of life to which it had pleased a Most High Providence to call them at birth." [14] Thus, the acceptance of an aristocratic class social order with an absolute monarchial political structure began to crystallize.

Official ideology was soon given its theoretical formulation by Count Uvarov, who became Minister of Education in 1833 and served until 1849.[15] Uvarov's formula was *Orthodoxy, Autocracy,* and *Nationality.* Returning from an assignment, given to him by the Tsar, to investigate Moscow University and other educational institutions in the provinces, Uvarov stated:

I firmly believe we shall be able to avoid those mistakes, and shall succeed in gradually capturing the minds of the youth and bringing them to that point where there must merge together—a regulated, fundamental education with a deep conviction and warm belief in the true-Russian conservative principles of *Orthodoxy, Autocracy,* and *Nationality,* which present the last anchor of our salvation and the surest pledge of the strength and majesty of our country.[16]

In the forties, revolutionary events in Europe thoroughly alarmed Nicholas. The proclamation of a republic in France, the Hungarian uprisings which Nicholas helped to quell, his sister's threatened position on the throne of Holland, Germany's attempt at unification—all helped to entrench the forces of conservatism more firmly than ever in Russia. The official regime now concentrated all its energies against any liberal activities. It regarded with apprehension the circles of the educated classes, which discussed political, social, educational and literary questions. The members of one such literary circle, Petrashevsky's, of which the young Dostoevsky was a participant, were arrested by the authorities. The press likewise was curtailed, and a strict censorship prevailed.[17] Even the Minister of Education, conservative Count Uvarov, resigned in 1849 as he could no longer tolerate the extreme restrictions of Nicholas I. In the universities philosophy itself was suspect, and, therefore, abandoned. Suppression and reaction reigned until the death of Nicholas I in 1855.

Political and intellectual radicalism had crystallized in the last years of the reign of Nicholas, and with Alexander II, who became Tsar in 1855, this radicalism entered the scene with full clarity and decisiveness.[18] In the forties socialism had already become an ingredient in the thought of the Russian intelligentsia; henceforth, it was to become the "secular equivalent of a religious world view." [19] Other tendencies in thought among the intellectuals were evident. The orthodox religious view of life was renewed by a group known as the Slavophiles. By the sixties two towering figures of wide influence emerged: Count Leo Tolstoy and Fyodor Dostoevsky, "who aroused all Russian society religiously with their passionate language. . . ." and thought.[20] Both Tolstoy and Dostoevsky took positions as mediators between the socialist group, known as the Westernizers, and the Slavophiles.

The first acts of the new official regime under Alexander II were liberal ones; he abolished university restrictions and again issued passports for Russians to study and to travel abroad. He lifted the censorship of the press; he began earnest preparations for the abolition of serfdom.[21] In the late fifties and early sixties a movement towards liberalism developed which moved in the direction of the establishment of a constitutional monarchy.

On February 19, 1861, after six years of study and debate, the Tsar signed the Act of Emancipation. With the bondage system eliminated, the entire administrative structure based on class principles was changed. New judiciary and educational reforms could now become possible.[22] The situation prevailing in the early sixties is described by one historian as follows:

During the first five years of Alexander's reign the public consciousness made big strides, and had gained initiative and definiteness of purpose. In connection with the peasant reform, there emerged concomitant questions concerning local self-government, judicial reorganization and jury-trials, publicity and freedom of speech, and numerous other questions regarding culture, education, and the satisfaction of the economic and industrial needs of the rejuvenated country. Those questions were formulated in projects of provincial committees, in speeches and addresses of delegates to the provincial assemblies in 1860, and were echoed in the press.[23]

It soon became evident that reforms were not enough for the radical intelligentsia, and the official regime found itself coping with a rising tide of outbursts and demonstrations by the revolutionary groups.[24]

A strong reaction against further liberalism now set in. In 1867, Count D. A. Tolstoy was appointed Minister of Education. Tolstoy was a conservative who opposed any liberal or democratic ideas. He was a classicist, and above all promoted the interests of the ruling class to which he belonged. In combatting the "revolutionary nihilism" among the university youth and among the circles of the intelligentsia, Tolstoy, together with the aid of two journalists, M. N. Katkov of the *Russian Messenger* and P. M. Leontiev of the *Moscow News,* favored a system of education which would "train young minds exclusively in the acquisition of exact information, and prevent them from excessive reasoning which led to Nihilistic ideas and materialistic teaching. They considered ancient languages, and next—mathematics, as the most important studies in the secondary schools." [25] Acting slowly, persistently, and efficiently, Tolstoy succeeded in having his plan realized to restore classicism to the curriculum, and in 1871 his full program went into effect.[26]

More firmly than ever adhering to the doctrine of *Orthodoxy, Autocracy,* and *Nationality,* the official regime continually strove to stem the tide of the radical revolutionary thought and action.[27] Those who advocated the return to classicism endeavored to keep young minds within bounds and to restore exact reasoning and clear thinking in support of the official national ideology.

The Westernizers and the Slavophiles

Alongside the ideology of the official regime, independent currents of thought developed throughout the nineteenth century in Russia. A striving after freedom and social justice permeated intellectual thought. The predominant themes in Russian philosophical thought were religious and ethical with social and educational corollaries.[28] We now turn to a brief study of these currents of thought which, by the forties, had crystallized into two movements which have come to be designated by the terms Westernizers and Slavophiles.

The stimulus and impetus for the awakening of philosophic thought among the young intellectuals was provided by the army officers' contact with the West in the Napoleonic wars. The Decembrist group represented the French influence in the twenties, but the failure of their coup broke their influence. In the thirties, German idealism prevailed, as Berdyaev has described: "German idealism, Kant, Fichte, Schelling, Hegel, had a determining significance for Russian thought. Russian creative thought began to show itself in an atmosphere of German idealism and romanticism. . . ." [29] One of the outstanding intellectuals of the period has left a description of the times. Prince Odoyevski in his *Russian Nights* says:

My youth was spent in a period when metaphysics was as much in the general atmosphere as the political sciences are now. We believed in the possibility of an absolute theory, by means of which one would be able to order all the phenomena of nature, just as men today believe in the possibility of a social order that will fully satisfy all human needs. . . . However that may be, at that time all of nature, all of human life, seemed very clear to us, and we rather looked down upon the physicists and chemists . . . who rooted about in 'vulgar matter.' [30]

In 1836, a young army officer and aristocrat, P. J. Chaadaiev, published his "Philosophical Letter" in a widely read journal, *Telescope*.[31] This letter brought about a sharp division of thought among the intellectuals. Chaadaiev's work criticized sharply the official doctrine of nationality. In contrast to the official regime's praise of Russian reality and history, Chaadaiev wrote:

At the very beginning we had savage barbarism, later rude superstition, then a cruel, humiliating domination of the conquerors, a domination the traces of which have not been erased from our mode of living to this day. Such is the sad history of our youth; we have not had that age of boundless activity, of the poetical display of the nation's moral forces. The epoch of our social life, corresponding to that age, was filled with a dark colour—less existence, without power, without energy.

We have no charming memories, no strong, instructive examples in popular legends. Cast a glance at all the centuries of our existence, at all the expanse that we are occupying now, and you will not find a single reminiscence which would arrest you, a single monument which would tell you about the past in a strong, vivid, picturesque way.

We live in indifference to all, in a narrow horizon, with no past or future. . . .[32]

He maintained that something had separated Russia from the universal life of mankind: "Russia must begin all over again the whole education of man. For this purpose we have before us the history of nations and the results of movements of ages. . . ."[33] The ideal of Chaadaiev was Western Europe.

Chaadaiev manifested an awakened and independent mind whether his contemporaries liked it or not. Nicholas I had him placed under house arrest; the "Philosophical Letter" was banned, and the publication of the journal *Telescope* ceased. Nevertheless, Chaadaiev had posed the fundamental problem for Russia: should she turn to the West, the Russia of Peter the Great, or to the East, Moscovy, in her line of further development and progress?[34] The crystallization of these two different "ways of life" came into clear focus with the emergence of the Westernizer and Slavophile movements.

WESTERNIZERS

The Russian intelligentsia which idealized the West formulated their ideological position in the forties. This group officially and articulately opposed the doctrine of the official regime. First, what is meant by the term *intelligentsia* which is applied to the Westernizers?

The singular phenomenon of the intelligentsia is not to be identified with those in the West who are known as intellectuals. As a social group intellectuals are people

of intellectual work and creativeness, mainly learned people, writers, artists, professors, teachers, and so on. The Russian intelligentsia is an entirely different group; and to it may belong people occupied in no intellectual work, and generally speaking not particularly intellectual. Many Russian scholars and writers certainly could not be reckoned as belonging to the intelligentsia in the strict sense of the word. The intelligentsia reminds one more of a monastic order or sect, with its very intolerant ethics, its own obligatory outlook on life, with its own manners and customs and even its own particular physical appearance, by which it is always possible to recognize a member of the intelligentsia and to distinguish him from other social groups.

Our intelligentsia were a group formed out of various social classes and held together by ideas, not by sharing a common profession or economic status. They were derived to begin with mainly from the more cultured section of the nobility, later from the sons of the clergy, small government officials, the lower middle class, and, after the liberation, from the peasants. That then is the intelligentsia; its members were of different social classes, and held together solely by ideas, and, moreover, by ideas about sociology.[35]

The typical features of the intelligentsia were

Lack of roots in the soil, a break with all class life and traditions, . . . but even these qualities in them took a characteristically Russian form.

The intelligentsia was always carried away by some idea or other, for the most part by social ideas, and devoted itself to them supremely. It acquired the power of living by ideas alone. Owing to Russian political conditions, the intelligentsia found itself divorced from practical social work, and that easily led to social day dreaming. In the Russia of autocracy and serfdom, the most radical socialist and anarchist ideas were developed. The impossibility of political action led to this, that politics were transferred to thought and literature. It was the literary critics who were the leaders of social and political thought and character. The intelligentsia assumed that sectarian character which is so natural to all Russians. It lived in schism from its actual environment, which it considered evil, and within it a fanatical sectarian ethic was elaborated.[36]

Possessing a particular faculty for "assimilating Western ideas and doctrines and giving them original form," the Russian intelligentsia embraced as dogma that which was in the West a hypothesis, or a relative truth.[37]

It must be kept in mind that both the Westernizers and the Slavophiles were dissatisfied with the way of life under the reigns of Alexander I and Nicholas I; both saw the need for reform and rejuvenation of Russia; both advocated freedom of intellectual thought and the dignity of man, and both strove for social and political justice. Their "ways" were different, however.

For the Westernizers the future of Russia lay on the path taken by the culture of Western Europe. In their idealization of the West, of course, they overlooked glaring dissonances. The extreme group among the Westernizers completely repudiated the past cultural tradition of Russia, including the national religion of Orthodox Christianity.

Ideologically the Westernizers adopted a materialistic philosophy. They were either indifferent to religion or atheistic. In repudiating any religious foundation, the Westernizers assimilated contemporary European philosophies of the nineteenth century; they strove to base their world-view on secular humanism. In associating themselves with Western secular culture, they attempted to link the problems of the West to the paths of Russian thought. They devoted their energies to writing on social and political themes; direct action was the desire and goal of their intellectual effort.[38]

The Westernizers moved from an idealistic position in utopian socialism (Fourier and Saint Simon) to materialistic socialism derived from Feuerbach in the sixties and seventies, finally culminating in scientific Marxist socialism.

The two influential personalities of the early Westernizers in the forties were Alexander Hertzen and Visarrion Belinsky. In periodicals which now began to appear, *Annals of the Fatherland* and the *Contemporary*, the Westernizers had means of expressing their point of view. Belinsky above all others was the intellectual leader of the younger generation.[39] Belinsky shifted his philosophical speculations from socialistic utopianism "in the name of the individual's emancipation from the oppression of the contemporary social order" to Enlightenment humanism, derived from Hegel.[40] Later he adopted materialism, became a revolutionary, an atheist, and a socialist. Berdyaev has called Belinsky the "intellectual ancestor of Russian communism." [41]

As the first significant representative of the Westernizers, what were Belinsky's ideas concerning education? He wrote no formal treatise on education, but scattered in his works one can find his leading ideas. He championed the idea that education should be available for all the people, and that the state should assume responsibility for the education of all its members. As a socialist he was against all class distinctions; he believed that nature is no respecter of classes in her gifts. Education should develop a man's moral powers. In championing individualism, Belinsky wrote: "The fate of the subject, the individual, the person, is more important than the fate of the whole world or the well being of the Chinese emperor." [42] Yet, Belinsky moved imperceptibly to a new general and abstract humanity in socialism. He believed in progress. Morality and education could perfect mankind.[43]

The second outstanding representative of the early Westernizers was Alexander Hertzen, who was a skeptic and a humanist. Hertzen was inspired by the French socialistic literature, and admired Western European culture. In 1847 he fled from the Russia of Nicholas I, and became active in London as the publisher of the *Polar Star,* later renamed *The Bell.* This periodical, though forbidden, had wide circulation in Russia. For Hertzen the higher value of personality was rooted in what he called socialist individualism. What he meant by this seeming contradiction was that the Russian peasant people held within their life the possibilities of both principles: personality and community which could fuse together without domination of one by the other.[44]

The implications of Belinsky's philosophical premises for educational philosophy led directly toward the formulation of the materialistic world outlook. Hertzen gave impetus to the populist movement of the sixties and seventies. With these early Westernizers the foundations were laid for a more definite movement which, by the sixties and in the seventies, fully developed into a new "Orthodoxy, Autocracy, and Nationalism" of its own which was in opposition to the official regime. It was a new orthodoxy of materialistic socialism (Feuerbach, Marx), an autocracy of the elite intelligentsia radical wing, and a nationalism of a new, future Russia. It took time for the elaboration of a political mission and "the realization that only a tightly-knit 'party' could effectively manage radical, political activity. . . ." [45]

However, by the sixties the younger generation had begun to speak, now defending *realism*. By this they meant a view of life based upon findings in the exact sciences. They felt that art should be utilitarian, and morality was also discussed in terms of British utilitarianism. The intellectual leaders of the younger generation now became Nikolai G. Chernyshevsky, Nikolai Dobroliubov, and Dmitri Pisarev. These men devoted all their talents and energies to advocating "the emancipation of the earthly man, the emancipation of laboring people from their excessive suffering, to establishing conditions of happy life and so on." [46] They "declared war against all historical traditions; they opposed 'reason' the existence of which as materialists they could not recognize, to all the beliefs and prejudices of the past." [47] These Russian materialists, unlike those in the West, were nihilists. The nihilist claimed that no objective ground for moral principles existed. Social organization was, in its present historical reality, evil, and the only solution was to destroy. The way of revolution thus became the ideal for the nihilists of the late sixties and seventies in Russia.

Both Chernyshevsky and Dobroliubov concurred in their educational theories. Education was, of course, to foster the revolutionary spirit. The teacher was to be a model for students to emulate. What was the ideal? It was the ideal revolutionary who would be trained to overthrow the regime. Once this revolution was accomplished, they all would have a general education. One serious young teacher, Nechaiev, carried the socialist ideal to its logical conclusion; he formulated the revolutionary catechism which will be discussed in detail shortly.[48]

In the seventies, the work of Chernyshevsky and Dobroliubov was carried on by two leaders who came forward to clarify the ideological foundation for the young generation. These leaders were Peter Lavrov and Nicholas Mihailovski. Lavrov held that "the development of the individual physically, mentally and morally, the embodiment of truth and justice in social forms, this short formula embraces everything that may be considered progress." [49]

Both Lavrov and Mihailovski embraced positivism, a philosophy which includes only natural phenomena or the properties of knowable things in their coexistence and relationships. They defended human personality, but to them "personality still remained the creation of the community, of its social environment, and it is not clear whence it found its power to fight against the community, which wants to turn personality into its own organ and function." [50] The ideology of Lavrov and Mihailovski was bound by the interests of the people, but not by their beliefs or opinions.[51] Believing that they held the truth, their method was to go directly to the people. This earned them the title *narodnik* or the *narodnichestvo,* which would be near the equivalent of *populist* in the West. The young intelligentsia who followed Lavrov and Mihailovski felt that it was their moral duty to serve the interests of the people, to wish for the peoples' freedom and to work toward this freedom.[52]

The *narodniki,* however, were doomed to disappointment. The Russian people still believed in the sacrosanct character of the autocracy, and were unmoved by these new "socialistic" views of the young "gentlefolk." By no means did the official government maintain its position by violence; its authority finally rested upon the religious convictions of the people.[53] Berdyaev has described the situation in the following way:

What happened was that the people did not welcome the intelligentsia, and the people themselves surrendered those who came desiring to serve them as unselfishly and disinterestedly into the hands of the authorities. The people—that is to say, chiefly the peasantry—found the point of view of the intelligentsia strange. The people still remained religious. Orthodox, and the lack of religion in the intelligentsia repelled them. The people saw a gentlefolk's pastime in the *narodnik* "going to the people." [54]

The radical wing of the intelligentsia was led by the anarchist, Michael Bakunin. He recommended going to the people, but not for the purpose of imparting knowledge and ideas, or literacy, but "in the direct sense of rebelling against the existing order of things, since until that order was overthrown and annihilated no proper social development was possible." [55] This call for terrorism culminated in the "Nechaiev affair." Bakunin set revolt as the first goal of life; man becomes man by revolt. He wanted to raise a world-wide revolt in the name of the free man.

Sergei Nechaiev went further than Bakunin. He "put into the foundation of his political system the principle of extreme jesuitism. In his opinion a revolutionist was justified in ignoring all moral principles, in deceiving, killing, and robbing; for the sake of holding the organization in a firm grip, Nechaiev allowed himself to compromise his co-workers, to steal their letters or documents, and to terrorize them in other ways." [56]

Nechaiev, the founder of the revolutionary society, "The Axe or the People's Justice," composed the "Revolutionary

Catechism." [57] In it he characterized the revolutionary as "the doomed man. He has no personal interests, business, feelings, connections, property, or even name. Everything in him is in the grip of the one exclusive interest, one thought, one passion, revolution." [58] The only science the revolutionary knows, according to Nechaiev, is destruction. "To the revolutionary everything is moral which serves the revolution—words which Lenin repeated later." [59]

Even Bakunin disowned Nechaiev after the murder of a student, Ivanov, in 1869, by one of Nechaiev's cell groups. After the publication of Dostoevsky's *The Possessed* (1871–72), Mihailovski took issue with the author, protesting that Peter Verhovensky in Dostoevsky's work (the Nechaiev type) was not the real characteristic ideal of revolutionary to be emulated and taught to the younger generation.

By the end of the seventies, with the failure of the peaceful *narodniki* who went to the people, all the active revolutionary forces were now concentrated in the terrorist struggle with the official regime. The ideal of the populist group was pushed into the background.[60] The assassination of Alexander II in March, 1881, "by the decision of the Peoples' Will Party was the end and disruption of the Russian revolutionary movement before the rise of Marxism. It was the tragic climax of the single combat between the Russian authority and the Russian intelligentsia." [61]

THE SLAVOPHILES

The Slavophiles were opposed to the Westernizers' ideology. By the forties they, too, had formulated their position. The historian, Kornilov, has made an adequate summary:

They were all pure, noble minds, who had worked out an original, solid, and well-proportioned system, their own historiosophy, which like that of Chaadaiev was based on theological principles, and they had also emphasized the contradictions and contrasts in the development of the two different worlds of contemporary mankind: the Western-Latin-German, and the Eastern-Byzantine-Slav, or Greco-Russian. . . .

In their conception the Orthodox faith and the Russian people had preserved the ancient principle of spiritual Christianity in all its purity, while in the West it had been distorted by the casuistry of Catholicism, by the Papal authority, and by the prevalence of material culture over spiritual. The consequent development of those circumstances had brought, in their opinion, at first Protestantism, and later the modern Materialism, and the denial of the Revelation and of all the truths of the Christian faith. The Slavophils asserted that in Russia the state and society had developed on principles of freedom, on the domination of democratic *communal* elements, while in the West the state and the society developed on principles of violence, of enslaving one class or nation by other classes or nations, which resulted in the Feudal aristocratic form of personal ownership of land, and the landlessness of the masses.[62]

Berdyaev described the Slavophiles as follows:

The Slavophils were originally Russian landowners, educated men, humanists, lovers of freedom, but they were deeply rooted in the soil, very closely connected with a particular type of life and suffered from the limitations which that type of life imposed . . . with all their animosity towards the empire they still felt the solid earth under their feet and had no premonitions of the catastrophes which were to come. . . . The patriarchal organic theory of society was peculiarly theirs; . . . society ought to be constructed upon the analogy of family relationships.[63]

In opposition to the Westernizers and Chaadaiev, the Slavophiles felt that the Europeanization of Russia by Peter the Great was a betrayal of Russia's destiny. Adopting Hegel's idea of a national people's vocation, the Slavophiles applied this to Russia. They associated Russia's destiny with her own unique history; they therefore idealized the past out of all proportion. The Slavophiles believed in the people's culture, and in its ideology, which was firmly grounded in Orthodox Christianity. In valuing the peasants' communal institutions like the *mir,* the Slavophiles worked for liberal reforms within the framework of the monarchy, holding that reform should come from the top, that is, from the government rather than by way of revolution.

The leader and inspirer of the early Slavophiles was Aleksei S. Khomyakov, a poet, dramatist, philosopher, and theologian. He attempted the construction of a Christian philosophy, that is, an integral world-view based upon the religious foundations of Orthodoxy.[64] Khomyakov rejected an individualism based on rationalism and elaborated an anthropology based on the idea of "organic togetherness" or *sobornost.* His social ideas also retained this principle. Khomyakov respected the principle of the *obshchina* or village commune among the people. While he held that sovereign power rests upon the acceptance by the people, he was no anarchist in the rejection of the state. The people should entrust their power to the Tsar.[65]

Other leaders among the Slavophiles were I. Kireyevski, Ivan and Constantine Aksakov, and Y. Sumarin. It is difficult to summarize the Slavophile position as a whole, because each thinker elaborated his philosophy uniquely. Nevertheless, the two elements common to all Slavophiles were: first, the striving to find in Orthodox Christianity an adequacy which would "satisfy and sanctify the basic and ineradicable searchings of the human spirit," [66] and second, while the Slavophiles were related to the genuine patristic tradition, they also "accepted everything of value that had matured in modern science, philosophy, and general culture." [67] They strove not for a synthesis of Western culture and Orthodoxy, but to construct "a new and creative cultural consciousness, growing organically out of the very foundations of the Orthodox ecclesiastical tradition." [68]

There were both liberal and conservative Slavophiles. The liberal group by no means repudiated the best in Western culture; further, they advocated an Orthodox popular democracy which would include freedom of speech and public opinion; serfdom was to be abolished as well. The conservative wing supported the monarchy closely, and later advocated Pan-Slavism, the uniting of all Slavs.[69]

One does not find direct theorizing on particular educational problems among the Slavophiles. However, on the basis of their ideological premises, one can see that they stood for the reintegration of a Christian culture, which would carry with it the religious and cultural enlightenment of the people.[70]

The voices of the leaders among both the Westernizers and the Slavophiles in nineteenth-century Russia did not develop particular philosophies of education as such. Rather they were concerned with the broader basis of philosophical inquiry, and they "almost invariably had something to say about education. And in this interest they had enough precedent to constitute almost a heritage. . . ." [71]

The implications of the Westernizer point of view, as already noted, would lead Russia toward the materialistic, and ultimately, revolutionary, world-view. The Slavophiles hoped to renew and to implement the Orthodox Christian view of life, rooted in the nation's historic tradition. They would combine Christian idealism with the best from Western culture.

The concern in this short study has been with ideological premises rather than with pedagogical aspects; philosophical ideas lead toward the forming of the minds of men. Westernizer ideology led to the formulation of the ideal of "the revolutionary fighter for democracy," in the view of the Soviet historian Medynskii.[72] The Slavophile ideology reformulated the religious ideal, rooted in the tradition of Russia.

LEADERS IN RUSSIAN THOUGHT OTHER THAN WESTERNIZERS AND SLAVOPHILES

We turn now to thinkers who stand apart from the movements of the Westernizers and the Slavophiles. Four outstanding personalities emerge: N. I. Pirogov (1810–81), Count Leo Tolstoy (1828–10), K. D. Ushinskii (1824–70), and Fyodor M. Dostoevsky (1821–81).

N. I. Pirogov was a world-famous surgeon. He and Tolstoy, as young men, were "adherents of a positivistic and naturalistic philosophy; both of them became profoundly disillusioned by it, and turned to a specific kind of religious world-view," Christianity.[73]

After his return from the Crimean War in 1856, Pirogov published his articles on educational themes, *Problems of Life*. He believed in educating the man rather than training technicians or emphasizing social position. In turning attention towards the whole individual, he has been hailed as a reformer in pedagogy.[74] Pirogov advocated higher and free education for all. In upholding the idea that work should be done for its own sake, Pirogov agreed with Tolstoy. Both were against coercion in learning; they advocated the voluntaristic approach to the student.[75]

Count Leo Tolstoy, world-renowned artist and ardent Christian moralist, began an experimental school on his estate, *Yasnaya Polyana* (The Clear Glade). Tolstoy studied pedagogy considerably, even making an extensive trip to Europe to observe the popular schools there.[76] During this period he confirmed his own pedagogical principles: study cannot be forced; one must enthusiastically kindle a child's longing to know. Tolstoy called this "unconscious education." [77]

Tolstoy held that teaching was an art and a talent; no one method sufficed, nor all of them together. He followed the psychological development of the child in age and ability. Learning should be something attractive, Tolstoy maintained, and the teacher had to love both his work and the students.

A special pedagogical journal, *Yasnaya Polyana,* was published by Tolstoy himself during the years of his educational activities, 1859–62. Here are printed his own articles which "later evoked a whole tendency toward 'Tolstoyan pedagogy' in various countries—in Russia last of all." [78] While Tolstoy's ideas and methods were practiced in a very limited way in Russia, his influence was much more widely felt in Europe.[79]

Konstantine Ushinskii was a professor of law in the Demidov Lycee during the reign of Nicholas I. His pioneer work in education was undertaken in the early sixties during the reign of Alexander II. Appointed Inspector of the Smolny Institute for Noble Girls in 1859, Ushinskii reorganized the entire curriculum, and greatly raised the standards of scholarship.

Ushinskii was closest to the Slavophiles. His philosophy can be called idealistic humanism; he was inspired by

Bacon, Locke, Mill, Spencer, Kant, and Descartes.[80] Ushinskii believed in the peaceful transformation and development of better men for a better society through education.
He agreed with Pirogov, Tolstoy, and Dostoevsky in seeing
the whole people of the nation as the "cornerstone of education." [81]

Ushinskii held that pedagogy in the broad sense meant
to "know man in all his relationships. Education must il-
luminate the conscience of man and show him clearly the
road to the good." [82] The aims of education should be
moral, mental, social, and physical, but chiefly moral. Education should devote itself primarily to the formation of
character.[83]

Ushinskii and Dostoevsky both stressed the importance
of the family and its duty in giving the child a strong,
sound, moral sensitivity, a love for his country, and a
respect for the dignity of work. Ushinskii wrote that work
was important in developing character; mental work was
no less labor than physical work. In fact, it was the highest
form of labor.[84] The habit of working was important in
itself: "Education must develop in the pupil a habit of
work and must make it possible for him to find for himself
a life work. The school must not only provide intellectual
development and a definite fund of knowledge, but must
arouse in the youth a thirst for serious work, without
which life can be neither worthy nor happy." [85]

Ushinskii was in agreement with the Slavophiles and
with Dostoevsky in insisting upon love and respect for
one's native land: "Love for the fatherland, present in
every person, provides a true key to the heart of man, and
education must accordingly rest upon nationalism." [86]
Both Ushinskii and Dostoevsky agreed that the native
Russian language should be the vehicle of expression in
the schools.[87]

It is significant that all these thinkers stressed the importance of the teacher. Ushinskii wrote:

The teacher feels that he is an active member of a great organism, which struggles against the ignorance and vices of humanity, a mediator between his own generation and everything noble and sublime in the past history of mankind, a keeper of the sacred legacy of the people who have struggled for truth and virtue. He feels that he is a living link between the past and the future . . . and understands that . . . kingdoms rest upon his work and that whole generations live by it.[88]

Agreeing with Tolstoy, Ushinskii also held that the teacher must learn each pupil's abilities and peculiarities. Teaching is also more of an art than a science. The art of teaching does, of course, require knowledge of the basic elements of anthropology, physiology, and psychology; but more than science is needed. Patience, understanding, and love are essential.[89] The ethical inspiration of the teacher must have a particular religious basis: "The public school teacher should have a devout belief in Christianity and his life should be one of example for others. Only in this way could the teacher have an ethical influence on children and youth and his work be 'truly educative.' " [90]

The valuable practical work of Ushinskii lay in his plans for a teacher-training program which included a curriculum and an administrative structure. In the seventies many of his proposals were widely applied. His plan for a Teacher's Seminary was in fact made the basis for the zemstvo schools for teachers.[91] His treatise Man as the Subject of Education became the "standard reference book of teachers and professors of education, and was used as a textbook in teachers' seminaries. A generation of teachers of education was brought up on this book and in the spirit of Ushinskii. They became teachers of teachers who cherished his instructions and passed them on to their successors." [92]

The following chapters are now concerned with exploring the views of F. M. Dostoevsky on educational problems. In addition, a study of the main aspects of his philosophy has been undertaken to discern his possible contribution toward the formulation of a philosophy of education for our times.

Chapter Two

Biography of Fyodor M. Dostoevsky

THREE RECOLLECTIONS

DOSTOEVSKY WROTE: "Man cannot even live without something sacred and precious carried away into life from the memories of childhood. Some people, apparently, do not even think about this; nevertheless, unconsciously, they do preserve such recollections." [1]

Two such "sacred and precious" events Dostoevsky recorded in his *Diary:*

I was only nine years old, I recall, when once, on the third day of Easter week, after five in the evening, all our family —father and mother, brothers and sisters—were sitting at a round table, at a family tea, and it so happened that the conversation revolved around our estate and how we should go there for the summer. Suddenly the door opened and at the threshold appeared our house-servant, Grigory Vasiliev, who just before had arrived from the estate. In the absence of the masters, he used to be entrusted even with the management of the estate. And now, instead of the "superintendent" who always wore a German suit and displayed a solid appearance, there appeared a man in an old shabby peasant's coat; with bast shoes on his feet. He had come from the estate on foot; he stepped into the room and stood without uttering a word.

"What is it?"—cried father, frightened.—"Look, what is it?"

"The estate has burned down!"—said Grigory Vasiliev, in a base voice.

I shall not describe what ensued: father and mother were working, not rich people—and such was their Easter present! It developed that everything had been destroyed by fire—everything: huts, granary, cattle-shed and even spring seeds, some of the cattle, and even our peasant Arkhip was burned to death. Owing to the sudden scare, we thought that it meant utter ruin. We threw ourselves on our knees and began to pray; mother was crying. Presently our nurse, Aliona Frolovna, went up to her; Aliona was a hired servant, not a serf, and belonged to the Moscow commoners' class. She had nursed and brought up all of us children. She was then about forty-five years old; she was a woman of serene and cheerful disposition, and she used to tell us such wonderful tales! For a number of years she had refused to draw her salary: "I don't need it." It had accumulated to the amount of some five hundred rubles, which were kept on deposit at a loan office: "It will come in handy in my old age." Suddenly, she whispered to mother: "If you should need money, take mine; I have no use for it; I don't need it. . . ." [2]

The second recollection, "one imperceptible moment in my early childhood" was recalled during his imprisonment in Siberia:

I will relate . . . just a remote reminiscence . . . when I was only nine years old. . . . I recalled the month of August in our village: a dry and clear day, though somewhat chilly and windy; the summer was coming to an end, and soon I should have to go to Moscow, again to be wearied all winter over French lessons; and I was so sad over the fact that I would have to leave the country I went beyond the barns and, having descended to a ravine, I climbed up to the "Losk"—thus was called a thick shrubbery on yonder side of the ravine, which extended as far as the grove. Presently I plunged deeper into the bushes, and then I heard not far off—some thirty steps away—in a field, a solitary peasant plowing. I knew that he was plowing steeply uphill, that it was difficult for the horse to get along, and, from time to time, I heard the man's halloos: "Giddap—giddap!" I knew virtually all of our peasants, but I didn't recognize the one now plowing; but this was of no concern to me, since I was absorbed in my task—I also was busy: I was trying to break a walnut whip for myself, to hit frogs; walnut whips are so pretty, though not solid —no comparison with birch ones! I was also interested in insects and beetles; I was collecting them—among them there are very neat ones. I was also fond of little agile lizards with tiny black dots; but I was afraid of little snakes; these, however, were found far more rarely than lizards. Here there were few mushrooms—to find mushrooms one had to go to the birch grove, and I intended to proceed thither. And in all my life nothing have I loved as much as the forest, with its mushrooms and wild berries, its insects and birds and little hedgehogs and squirrels; its damp odor of dead leaves, which I so adored. Even now, as I am writing these lines, it seems that I can smell the odor of our country birch grove: these impressions remain intact throughout one's whole life. Suddenly, amidst the profound silence, clearly and distinctly, I heard the cry: "A wolf's running!" I let out a scream and, beside myself with fright, and vociferating, I ran out into the field, straight up to the plowing peasant.

This was our peasant Marei. I don't know if there is such a name, but everybody called him Marei; he was almost fifty years old, stocky, pretty tall, with much gray hair in his bushy flaxen beard. I knew him, but up to that time I had never had occasion to talk to him. When he heard my cries, he stopped his little filly, and when I, in the heat of running, seized the plow with one hand, and with the other—his sleeve, he sensed my dread.

"A wolf's running!"—I shouted, quite out of breath.

He raised his head and impulsively looked around, for an instant almost believing my words.

"Where's the wolf?"

"Shouted . . . someone had just shouted: 'a wolf's running!' "—I lisped.

"What's the matter with you?—What wolf?—This appeared

to you in a dream! Look! How can a wolf be here!"—he muttered, trying to enhearten me. But my whole body was trembling and I was clinging ever so fast to his coat. I must have looked very pale. He looked at me with an uneasy smile, apparently alarmed on my account.

"See, how thou are frightened! Oh, oh!"—he said, shaking his head. "Never mind, dear. See, little kid! Oh!"

He extended his hand and stroked me on my cheek. "Do stop fearing! Christ be with thee. Cross thyself."

But I did not cross myself; the corners of my lips quivered and, I believe, this was what impressed him most. Slowly he stretched out his thick finger, with the black nail soiled with earth, and gently touched my trembling lips.

"See! Oh!"— And he looked at me with a long motherly smile.—"Good Lord! What's this? Oh, oh!"

Finally, I grasped the fact that there was no wolf, and that the cry "a wolf's running" must have been falsely heard by me. Still, there was a clear and distinct cry, but pseudo cries of this kind had been heard by me two or three times before, and I was aware of this. (Later, with childhood, these hallucinations disappeared.)

"Why, I'll go!"—I said, questioningly and timidly looking at the peasant.

"All right, go! And I shall be keeping thee in sight! Be sure, I shall not surrender thee to the wolf!"—he added with the same motherly smile.—"Well, Christ be with thee. Now, go!" — And he crossed me with his hand and then crossed himself. I started, but every ten steps I kept looking back. To be frank, I was a little ashamed that I got so frightened in his presence. Yet, on my way I was still quite afraid of the wolf till I had reached the slope of the ravine, and then the first barn. There, fright left me altogether. Presently, as if from nowhere, our house dog Volchok rushed to me. Well, of course, with Volchok I felt quite safe, and so, for the last time, I turned back toward Marei. No longer was I able to discern him distinctly, but I felt that he still kept tenderly smiling at me and nodding. I waved my hand to him; he waved his hand, too, and stirred his filly. . . . And now suddenly—twenty years later, in Siberia—I was recalling that meeting . . . it had hidden in my soul imperceptibly, of its own accord, without any effort of my will, and then it came to my mind at the needed time: . . . No doubt, anyone would have cheered up a child —but here, at this solitary meeting, something, as it were, altogether different had happened; and if I had been his own son, he could not have bestowed upon me a glance gleaming with more serene love. And yet, who had prompted him? . . .[3]

To the child of nine, two people radiated active love, and at a time when Dostoevsky was surrounded by desperate men in the Siberian prison, the memory of Marei restored the spirit of the young man.

A child, a youth experiences sufferings, too. The third reminiscence is a painful one. However, Dostoevsky says:

They may even be painful and bitter; however, even suffering endured in one's life may subsequently transform itself into a sanctuary of the soul. Generally speaking, man has been so created that he loves his past suffering. Besides, man, of necessity, is inclined to mark points, as it were, in his past in order to be subsequently guided by them and to deduce from them something whole—as a matter of routine and for his own edification.[4]

The third begins:

. . . enroute from Moscow to Petersburg. My elder brother and I were going with our late father to Petersburg for matriculation in the Chief Engineering School. It was in May and it was hot. We drove with hired horses almost at a foot-pace, halting at stations for as long as two or three hours. I remember how, at length, we had grown weary of this journey which had lasted almost a whole week. My brother and I were then longing for a new life; we were meditating intensely about something, about everything "beautiful and lofty": in those days these were still novel words and they used to be uttered without irony. And, at the time, how many beautiful little words were in use! We passionately believed in something, and although we knew very well everything that was required for the examination in mathematics, we dreamed only about poetry and poets. My brother wrote verses, three poems every day, even during our journey, while I kept busy planning in my mind a novel dealing with Venetian life. Only two months before, Pushkin had died, and en route brother and I agreed to visit without delay the place of the duel and to try to make our way into the former apartment of Pushkin, in order to behold the room in which he had passed away. One evening we were stopping at a station, an inn, in some village—the name of which I have forgotten—in the province of Tver, if I correctly recall. It was a large and well-to-do village. In half an hour we were to resume our journey and, meanwhile, I was looking through the window, and I saw the following:

Across the street, directly opposite the inn, was the station building. Suddenly a courier's troika speedily drove up to the station's platform; a courier jumped out of the carriage; he was in full uniform, with narrow little flaps on the back, as was the fashion in those days, and he wore a large three-cornered hat with white, yellow and, I think, green plumes. (I have forgotten this detail, which I could check; but I seem to recall the glimpse of green plumes, too.) The courier was a tall, very stout and strong chap, with a livid face. He ran into the station house and there, surely, must have "swallowed" a glass of vodka. I recall that our coachman then told me that such couriers always drink a glass of vodka at every station, for without it they would be unable to endure "such a torment."

Meanwhile, a fresh, spirited, substitute troika drove up to the postal station, and the yamschik, a young lad of about twenty, in a red shirt and holding an overcoat in his hands, jumped into the coachman's seat. Forthwith, the courier came running down the staircase and seated himself in the carriage. The yamschik stirred on, but hardly had he started to move than the courier rose up and silently raised his hardy right fist and, from above, painfully brought it down on the back of the yamschik's head. He jolted forward, lifted his whip and, with all his strength, lashed the wheel horse. The horses dashed forward but this in no way appeased the courier. Here there was method and not mere irritation—something preconceived and tested by long years of experience—and the dreadful fist soared again and again and struck blows on the back of the head. And then, again and again, and thus it continued until the troika disappeared out of sight. Of course, the yamschik, who could hardly keep his balance, incessantly, every second, like a madman, lashed the horses and, finally, he had whipped them up to the point where they started dashing at top speed, as if possessed.

Our coachman explained to me that virtually all couriers are riding in approximately the same manner, but that this one is particularly notorious and everybody knows him; . . . This disgusting scene has remained in my memory all my life. Never was I able to forget it, or that courier, . . .[5]

Experiencing the cruelty of man which lacerated his soul, and the illuminating good which gave him support in times of crisis, Dostoevsky's principle that the "strongest and most influential recollections are those produced in childhood"[6] was verified in his own life.

FAMILY, CHILDHOOD, AND YOUTH

In the parish of St. Peter and Paul at Moscow was born on October 30 of the year 1821, in the dwelling-house of the Workman's Hospital, to Staff-Physician Michail Andreyevitch Dostoevsky, a male child, who was named Fyodor. Baptised on November 4.[7]

Dostoevsky's father, Michail Andreyevitch, came to Moscow in the early years of the nineteenth century to study medicine at the University. During the 1812 campaign he was a military physician. In 1819 he married, and soon obtained the appointment as a staff physician in the Marinsky Hospital in Moscow. Fyodor's father and his mother, the quiet and pious, kind Maria Timofeevna Nechaeva, belonged to the intelligentsia and to the nobility. The boy was the second son in a family of seven brothers and sisters: Varvara, Andrei, Vera, Nicholas, Mihail, and Alexandra.

The Dostoevskys lived in a small apartment attached to the hospital. In the evenings the family met together, and, as was a favorite pastime of Russian families of that time, Pushkin, Karamzin's *History*, and the Bible were read aloud. The children's nurse Aliona told them tales and legends of the Russian people. Dostoevsky wrote about these early years in his *Diary of a Writer:*

I descended from a pious Russian family. As far as I can remember myself, I recall my parents' affection for me. We, in our family, have known the Gospel almost ever since our earliest childhood. I was only ten when I already knew virtually all the principal episodes in Russian history—from Karamzin whom, in the evenings, father used to read aloud to us. Every visit to the Kremlin and the Moscow cathedrals was, to me, something solemn.[8]

The intimate family life during the early years is reflected in Dostoevsky's fiction. "Human intercourse was always conceived by Dostoevsky in later life in terms of the intense, intimate relations of the family hearth." [9]

Zenta Maurina discerns correctly Dostoevsky's nature:

Dostoievsky was of the kind who never forgot. Light-hearted, transparent natures can behold or experience gloom, pass on and forget. If we pass lightly by, if we forget easily, then the sunlight easily irradiates us again. Dostoievsky could not pass on; he absorbed everything, and when his soul was loaded to the full its fruit fell of itself.

This wretched hospital was his first childhood impression. The second was when he was eight years old. He had gone with his mother to the cathedral in Holy Week and heard in the heavy atmosphere of the dim, incense-perfumed building, a young priest reading the Book of Job. As he listened tears stole down his thin, sallow cheeks. Deep into his memory sank Job's cry of despair: "Wherefore is light given to him that is in misery, and life unto the bitter in soul? . . . I was not in safety, neither had I rest, neither was I quiet: yet trouble came. . . . For the arrows of the Almighty are within me, the poison whereof drinketh up my spirit: the terrors of God do not set themselves in array against me. . . ." [10]

When he was over fifty years of age, Dostoevsky wrote to his wife from abroad: "I am reading again the book of Job, and it stirs up in me such an ecstasy of anguish, such a turmoil of emotion that for long hours I pace my room, well-nigh groaning aloud." [11]

In 1831 when Dostoevsky was ten years old, the family purchased the summer estate of Daravoe in the province of Tula.[12] The family spent their summers there, away from the heat of the city. The children lived close to nature and came to know some peasants. "To the children it meant deliverance from the confinement of Moscow and, perhaps also, from their father's stern control." [13] In the clear, fresh air these children hunted mushrooms and played games inspired by *Robinson Crusoe* and *The Last of the Mohicans*. They had horses to ride, countryside to explore, peasants to talk with, and time for leisurely reading. Dostoevsky wrote to a friend in later years: "At twelve, I read right through Walter Scott during the summer holidays; certainly such reading did extraordinarily stimulate my imagination and sensibility, but it led them into good, not evil, paths; I got from it many fine and noble impressions, which gave my soul much power of resistance against others which were seductive, violent, and corrupting." [14]

Andrei, the youngest brother, has left us an impression about his brother who loved going to Tula:

During those journeys my brother Thedor would be in a state bordering upon delirium. He would perch himself upon the splash-board of the britchka, and, should the vehicle happen to stop anywhere, even for the briefest of halts, he would leap down and scamper around the vicinity, or else walk beside the driver while the latter led the horses. . . . At our country house, we were almost constantly in the open air; and, except when at play, we would spend the whole day in watching and superintending the labours of the field. All the peasantry liked us, but especially so our brother Thedor, whose lively disposition would lead him to bear a hand in everything—to ask to be allowed to lead the horses when harrowing, and to drive them when ploughing. Also he loved entering into conversation with the peasants, who would speak to him freely whenever he did so. But his greatest delight of all was to be entrusted with some task which enabled him to make himself useful. For instance, one day a peasant woman, when going out to reap with her baby, happened to upset her zhbantchik [wooden can] of water, so that the poor infant would have nothing to drink. Upon that my brother caught up the zhbantchik, ran to the house, and brought thence a fresh canful of water.[15]

Dostoevsky wrote the following to his friend Vladimir Solovyev: "That little insignificant spot bequeathed to me a strong and a profound impression which will abide with me to the end of my life. Everything connected with the place has for me the dearest of recollections."[16]

From 1827 on the children's education was begun. They heard the works of the poets Derzhavin and Zhukovsky, as well as Pushkin. They knew of Gogol, and Dostoevsky declaimed lines from him. Their father taught the children Latin. In 1831 Mihail and Fyodor attended a small private day school under the directorship of Monsieur Souchard. In 1834 and for the next three years, the boys attended the private boarding school of Chermak. "The curriculum was conceived on the generous lines then current—eight hours of school work in the day, not counting preparation; but the school seems to have been a good one in most respects." [17]

Early in 1837, the first crisis of Fyodor's life occurred: his mother died. Dostoevsky had always spoken of his mother with affection and love. She left him a little miniature inscribed *J'ai le coeur tout plein d'amour;* he cherished it all his life.[18] Maria Timofeevna had been the children's first teacher; she taught them the alphabet, took them to church, and joined with them in their prayers. She watched over their health and their moral welfare.[19] Near the time of his mother's death the great poet Pushkin died. Dostoevsky's younger brother, Andrei, wrote: "My brothers nearly went off their heads. Fyodor in conversations with his elder brother several times said that, if we had not had our family mourning, he would have asked father's permission to wear mourning for Pushkin." [20]

In May of the same year, Fyodor, with his brother Mihail, prepared to enter the Military Engineering Academy at St. Petersburg. In September the examinations were passed, and in January of 1838 Fyodor entered—but alone. Mihail was rejected on account of his health; he later entered the Engineering Academy at Revel. With the separation of the brothers their invaluable correspondence began.

Now in the capital city of the empire, this youth was about to begin his studies. What was his mind and soul to find, to endure? The letters to Mihail give us an insight into the young Dostoevsky. The following excerpts reveal the seriousness and the perspective:

I don't know if my gloomy state will ever leave me. And to think that such a state of mind is allotted to man alone—the atmosphere of his soul seems compounded of a mixture of the heavenly and the earthly. What an unnatural product, then, is he, since the law of spiritual nature is in him violated. . . . This earth seems to me a purgatory for divine spirits who have been assailed by sinful thoughts. I feel that our world has become one immense Negative, and that everything noble, beautiful, and divine, has turned itself into a satire.[21]

He continues:

If in this picture there occurs an individual who neither in idea nor effect harmonizes with the whole—who is, in a word, an entirely unrelated figure—what must happen to the picture? It is destroyed, and can no longer endure.

Yet how terrible it is to perceive only the coarse veil under which the All doth languish! To know that one single effort of the will would suffice to demolish that veil and become one with eternity—to know all this, and still live on like the last and least of creatures. . . . How terrible! How petty is man! Hamlet! Hamlet! When I think of his moving wild speech, in which resounds the groaning of the whole numbed universe, there breaks from my soul not one reproach, not one sigh. . . . That soul is then so utterly oppressed by woe that it fears to grasp the woe entire, lest so it lacerate itself. Pascal once said: He who protests against philosophy is himself a philosopher. A poor sort of system![22]

In the same letter we learn that he has read the whole of Hoffman in Russian and German, nearly all of Balzac, and works of Goethe, Victor Hugo, and others.

His letter of October 21, 1838, gives us insight into his own thinking:

My friend, you philosophize like a poet. And just because the soul cannot be for ever in a state of exaltation, your philosophy is not true and not just. To *know* more, one must *feel* less, and *vice versa*. . . . What do you mean precisely by the word *know?* Nature, the soul, love, and God, one recognizes through the heart, and not through the reason. Were we spirits, we could dwell in that region of ideas over which our souls hover, seeking the solution. But we are earth-born beings, and can only guess at the Idea—not even grasp it by all sides at once. The guide for our intelligence through the temporary illusion into the innermost centre of the soul is called *Reason*. Now, Reason is a material capacity, while the soul or spirit lives on the thoughts which are whispered by the heart. Thought is born in the soul. Reason is a tool, a machine, which is driven by the spiritual fire. When human reason (which would demand a chapter for itself) penetrates into the domain of knowledge, it works independently of the *feeling*, and consequently of the *heart*. But when our aim is the understanding of love or of nature, we march towards the very citadel of the heart. . . . Philosophy cannot be regarded as a mere equation where nature is the unknown quantity! Remark that the poet, in the moment of inspiration, comprehends God, and consequently does the philosopher's work. Consequently poetic inspiration is nothing less than philosophical inspiration. Consequently philosophy is nothing but poetry, a higher degree of poetry! [23]

In the same letter Dostoevsky states his view on the contemporary philosophical systems: "It is odd that you reason quite in the sense of our contemporary philosophy. What a lot of crazy systems have been born of late in the cleverest and most ardent brains! To get a right result from this motley troop one would have to subject them all to a mathematical formula. And yet they are the 'laws' of our contemporary philosophy." [24]

In conclusion Dostoevsky writes of his father: "I pity our poor father! He has such a remarkable character. What trouble he has had. It is so bitter that I can do nothing to console him! But, do you know, Papa is wholly a stranger in the world. He has lived in it now for fifty years, and yet he has the same opinions of mankind that he had thirty years ago. What sublime innocence! Yet the world has disappointed him, and I believe that that is the destiny of us all." [25]

In the summer of 1839, Dostoevsky received the news from Moscow of his father's death. The Dostoevsky family maintained silence on the circumstances of their father's death; nowhere in extant correspondence can one find information. However, one surviving letter of Dostoevsky refers to the event. He wrote to Mihail: "Dear brother, I have shed many tears over the death of our father, but now our position is still more appalling! I speak not of myself, but of our family." [26] The main problem besetting the family was financial. Their father had only begrudgingly and partially supported the boys in school; now their situation was more distressing.

During the next few years, however, Dostoevsky managed to continue and to complete his studies. At school he was diligent and precise in his work. The school director's report stated: "What are his gifts? Good." [27] Dostoevsky won and held his classmates' attentions by his inspired lectures or readings of European and Russian classical literature. A close friend and later, a young writer, D. V. Grigorovitch, has written in his *Reminiscences:*

I made friends with Fyodor Dostoevsky the very first day that he entered the College. . . . Despite his reticent nature and general lack of frankness and youthful expansion, he appeared to reciprocate my affection. Dostoevsky always held himself aloof, even then, from others, never took part in his comrades' amusements, and usually sat in a remote corner with a book; his favourite place was a corner in Class-Room IV, by the window. . . . Dostoevsky was much more advanced in all knowledge than I was, and the extent of his reading amazed me. . . . His literary influence was not confined to me alone; . . . a little circle was formed, which gathered round Dostoevsky in every leisure hour.[28]

In 1843 Dostoevsky obtained his commission as lieutenant and was appointed to the Engineering Department of the Ministry of War.

Literature was for him still the predominant interest. He read and studied thoroughly French literature: the classics and contemporary works, from Lamartine and Victor Hugo to Soulie and Paul de Kock. He knew pages of Gogol by heart, and read Russian literature extensively; he knew his Shakespeare and Dickens, as well as the German classics.[29]

Soon his brother Mihail graduated from the Academy at Revel and married. Meanwhile Andrei had come to St. Petersburg to prepare for the Academy, and for a while lived with Fyodor. It was one year after his commission that Dostoevsky decided to resign from the Army to devote himself to literature. He wrote to Mihail:

Yes, brother, indeed I know that my position is desperate. I want to lay it to you now, just as it is. I am retiring because I can serve no longer. Life delights me not if I am to spend the best part of it in such a senseless manner. Moreover, I never did intend to remain long in the service—why should I waste my best years? But the chief point is that they wanted to send me to the provinces. . . . I am just finishing a novel, about the length of *Eugenie Grandet*. It is most original. I am now making the fair copy; by the 14th I ought certainly to have an answer from the editor. I want to bring it out in the *Otetchestvennia Zapiski* [Annals of the Fatherland]. . . . That is the way I wish to make a living.[30]

DOSTOEVSKY'S EARLY LITERARY ACTIVITY

From 1844 to the spring of 1845, Dostoevsky worked on his first novel *Poor Folk*. He altered it, cut, polished, and reworked it. His letters tell us that financially he was constantly in debt, but still had income from his father's estate. At one point he had hopes of publishing the novel himself. This would have been a hazardous undertaking for a writer of that time. He wrote about *Poor Folk:* "I am really pleased with my novel. It is a serious and well-constructed work. But it has terrible short-comings, too. . . . These two years of hard study have taken much from me, and brought much to me." [31] Two months later he was still hard at work on the novel. He wrote to Mihail: "My novel, which I simply can't break loose from, keeps me endlessly at work. . . . I decided to do it all over again, and by God! that has improved it a lot." [32]

The city of St. Petersburg was the locale of this novel. This "intentional and theoretical" town remained an unreal magical vision that gave him the first "hints of the strange human scene of whose description he was to become a master." [33]

Dostoevsky's first work, *Poor Folk,* and its reception by the literary world, was an event in literary history. "It is a simple story," he said, "like everyday reality. And the hero is not a great man or a historical figure. . . . He is a humble civil servant, a drudge, even something of a simpleton, with several buttons missing on his uniform!" [34] The two main characters who write letters to one another (Dievushkin and Varena) took Russia by storm; their story skyrocketed Dostoevsky to literary fame.

In May the manuscript was confided by Dostoevsky to Grigorovich, a literary aspirant like himself whom he had met at the Engineering Academy. Grigorovich took it to his friend Nekrasov, a young writer whose poems had already brought him a certain success and standing in the world of letters. The two sat down to read it together, went on reading it through the twilight of the May night, and at four o'clock in the morning came to wake Dostoevsky and congratulate him on having written a masterpiece. The manuscript continued its ascent through the literary hierarchy. It was brought by Nekrasov to Belinsky with the tidings that "a new Gogol had appeared", and the famous critic, after a moment of initial scepticism, endorsed the verdict of Nekrasov and Grigorovich. Three days later Dostoevsky was presented to Belinsky. "Do you understand," shouted the latter, impetuously, "what is it that you have written? . . . It is impossible that you at twenty should understand." And he proceeded to explain to the enraptured and open-mouthed author the significance of his work. "Am I really so great?" Dostoevsky began to ask himself.[35]

Poor Folk was published the following January of 1846 in Nekrasov's *Petersburg Almanac*. His career as a novelist seemed secure as he was welcomed to the literary circles of the capital.[36]

While awaiting the publication of his novel, Dostoevsky spent the summer with his brother in Revel, and upon his return to St. Petersburg began working on a new novel throughout the autumn of 1845. To Mihail he wrote:

Jakov Petrovich Goliadkin is a bad hat! He is utterly base, and I positively can't manage him. He won't move a step, for he always maintains that he isn't ready; that he's mere nothingness as yet, but *could*, if it were necessary, show his true character; then why won't he? After all, he says, he's no worse than the rest. What does he care about my toil? Oh, a terribly base fellow! In no case can he bring his career to a finish before the middle of November. . . .[37]

Dostoevsky did finish *The Double*, which introduced the theme of the split personality into Russian literature.

Throughout 1845–46 he completed the short stories "Novel in Nine Letters," "Mr. Prokhartchin," and "The Landlady."

During this period, however, fame went to the young author's head. He himself felt in a whirl of events:

Well, brother, I believe that my fame is just now in its fullest flower. Everywhere I meet with the most amazing consideration and enormous interest. I have made the acquaintance of a lot of very important people. Prince Odoyevsky begs me for the honor of a visit, and Count Sollogub is tearing his hair in desperation. Panayev told him that a new genius had arisen who would sweep all the rest away. . . . Everybody looks upon me as a wonder of the world.[38]

Everyone was splendid, he thought. With the actual publication of *Poor Folk,* criticism ensued. In February he wrote to Mihail:

If you only knew, brother, how bitterly the book has been abused! . . . Even the public is quite furious: three-fourths of my readers abuse, and a quarter (or even less) praise the book beyond measure. It is the subject of endless discussion. They scold, scold, scold, yet they read it. . . . And it was the same with Gogol. They abused, abused, but read him. Now they've made up *that* quarrel, and praise him. I've thrown a hard bone to the dogs, but let them worry at it—fools! . . . Only think, all our lot, and even Belinsky consider that I have far surpassed Gogol. . . .[39]

He continued: " . . . Every day brings me so much that is new, so many changes and impressions, agreeable and disagreeable, lucky and unlucky, matters that I have no time to reflect upon them." [40] He bragged outlandishly, and he himself recognized this:

. . . My fame has reached its highest point. In the course of two months I have, by my own reckoning, been mentioned five-and-thirty times in different papers. In certain articles I've been praised beyond measure, in others, again, frightfully abused. What could I ask for more? But it does pain and trouble me that my own friends, Bielinsky and the others, are dissatisfied with my "Goliadkin." The first impression was blind enthusiasm, great sensation, and endless argument. The second was the really critical one. They are—that is, my friends and the whole public—declare with one voice that my "Goliadkin" is tedious and thin, and so drawn-out as to be almost unreadable. . . . As to myself, I was for sometime utterly discouraged." [41]

He was self-critical: "I have one terrible vice: I am unpardonably ambitious and egotistic. The thought that I had disappointed all the hopes set on me, and spoilt what might have been a really significant piece of work, depressed me very heavily." [42] A few years prior, Dostoevsky had written to his brother his thoughts on the poet's gift and responsibility:

. . . The mere thought that through one's inspiration there will one day lift itself from the dust to heaven's heights, some noble, beautiful human soul; the thought that those lines over which one has wept are consecrated as by a heavenly rite through one's inspiration, and that over them the coming generation will weep in echo . . . . That thought, I am convinced, has come to many a poet in the very moment of his highest creative rapture. [43]

Knowing that he felt this, one can understand Dostoevsky's conflict within himself.

During the next two years Dostoevsky continued his literary work. This period was a critical one. He had to work himself out of the malady of conceit in fame. To Mihail he wrote:

. . . the artist must be independent; and finally, he must consecrate all his toil to the holy spirit of art—such toil is

holy, chaste, and demands single-heartedness; my own heart
thrills now as never before with all the new imaginings that
come to life in my soul. Brother, I am undergoing not only
a moral, but a physical, metamorphosis. Never before was there
in me such lucidity, such inward wealth; never before was my
nature so tranquil, nor my health so satisfactory, as now.[44]

And then a reverse:

You will scarcely believe it. Here is the third year of my
literary activity, and I am as if in a dream. I don't see the
life about me at all, I have no time to become conscious of it;
no time, either, to learn anything. I want to attain to something steadfast. People have created a dubious fame for me,
and I know not how long this hell of poverty and constant
hurried work will last. Oh, if I could but once have rest! [45]

The early part of 1849 saw the work *Netochka Nezvanovna*, a full length novel, begun. However, in April, Dostoevsky, along with other members (including his brother,
Mihail) of the literary circle of Petrashevsky, was arrested.
This circle met to discuss idealistic and socialistic philosophy; they drank tea, discussed Fourier's theories, read
literary works, protested against serfdom, and so on.

Dostoevsky's activity in the circle was literary. He interpreted the criticisms of Belinsky, declaimed Pushkin,
read his novel upon which he was working, and also read
the famous "Letter to Gogol" of Belinsky (the sole charge
brought against him.) [46]

The outcome of the trial sent Dostoevsky at twenty-eight
years of age into penal servitude for four years and another five years in Siberian exile. Meanwhile, waiting, he
spent eight months in the Fortress of Peter and Paul.
From the Fortress he wrote to his brother all during the
summer of 1849. He was joyous that Mihail had been
released and told about himself:

At last you are free, and I can vividly imagine how happy you were when you saw your family again. How impatiently they must have awaited you! . . . Have you work, and of what sort?

I rejoice that I may answer you, dear brother . . . I rejoice also that you are well, and that the imprisonment had no evil effects upon your constitution.

You write, my dear fellow, that I must not lose heart. Indeed, I am not losing heart at all; to be sure, life here is very monotonous and dreary, but what else could it be? And after all, it isn't invariably so tedious. The time goes by most irregularly, so to speak—now too quickly, now too slowly. . . . I have occupation, however, I do not let the time go by for naught; I have made out the plots of three tales and two novels; and am writing a novel now, but avoid over-working. . . .[47]

His health was on the whole fairly good. However, the incarceration severely taxed him. He suffered from time to time physically. But, he wrote: "At any rate I'm alive, and comparatively well." He asked his brother to send him Shakespeare, historical works, and the Bible; he comments on the endurance of man: "Human beings have an incredible amount of endurance and will to live; I should never have expected to find so much in myself; now I know it from experience." [48]

In August he wrote that life was as monotonous as ever, but that he had permission to walk in the garden, "where there are almost seventeen trees! Moreover, I am given a candle in the evenings—that's my second piece of luck . . .[49]

In his letter of September 14, Dostoevsky thanked his brother for the requested books. Spiritually he suffered from the prison life:

For almost five months I have been living exclusively on my own provision—that is to say, on my own head alone and solely. But it is unspeakably hard to think *only*, everlastingly to think, without any external impressions which renew and nourish the soul. I live as though under the bell of an air-pump, from which the air is being drawn. My whole existence has concentrated itself in my head, and from my head has drifted into my thoughts, and the labour of those thoughts grown more arduous every day. Books are certainly a mere drop in the ocean, still they do always help me; while my own work, I think consumes my remains of strength. Nevertheless it gives me much happiness.[50]

On the fateful day of December 22, the following was written by Dostoevsky:

To-day, the 22nd of December, we were all taken to Semjonov-sky Square. There the death-sentence was read to us, we were given the cross to kiss, the dagger was broken over our reads, and out funeral toilet (white shirts) was made. Then three of us were put standing before the palisades for the execution of the death-sentence. I was sixth in the row; we were called up by groups of three, and so I was in the second group, and had not more than a minute to live. I thought of you, my brother, and of yours: in that last moment you alone were in my mind; then first I learnt how very much I love you, my beloved brother! I had time to embrace Plestcheiev and Dourov, who stood near me, and to take leave of them. Finally, retreat was sounded, those who were bound to the palisades were brought back, and it was read to us that His Imperial Majesty granted us our lives. Then the final sentences were recited. . . .[51]

One cannot know what Dostoevsky experienced spiritually from this shattering experience. He did write to Mihail:

. . . I am not dejected, I have not lost courage. Life is life everywhere, life is in us and not in the world that surrounds

us. There will be people near me, and to be a man among
men, and to remain one forever, under whatever circumstances, not to weaken, not to fail, that is what life is, that is
the real meaning of life. I have realized this, and this idea has
entered into my flesh, my blood . . .[52]

Two days following, on Christmas Eve, Mihail visited
his brother to take his farewell. About midnight fetters
were put on the prisoners; and the party, consisting of
Dostoevsky, Dourov, and a Polish political prisoner, Jastrzembski, started to Siberia.

They drove for many days, finally crossing the Urals
where at one point the thermometer fell to forty degrees
below zero. At Tobolsk they halted for six days. Here the
prisoners were visited by the wives of survivors of the
Decembrists. Dostoevsky later described this meeting at
Tobolsk in his *Diary of a Writer:*

In Tobolsk, when we, awaiting our further lot, were assem-
bled in a prison courtyard, the wives of the Decembrists prevailed upon the superintendent to arrange a secret meeting
with us in his apartment. We saw these great sufferers who
had voluntarily followed their husbands into Siberia. They
had renounced everything: eminence, wealth, connections and
relatives; they sacrificed everything for the sublime moral duty,
the freest duty that can ever exist. Guilty of nothing, they
endured over a long period of twenty-five years everything
which their convicted husbands were forced to endure.

The interview lasted one hour. They blessed us who were
about to start on a new journey; they crossed us and gave us
copies of the New Testament—the only book permitted in
prison. It lay four years under my pillow in penal servitude.
Sometimes I read it to myself and sometimes—to others. I
used to teach a convict how to read.[53]

Three days of further traveling brought Dostoevsky and
Dourov to the convict prison at Omsk.

HIS LIFE IN SIBERIAN EXILE

For the next four years Fyodor Dostoevsky served at hard labor in Siberia. His sentence was completed on February 15, 1854. He was not thirty-three years old. His letters to his brother Mihail, and occasionally to Andrei and Apollon Maikov, written after his release, give us the most vivid and objective view of what he had lived through. He was faced with the enormous task of setting down four years of his life. The following excerpts describe some of the conditions of the life in prison, the nature of the prisoners, Dostoevsky's epilepsy, the books he so much wished for, the convictions he gained:

. . . It is a week now since I left the prison. . . . What *is* the most important? What was the most important to me in the recent past? When I reflect, I see that even to tell that, this sheet is far too small. How can I impart to you what is now in my mind—the things I thought, the things I did, the convictions I acquired, the conclusions I came to? I cannot even attempt the task. . . . It is my duty to tell you all, and so I will begin with my recollections. Do you remember how we parted from one another, my dear beloved brother? You had scarcely left me when we . . . were led out to have the irons put on. Precisely at midnight on that Christmas Eve (1849), did chains touch me for the first time. They weigh about ten pounds, and make walking extraordinarily difficult. Then we were put into open sledges, each alone with a gendarme, and so, in four sledges, the orderly opening the procession—we left Petersburg. I was heavy-hearted, and the many different impressions filled me with confused and uncertain sensations. My heart beat with a peculiar flutter and that numbed its pain. Still, the fresh air was reviving in its effect, and, since it is usual before all new experiences to be aware of a curious vivacity and eagerness, so *I* was at bottom quite tranquil. I looked attentively at all the festively-lit houses of Petersburg, and said good-bye to each. They drove us past your abode, and at Krayevsky's the windows were brilliantly lit. You had told me that he was giving a Christmas party and tree, and that your children were going to it, with Emilie Fyodorovna; I did feel dreadfully sad as we passed that house. . . .

Strange to say, the journey completely restored me to health. . . . Mournful was the moment when we crossed the Ural. The horses and sledges sank deep in the snow. A snow-storm was raging. We got out of the sledges—it was night—and waited, standing, till they were extricated. All about us whirled the snow-storm. We were standing on the confines of Europe and Asia; before us lay Siberia and the mysterious future—behind us, our whole past; it was very melancholy. Tears came to my eyes. . . .

On January 12 (1850) we came to Tobolsk. . . . I will only tell you that the great compassion and sympathy which were shown us there, made up to us, like a big piece of happiness, for all that had gone before. The prisoners of former days (and still more their wives) cared for us as if they had been our kith and kin. Those noble souls, tested by five-and-twenty years of suffering and self-sacrifice! We saw them but seldom, for we were very strictly guarded; still they sent us clothes and provisions, they comforted and encouraged us. I had brought far too few clothes, and had bitterly repented it, but *they* sent me clothes. Finally, we left Tobolsk, and reached Omsk in three days. . . .[54]

About the prison and the convicts, he wrote:

I had made acquaintance with convicts in Tobolsk; at Omsk I settled myself down to live four years in common with them. They are rough, angry, embittered men. Their hatred for the nobility is boundless; they regard all of us who belong to it with hostility and enmity. They would have devoured us if they only could. . . . "You nobles have iron beaks, you have torn us to pieces. When you were masters, you injured the people, and now, when it's evil days with you, you want to be our brothers."

This theme was developed during four years. A hundred and fifty foes never wearied of persecuting us—it was their joy, their diversion, their pastime; our sole shield was our indifference and our moral superiority, which they were forced to recognize and respect; they were also impressed by our never yielding to their will. . . . We had to let the whole of the vindictiveness, the whole of the hatred, that they cherish against the nobility, flow over us. We had a very bad time there. A military prison is much worse than the ordinary ones. I spent the whole four years behind dungeon walls, and only left the prison when I was taken on "hard labour." The labour was hard, though not always; sometimes in bad weather, in rain, or in winter during the unendurable frosts, my strength would forsake me. . . . We all lived together in one barrack-room. Imagine an old, crazy wooden building, that should long ago have been broken up as useless. In the summer it is unbearably hot, in the winter unbearably cold. All the boards are rotten. On the ground filth lies an inch thick; every instant one is in danger of slipping and coming down. The small windows are so frozen over that even by day one can hardly read. The ice on the panes is three inches thick. The ceilings drip, there are draughts everywhere. We are packed like herrings in a barrel. The stove is heated with six logs of wood, but the room is so cold that the ice never once thaws; the atmosphere is unbearable—and so through all the winter long.
. . . I was often in hospital. My nerves were so shattered that I had some epileptic fits—however, that was not very often . . . it was almost impossible to get one's-self a book, and that when I did get one, I had to read it on the sly; that all around me was incessant malignity, turbulence and quarreling; then perpetual espionage, and the impossibility of ever being alone for even an instant—and so without variations for four long years; . . .

I won't even try to tell you what transformations were undergone by my soul, my faith, my mind, and my heart in those four years. . . . Still, the eternal concentration, the escape into myself from bitter reality, did bear its fruit. I now have many new needs, and hopes of which I never thought in other days. . . .

. . . Brother, there are very many noble natures in the world. For that matter, men everywhere are just—men. Even among the robber-murderers in the prison, I came to know some men in those four years. Believe me, there were among them deep, strong, and beautiful natures, and it often gave me great joy to find gold under a rough exterior. And not in a single case, or even two, but in several cases. Some inspired respect; others were downright fine. I taught the Russian language and reading to a young Circassian. . . . Another convict wept when I said good-bye to him. Certainly I had often given him money, but it was so little, and his gratitude so boundless. My character, though, was deteriorating; in my relations with others I was ill-tempered and impatient. They accounted for it by my mental condition, and bore all without grumbling. Apropos: what a number of national types and characters I became familiar with in the prison! I lived *into* their lives, and so I believe I know them really well. Many tramps' and thieves' careers were laid bare to me, and, above all, the whole wretched existence of the common people. Decidedly I have not spent my time there in vain. I have learnt to know the Russian people as only a few know them. I am a little vain of it. I hope that such vanity is pardonable.[55]

Dostoevsky asked for an assortment of books; ancient and modern historians, and the Fathers of the Church; the Koran, Kant's *Critique of Pure Reason,* Hegel, and the national studies and newspapers.

In March, while still at Omsk, Dostoevsky wrote to Madame Fonvizin, the wife of one of the Decembrists. In this letter we have the direct statement of Dostoevsky's religious beliefs:

. . . no one can really know exactly his fellow-mortal's life; still, human feeling is common to us all, and it seems to me that everyone who has been banished must live all his past grief over again in consciousness and memory, on his return home. It is like a balance, by which one can test the true gravity of what one has endured, gone through, and lost. God grant you a long life! I have heard from many people that you are very religious. But not because you are religious, but because I myself have learnt it and gone through it, I want to say to you that in such moments, one does, "like dry grass," thirst after faith, and that one finds it in the end, solely and simply because one sees the truth more clearly when one is unhappy. I want to say to you, about myself, that I am a child of this age, a child of unfaith and scepticism, and probably (indeed I know it) shall remain so to the end of my life. How dreadfully has it tormented me (and torments me even now)— this longing for faith, which is all the stronger for the proofs I have against it. And yet God gives me sometimes moments of perfect peace; in such moments I love and believe that I am loved; in such moments I have formulated my creed, wherein all is clear and holy to me. This creed is extremely simple; here it is: I believe that there is nothing lovelier, deeper, more sympathetic, more rational, more manly, and more perfect than the Saviour; I say to myself with jealous love that not only is there no one else like Him, but there could be no one. I would even say more: If anyone could prove to me that Christ is outside the truth, and if the truth really did exclude Christ, I should prefer to stay with Christ and not with truth.[56]

Dostoevsky asked her whether she knew when he should be free, "at any rate free as other people." He felt himself to be the same prisoner in his soldier's uniform. Still, he wrote: "I rejoice greatly that I find there is patience in my soul for quite a long time yet, that I desire no earthly possessions, and need nothing but books, the possibility of writing, and of being daily for a few hours alone." [57] For five years he had not had one hour alone, and the concentrated communism of the prison life evoked these words:

. . . to be alone is a natural need, like eating and drinking; for in that kind of concentrated communism one becomes a whole-hearted enemy of mankind. The constant companionship of others works like poison or plague; and from that unendurable martyrdom I most suffered in the last four years. There were moments in which I hated every man, whether good or evil, and regarded him as a thief who, unpunished, was robbing me of life. The most malignant, and evil, is aware of it, even reproves one's-self, and yet has not the power to control one's-self. I have experienced that. . . .[58]

Soon Dostoevsky left Omsk for the small provincial town of Semipalatinsk, near the Mongolian frontier. For the next five years he served as a private in the Russian Army, the Seventh Siberian Infantry Division.

In November of 1854 Dostoevsky made the acquaintance of the new district attorney, Baron Vrangel; the two men became fast friends. Vrangel has left us in his memoirs a valuable and interesting account of his friendship with Dostoevsky.[59] The two read together, gardened, rode across the steppes, and planned translations of Carus' *Psyche* and Hegel's philosophy. Life was monotonous at times but more than bearable. Dostoevsky himself had begun his work on *The House of the Dead*. His friend wrote:

. . . I had the great good luck to see Dostoevsky in his inspired state, and to hear the first drafts of that incomparable work from his own lips; even now, after all these years, I recall those moments with a sense of exaltation. I was always amazed by the superb humanity that glowed in Dostoevsky's soul, despite his grievous destiny, despite the prison, the exile, the terrible malady, and the eternal want of money. Not less was I astonished by his rare guilelessness and gentleness, which never left him even in his worst hours.[60]

Dostoevsky's letters to friends after his release from prison reveal his gratitude to those who extended him spiritual support. In one letter to Madame Maria Dimitryevna Issayev, who later became his wife, he wrote: "Woman's heart, woman's compassion, woman's sympathy, the endless kindness of which we have no clear perception, and which, in our obtuseness, we often do not even notice—these are irreplaceable. All *that* I found in you: even apart from my many failings, a sister could not have been kinder and more tactful to me than you were." [61] And in his letter to Madame Praskoya Annenkov, the wife of the Decembrist who befriended him at Tobolsk, he wrote:

I shall ever remember the full, cordial sympathy which you and your whole excellent family showed to me and my companions in misfortune on my arrival in Siberia. I think of that sympathy with a quite peculiar sense of solace, and shall never, I think, forget it. He who has learnt by his own experience what "hostile destiny" means, and in certain moments has savoured the full bitterness of such a lot, knows also how sweet it then is to meet, quite unexpectedly, with brotherly compassion.[62]

He recalled his month's stay with her daughter and son-in-law, and describes himself as "a man who for four years, adapting myself, as I did, to my fellow-prisoners, had lived like a slice cut from a loaf, or a person buried underground." [63] And in the same letter, Dostoevsky's definition of happiness: "I believe that happiness lies in a clear conception of life and in goodness of heart, not in external circumstances." [64]

By January 15, 1856, Dostoevsky received promotion to a noncommissioned rank. Later in October he received the rank of ensign. By an Imperial Minute on April 18, 1857, Dostoevsky and his heirs were restored to the ancient title of nobility. At the end of the year he petitioned the new Tsar Alexander II that he might be allowed to return to Moscow. By this time he had become engaged to the widow Maria Dimitryevna Issayev.

Again in the beginning of 1858, Dostoevsky petitioned the Tsar. Another year of suspense followed. Finally, in the spring of 1859, he learned from his brother that the government had accepted his resignation and fixed the town of Tver, some 150 kilometers north of Moscow as his dwelling place.

The ban was lifted upon his publications in 1857. His story "The Little Hero" was published in *O. Z. (Annals of the Fatherhood.)* The year 1859 saw the publication of two short works: "Uncle's Dream" (*Roussky Viestnik*) and "The Village of Stepanchikovo" (*O. Z.*).

By the middle of August, Dostoevsky, with his wife, Maria Dimitryevna, together with her young son, Paul Issayev, were in Tver. His brother Mihail visited him shortly after his arrival.

In a final petition to the Tsar, Dostoevsky requested permission to return to Moscow, and for the admission of his stepson to a free place in one of the Petersburg schools. These requests were granted. By mid-December Dostoevsky was on his way to St. Petersburg.

RETURN TO THE CAPITAL: RENEWAL OF HIS LITERARY WORK

During Dostoevsky's ten-year absence, Russia had lost the Crimean War, Nicholas I had died, and the young Liberal Alexander II had ascended the throne. The railway from St. Petersburg to Berlin had been completed.

Having made housing arrangements for his family, Dostoevsky settled down to make preparations for a collected edition of his works, as this was his sole financial resource. He renewed his acquaintances and met Vrangel again although both were caught up in the whirl of events. He gave readings on literature. Mihail gave up his venture in business, a tobacco factory, and the two brothers now embarked on the publication of a literary journal, *Vremya* (Time). In the first issue of January, 1861, Dostoevsky published the first installment of the novel *The Insulted and Injured*. His *Memoirs from the House of the Dead,* which had appeared in another periodical, was transferred to *Vremya.*

What was the policy of *Vremya?* It was set forth in the word *pochva* or soil. It suggested devotion to the Russian people and to the quality of thought "rooted in the soil," that is, organic, wholesome, native growth. Together with Apollon Grigorev, literary critic, and his brother, Mihail, Dostoevsky worked towards a synthesis which would reconcile and transcend the opposed groups, the Westernizers and Slavophiles.

At this time Dostoevsky met the young writer whose story he had published, Apolinaria Suslova. Soon afterwards the two became close friends. Dostoevsky's wife was dying of consumption, and their marriage was fraught with tragedy. This new friendship and love with Suslova was a difficult personal trial for Dostoevsky.

For the next four years Dostoevsky continued his writing: articles, novels, and short stories. Throughout the 'sixties, he criticized the utilitarian and moral rationalism of Dobroliubov and the radical Westernizers. *The Notes From Underground,* a biting parody on "imported" Western ideas, was published in 1864. Many felt it was Dostoevsky's answer to the Westernizer Chernishevsky.

Early in June of 1862 Dostoevsky made his first trip abroad, visiting Paris, London, Berlin, Cologne, and Dresden, and in Italy: Turin, Genoa, Florence. He met Hertzen in London, and he said of their meeting: Dostoevsky is "naïve, not at all clear, but very agreeable; is an enthusiastic believer in the Russian people." [65] During the journey Dostoevsky also visited London's Universal Exhibition with its famed "crystal palace" on Sydenham Hill. Here was the symbol of the scientific and technological achievements of the century. Upon his return to Russia, Dostoevsky wrote his *Winter Notes on Summer Impressions,* a work which presaged the main theme of *Notes from Underground.*

Political turmoil with Poland in 1863 evoked a sharp article by Strakhov in *Vremya.* The consequences of his article brought about the suspension of the journal. At one stroke the Dostoevsky brothers lost their livelihood. Up to that time the journal had been a success, and had even made a profit. However, Dostoevsky borrowed funds and made a second trip abroad, visiting Wiesbaden, Paris, and Italy. He planned his novel *The Gambler,* and wrote to Strakhov: "My story will depict a typical figure, a Russian living abroad. You know of course that last summer there was a great deal of talk in our journals about the absentee Russian. . . . The main character would be a man of the people who has lost faith and who has wasted his talents on roulette; it will be a psychological and faithful portrait." [67]

The year 1864 brought new tragedies to Dostoevsky's life. For months he attended his dying wife. And he was busy with a new journal, *Epoch,* and the writing of *Notes from Underground.* In April Maria Dimitryevna died. A second blow was dealt, when, in June, Mihail suddenly died. Later that same year, in December, his close friend and collaborator Apollon Grigoryev died.

Somehow Dostoevsky managed to edit the *Epoch* through 1864–65. He published his *Notes,* and assumed the support of his brother's family and other relatives. However, his efforts to try to pay off debts were not successful, and up to the last year of his life he was to have constant financial worries.

In 1865 Dostoevsky made a third trip to Europe, visiting his friend Baron Vrangel in Copenhagen. Ridden by debt, he gambled at Wiesbaden, hoping somehow to win. At that time, meeting Turgenev, he borrowed from him, too. He tried hard to save *Epoch,* but upon his return to Petersburg he found the journal bankrupt. "Dostoevsky saw only one way to overcome these difficulties: this was to write as much and as quickly as possible and thus find money which he so desperately needed." [68] Throughout the summer and autumn of 1866, he was hard at work on the novel *Crime and Punishment.*

Autumn 1866 began a new "epoch" in Dostoevsky's personal life. He met his closest friend, Anna Grigorievna Snitkin. She became his second wife later, but at this time Anna Grigorievna was his secretary in the writing of *The Gambler.* In her *Reminiscences* she has left us an account of the difficult conditions under which Dostoevsky had to live and to write:

He began telling me that it was incumbent on him to finish the novel by 1st November [1866]. . . . To my question as to whether the novel was to appear in a monthly magazine, he gave me a detailed account of his business relations with Stellovsky, the publisher. The story was, indeed, a revolting one. It must be said that Dostoevsky owed much money; debts taken over by him after his brother's death and after his review *Epocha* had stopped publication. The creditors worried him terribly; they threatened to put him in prison. The urgent debts he had to meet amounted to three thousand rubles, and he had been trying to find the money, but with no success. When all attempts to persuade the creditors to wait some time longer had failed and Dostoevsky was driven almost to despair, then the publisher Stellovsky came forward with the offer to buy the copyright of all Dostoevsky's works for publication in three large volumes. For the copyright Stellovsky offered to pay 3,000 rubles, on condition that Dostoevsky give him a new novel, of seven folios large size, in a two columned page. Dostoevsky's position was critical, and he agreed to all conditions, just to save himself from the debtors' prison. The agreement was made in April, 1866, and Stellovsky deposited three thousand rubles with a Notary Public to be paid to Dostoevsky's order. The three thousand rubles Dostoevsky handed over the very next day to the creditors. Thus out of the three thousand rubles obtained for his copyright he received no ready cash at all. But the most revolting thing was this: quite soon it became clear that the three thousand rubles had passed again into Stellovsky's pocket. Having then bought up for a mere trifle Dostoevsky's bills from the creditors, Stellovsky forced him to accept extremely bad terms. The price for the copyright of all the works, three thousand rubles was in itself scandalously small, in view of the success of Dostoevsky's novels, especially after the publication of *Crime and Punishment.* But the cruelest thing of all was the clause requiring Dostoevsky to deliver the new novel by 1st November, 1866. In case of non-delivery Dostoevsky was to pay a heavy fine; and should the novel not be delivered by 1st December of the same year, Dostoevsky was to lose his copyright, which would then pass to Stellovsky in perpetuity. That man was a cunning and astute exploiter of our authors and musicians (as for instance of Pisemsky, Krestovsky, Glinka). He was always looking out for people who were in a difficult position and used to catch them in his net. I think that by stipulating for the delivery of the new novel at a fixed date with a heavy fine for non-delivery, Stellovsky was certainly calculating on appropriating the copyrights of Dostoevsky's books. Dostoevsky at that time had been absorbed by his work on *Crime and Punishment* (running as a serial then), and in view of the great interest it aroused among the public, he wished to complete it to the best of his ability. And then to deliver ten folios of a new novel! Knowing the sickly state in which Dostoevsky nearly always was, Stellovsky counted on the chance that he would not have the time or the energy to execute two works simultaneously, and then, according to the agreement, he would acquire the copyright of Dostoevsky's works forever. And this would certainly have happened had not God given Dostoevsky the strength to finish his new novel in time. That was the state of Dostoevsky's affairs then. He also told me, as it seemed almost impossible to write the novel during that one month of October, his friends, Maikov, Milyukov and others —had suggested that he should give them the plan of his novel, and each of them would write a part of it, so that the three or four of them in combination could manage to have it done on time. But Dostoevsky preferred paying a fine or even losing his copyrights to signing his name to a work which he had not written.[69]

The new novel was written and delivered to the publisher by November 1st: "On 29th October the last dictation took place: the novel, *The Gambler*, was finished. Thus, from 4th to 29th October in twenty-six days, a novel of seven folios . . . had been written." [70]

On February 15, 1867, Anna Grigorievna and Fyodor Dostoevsky were married. By April 14 they were on their way abroad. Until the summer of 1871, for four years, debt delayed their return to Russia.

DOSTOEVSKY'S SOJOURN IN EUROPE: 1867–71

There are numerous letters written by Dostoevsky to his family and friends during his years abroad. Correspondence is addressed to relatives: his step-son Pasha, Vera his sister, his niece Sofia Alexandrovna, and to his friends Nicholas Strakhov and Apollon Maikov. His letters are vivid, passionate. The weight in all the letters is on literary matters: his projects, writing, literary criticism, contemporary affairs, his ideas—religious, artistic, political, cultural. One also finds the recurring themes of homesickness, poor health, and always the financial worries. To Sofia and to Maikov he confided these personal affairs. He also made keen observations of the peoples, lands and cities visited.

These four years abroad were chaotic, harassed ones. Under the burden of debts, Dostoevsky lived through a gambling passion. He suffered epileptic fits. In May, 1868, his first child, Sonia, died of pneumonia at the age of one month. Madame Dostoevsky recorded in her diary their first months abroad. She details the days minutely; one has the impression of a hectic life of turmoil and troubles.

These years spent abroad in Germany, Italy, and Switzerland, however, constitute the period of Dostoevsky's artistic maturity. The years of ferment after his return from Siberia were now followed by this voluntary exile in "isolation and monotony," and were, perhaps, "necessary to bring his genius to its full mellowness." [71]

One significant event in Geneva in the fall of 1867 was the Peace Congress held by the European socialists. Dostoevsky now had the opportunity to listen to these idealists first hand. While he was disheartened by "this rabble which is stirring up the whole unfortunate working-class," he gained valuable experience which provided him with evidence for his later analyses of the developing socialist movement in Europe and in Russia.[72]

During the years abroad, several major works were written by Dostoevsky. In *The Idiot,* he attempted to por-

tray the truly perfect and noble man which, according to
him, was the most difficult task, for "the beautiful is the
ideal."

From the letter to his niece Sofia, we have Dostoevsky's
plan for this important novel:

Three weeks ago (December 18 by the Style here) I attacked
another novel, and am now working day and night. The idea
of the book is the old one which I always have so greatly liked;
but it is so difficult that hitherto I never have had the courage
to carry it out; and if I'm setting to work at it now, it's only
because I'm in a desperate plight. The basic idea is the representation of a truly perfect and noble man. And this is more
difficult than anything else in the world, particularly nowadays. All writers, not ours alone but foreigners also, who have
sought to represent Absolute Beauty, were unequal to the task,
for it is an infinitely difficult one. The beautiful is the ideal;
but ideals, with us, as in civilized Europe, have long been
wavering. There is in the world only one figure of absolute
beauty: Christ. That infinitely lovely figure is, as a matter of
course, an infinite marvel (the whole Gospel of St. John is full
of this thought: John sees the wonder of the Incarnation, the
visible apparition of the Beautiful). I have gone too far in my
explanation. I will only say further that of all the noble figures in Christian literature, I reckon Don Quixote as the most
perfect. But Don Quixote is noble only by being at the same
time comic. And Dickens' Pickwickians (they are certainly
much weaker than Don Quixote, but still it's a powerful work)
are comic, and this it is which gives them their great value.
The reader feels sympathy and compassion with the Beautiful,
derived and unconscious of its own worth. The secret of humour consists precisely in this art of wakening the reader's
sympathy. Jean Valjean is likewise a remarkable attempt, but
he awakens sympathy only by his terrible fate and the injustice
of society towards him. I have not yet found anything similar
to that, anything so *positive,* and therefore I fear that the book
may be a "positive" failure.[73]

The Idiot was completed in January, 1869. Already Dostoevsky had been planning anew. He wrote to Maikov in December 1868:

Now here's what I propose: 1. A long novel entitled *Atheism* . . . before I attack it I shall have to read a whole library of atheistic works by Catholic and Orthodox-Greek writers. Even in the most favorable circumstances, it can't be ready for two years. I have my principle figure ready in my mind. A Russian of our class, getting on in years, not particularly cultured, though not uncultured either, and of a certain degree of social importance, loses *quite suddenly,* in ripe age, his belief in God. His whole life long he has been wholly taken up by his work, has never dreamed of escaping from the rut, and up to his forty-fifth year has distinguished himself in no wise. (The working out will be pure psychology: profound in feeling, human, and thoroughly Russian.) [74]

Also to his niece Dostoevsky wrote, concerning the proposed work, *Atheism*: ". . . my whole literary activity has embodied for me but one definite ideal value, but one sin, but one hope—and that I do not strive for fame and money, but only and solely for the synthesis of my imaginative and literary ideals, which means that before I die I desire to speak out, in some work that shall as far as possible express the whole of what I think." [75] A second work, *The Eternal Husband* was his lightest novel, an interim one. The complex work, *The Possessed,* then followed. This latter work was rewritten twice by Dostoevsky, and it was not until his return to Russia that he completed this study of anarchistic socialism.

In one letter to Strakhov Dostoevsky spoke about his own creative works:

I have never yet sought a theme for the money's sake, nor even from a sense of duty, so as to have promised work ready by the appointed time. I have undertaken commissions only when I already had a theme ready in my head, one that I really desired to work out, and the working-out of which I considered necessary. Such a theme I have now. I won't enlarge upon that; I will only say that I have never had a better or more original idea. I may say this without incurring the reproach of lack of modesty, because I speak only of the idea, not of the execution of it. *That* lies in God's hand; I may indeed spoil all, as I have so often done; still, an inward voice assures me that inspiration will not fail in the execution, either.[76]

The "idea" which he had thought about for three years Dostoevsky called *The Life of a Great Sinner*. The fundamental idea which he sketched in other letters to Maikov was later worked out in *The Brothers Karamazov*. "Perhaps," he said, "I shall succeed in creating a majestic, authentic, saint." [77]

Of their four year sojourn abroad, Madame Dostoevsky later wrote:

I must say that I remember it with the most profound gratitude. True, in the course of the four years spent by us in voluntary exile, we passed through hard trials: the death of our first-born daughter, Fiodor's illness, our constant lack of money and insecurity of work, Fiodor's unfortunate passion for roulette, and the impossibility of returning to Russia. But those trials were for our good: they brought us closer together, made us understand and appreciate one another. . . . In spite of many troubles, continual lack of money and moments of depressing boredom, that long isolated life had a good influence on the growth and manifestation in my husband of his Christian ideas and feelings.[78]

Six months after their return to Russian soil, Dostoevsky wrote to his friend, S. D. Yanovsky, a physician who had attended Dostoevsky in his youth: "I spent four years abroad—in Switzerland, Germany, and Italy, and got terribly sick of it in the end. . . . I was falling behind Russia. . . . Well, I've returned, and found nothing particularly puzzling; in a couple of months I shall understand everything again!" [79]

Fruitful Last Ten Years (1871–81)

Leaving Dresden at the end of June, 1871, the Dostoevskys were back in St. Petersburg by July. Thus began a new period for Dostoevsky, a period in which he was to bring his life's work to final fruition. Anna Grigorievna wrote in her reminiscences:

Our return to Petersburg, after an absence abroad for over four years, took place on a hot summer day on July 8, 1871.

From the Warsaw station we drove past the cathedral of Holy Trinity, in which our wedding had taken place. Both Fiodor Mihailovich and myself crossed ourselves, and seeing us do this our little baby daughter (Lubov) also made the sign of the cross. I remember Fiodor Mihailovich saying: "Well, Anochka, we have lived happily these four years abroad, despite the fact that at times life had been hard. What is life in Petersburg going to give us? Everything is in a mist before us! I foresee a good many troubles, difficulties, and worries before we stand on our own feet. On God's help only do I rely! "Why worry beforehand." I remember answering him, "Let us rely on God's mercy. The chief thing now is that our long-cherished dream has been realized, and we are again in Petersburg, again in our mother country.[80]

The Dostoevskys found an apartment and settled down. While Dostoevsky had become one of the most prominent figures in Russian letters during his absence abroad, nevertheless his financial position was still precarious. "The battle for financial recovery was organized and fought by Anna singlehanded, and fought with extraordinary success. She took a flat in St. Petersburg, furnished it, and held off creditors all with nothing more substantial than plans, promises, and a little borrowed money." [81] During this summer, their third child, a son, Fyodor, was born.

Dostoevsky now resumed work on *The Possessed* (*The Devils*), and at the end of the year completed it. This novel was a penetrating study of the contemporary radical movement among the new intelligentsia of the 'sixties.

During the following two years Dostoevsky as editor of the weekly *Grazhdanin* (*The Citizen*) resumed his journalistic writings.

In 1873 the Dostoevskys began their independent publishing activities, and with success. At that time no author undertook to publish his own works. Thus, the adventure was a risk. Madame Dostoevsky's sense of humor on this project is delightful. By January 20, *The Devils* in book form was ready for sale.

The Devils had had great success when it was running as a serial in the *Russky Vestnik,* and now there appeared to be a number of people who wanted to have the novel in book form; and the booksellers who bought copies in the morning sent again for fresh supplies. I was more triumphant than ever, especially seeing that Fiodor was greatly interested in the success of the book and that he was very glad. . . . In a word, our publishing activity started brilliantly, and the first three thousand copies were sold before the year was out. . . . I must say that the title of the novel served to those who came to buy it as an excuse for calling the book all sorts of names. Not to distract myself from my secretarial work, I only counted the copies and reckoned up the amounts; and the customers were attended to by my cheerful maid. They would come in and say to her: "Let us have a dozen devils," or "I've come to fetch a half a dozen demons," or "Give me five fiends, etc." They called it either "demons," or "fiends," or "Satan." Our old nurse who frequently heard these appellations complained to me and assured me that since "Satan" got into our house, her charge (my boy) had become restless and did not sleep so well at night.[82]

Succeeding years brought gradual financial security to the Dostoevskys. Fyodor made several trips abroad to Ems for his health. In June, 1874, he visited Ems for cure, and upon his return his wife persuaded him to rent a country house for the winter in Staraya Russa, some distance from Petersburg. His next novel, *The Raw Youth,* was written in this quiet country retreat.

In his *Diary of a Writer* for 1874 Dostoevsky tells us something about the genesis of this work. Nekrasov had asked him to write a new work:

. . . I have written merely *A Raw Youth*—this first proof of my thought. But there the child has already out-lived his childhood and appears merely as an unready man, timidly and yet boldly seeking to take the first steps on the path of his life. I took an innocent soul, but one already polluted with the dreadful possibility of depravity, early hate, because of his nothingness and "accidentalness," and that breadth with which a still chaste soul already admits vice to his thoughts, fondles it in his still bashful but already daring and tempestuous visions—all this left solely to his own forces, his own reasoning and, perhaps, in truth, to the will of God. They are all cast-offs of society, "accidental" members of "accidental" families.[83]

In this novel Dostoevsky unfolded and traced the psychological growth of the adolescent on the threshold of adulthood; one can find many of his basic educational ideas in this work. The 1870's saw Dostoevsky's attention drawn especially to educational problems concerning youth and children. In his letters of the time and in *The Diary of a Writer* can be found Dostoevsky's views and analyses of educational issues.

Dostoevsky did not undertake another major work for several years after the completion of *The Raw Youth*. "These were quiet years, alternating between the pleasures of a happy family life and occasional and regretted trips to Ems to take the cure." [84] He found himself a celebrity now, and was invited to literary gatherings and to the homes of aristocratic families.

In 1876 their second son, Alexey, was born. This year Dostoevsky also realized his long-cherished dream, the independent publishing of *The Diary of a Writer*, a journal on contemporary affairs. After the first year of publication, Dostoevsky wrote: "The chief purpose of *The Diary* has been to explain, as far as possible, the idea of our national spiritual independence, and to point out, as far as possible, in the current time, facts as they present themselves." [85] *The Diary* was the vehicle for the expression of Dostoevsky's own ideas on broad questions which meant so much to him: social and political, religious, educational, literary, and cultural matters. He interspersed among these autobiographical material—*The Peasant Marei*—and stories like "The Dream of a Ridiculous Man," "The Heavenly Christmas Tree," and "A Gentle Spirit." The journal was extremely successful, and "at its height it had some six thousand subscribers, a convincing testimony of Dostoevsky's popularity." [86]

During the next years many people—fathers, mothers, students—came to see Dostoevsky or wrote him asking advice, especially on educational matters. The following excerpts give us some idea of his views.

In a letter to a Mrs. Altschevsky, Dostoevsky defended his *Diary*, and stated his concern about Russian family life:

I have been driven to the conviction that an artist is bound to make himself acquainted, down to the smallest detail, not only with the technique of writing, but with everything—current no less than historical events—relating to that reality which he designs to show forth. We have one writer who is really remarkable in that respect: it is Count Leo Tolstoy. . . . As I am now proposing to write a very big novel, I must devote myself most especially to the study of actuality: I don't mean actuality in the literal sense, for I am fairly well versed in that, but certain peculiarities of the present moment. And in this present moment the younger generation particularly interests me, and, as akin to it, the question of Russian family-life, which, to my *thinking,* is to-day quite a different thing from what it was twenty years ago. . . .[87]

The Diary was a study for his impressions so that "nothing may be wasted." As an illustration he recounted visits from youths who had wished to make his acquaintance:

They told me that they were students at the Academy of Medicine, that there were at that Academy as many as five hundred women-students, and that they had entered there "to obtain higher education, so as later to be able to do useful work." I had never before seen girls of that sort (of the earlier Nihilists I know a number, and have studied them thoroughly.) Believe me, I have seldom passed my time so agreeably as in the company of those two girls, who remained with me a couple of hours. Such wonderful spontaneity, such freshness of feeling, such purity of heart and mind, such *grave sincerity, and such sincere mirth!* [88]

Then he wrote of a young man whose character is the reverse of the girl students: The young man visits friends, and "goes accidentally into the tutor's room, and sees a *forbidden* book, lying on the table; he instantly tells the master of the house, and the tutor is instantly dismissed. When, in another household, someone told this young man that he had been guilty of a *base action,* he could not in the least see it." [89] Now, asked Dostoevsky, how is he to write about these, for at once these are personal matters, and yet they are typical, and deeply moral.

In a letter of 1878, Dostoevsky wrote about his own religious convictions:

Least of all by words and argument does one convert an unbeliever. Would it not be better if you would read, with your best possible attention, all the epistles of St. Paul? Therein much is said of faith, and the question could not be better handled. I recommend you to read the whole Bible through in the Russian translation. The book makes a remarkable impression when one thus reads it. One gains, for one thing, the conviction that humanity possesses, and can possess, no other book of equal significance. Quite apart from the question of whether you believe or don't believe, I can't give you any sort of idea. But I'll say just this: Every single organism exists on earth but to live—not to annihilate itself. Science has made this clear, and has laid down very precise laws upon which to ground the axiom. Humanity as a whole is, of course, no less than an organism. And that organism has, naturally, its own conditions of existence, its own laws. Now suppose that there is no God, and no personal immortality (Personal immortality and God are one and the same identical idea). Tell me then: Why am I to live decently and do good, if I die irrevocably here below? If there is no immortality, I need but live out my appointed day, and let the rest go hang. And if that's really so (and if I am clever enough not to let myself be caught by the standing laws), why should I not kill, rob, steal, or at any rate live at the expense of others? For I shall die and all the rest will die and utterly vanish! By this road, one would reach the conclusion that the human organism alone is not subject to the universal law, that it lives but to destroy itself—not to keep itself alive. For what sort of society is one whose members are mutually hostile? Only utter confusion can come of such a thing as that. And then reflect on the "I" which can grasp all this. If the "I" can grasp the idea of the universe and its laws, then that "I" stands above all other things, stands aside from all other things, judges them, fathoms them. In that case, the "I" is not only liberated from earthly axioms, the earthly laws, but has its own law, which transcends the earthly. Now, whence comes that law? Certainly not from earth, where all reaches its issue, and vanishes beyond recall. Is *that* no indication of personal immortality? If there were no personal immortality would you, Nikolay Lukitch, be worrying yourself about it, be searching for an answer, be writing letters like this? So you can't get rid of your "I," you see; your "I" will not subject itself to earthly conditions, but seeks for something which transcends earth, and to which it feels itself akin. . . .[90]

Dostoevsky's inspiration, support, and wisdom to many people is testified to by his daughter:

When he began the publication of the *Journal of the Writer,* Dostoevsky hoped to reunite this handful of wrong-headed intellectuals with the great popular masses by awakening in them the sentiments of patriotism and religion. His ardent voice was not lost in the wilderness; many Russians saw the danger of this moral abyss which separated our peasants from our intellectuals and tried to fill it in. The fathers were the first to respond to Dostoevsky's appeal. They came to see him, consulted him as to the education of their children, and wrote to him from the depths of the provinces, asking for advice. These conscientious fathers belonged to all classes of Russian society. Some were humble folks of the lower classes of Russian society, who had deprived themselves to give their children a good education, and saw with terror that they were becoming atheists and enemies of Russia. At the other end of the scale there was the Grand Duke Costantine Nicolaievitch, who begged my father to exercise his influence on his young sons. . . . After the fathers came the sons. No sooner did Dostoevsky begin to speak of patriotism and religion than the boy and girl students of Petersburg flocked to him, forgetting their former grievances against him. . . .

The Russian girl-students in particular were warm admirers of Dostoevsky, for he always treated them with respect. . . .[91]

What was Dostoevsky like at home? His daughter, Aimée, has given us glimpses:

Russian students are not very orderly in their habits. They interfered with my father's work by coming to see him at all hours of the day, and thus Dostoevsky, who never refused to receive them, was obliged to sit up at night writing. Even before this, when he had any important chapters on hand, he preferred working at them when everyone was asleep. This nocturnal toil now became a fixed habit. He would write until four or five in the morning, and would not get up till eleven o'clock. He slept on a sofa in his study. This was then the fashion in Russia. . . . On the wall over the sofa there was a large and beautiful photograph of the Sistine Madonna, which had been given to my father by friends who knew how much he loved the picture. His first glance when he awoke fell upon the sweet face of this Madonna, whom he considered the ideal of womanhood.[92]

The children gathered around him and chatted while he breakfasted. Afterwards, he and Anna Grigorievna worked together on chapters he had written the night before. Aimée writes about her father's handwriting: "I called it 'Gothic writing' because all his manuscripts were adorned with Gothic windows, delicately drawn with pen and ink. Dostoevsky traced them mechanically as he pondered on his work; it seems as if his soul had craved for these Gothic lines which he had admired so much in the cathedrals of Milan and Cologne." [93]

During the summers, the family went to the country estate at Staraya Russa. When, later, Dostoevsky went to Ems for health cures, he brought presents to everyone upon his return.

On family festivals he loved to collect his own relatives and his wife's around the table. "He was always very pleasant to them, talking of things which they were interested in, laughing, jesting, and even playing cards, an amusement he disliked." [94]

Dostoevsky read his children the legends and tales of the Russian people, and they listened entranced, "weeping over the misfortunes of the errant knights and rejoicing at their victories." [95] Passing from the legends, he read Pushkin's stories, Lermontov's Caucasian tales, and Gogol's *Taras Bulba*. He took the children to the ballet and to the opera, particularly to *Russlan and Ludmilla*.[96]

Their mother read to them two of Dostoevsky's favorites: Sir Walter Scott's works and Dickens' works.

About the children's religious education, Aimée wrote:

Dostoevsky superintended our religious education and liked to worship in company with his family. In Russia we communicate once a year, and we prepare for this solemn event by a week of prayer. My father performed his religious duties reverently, fasted, went to church twice a day, and laid aside all literary work. He loved our beautiful Holy Week services, especially the Resurrection Mass with its joyful hymns. Children do not attend this mass, which begins at midnight, and ends between two and three in the morning. But my father wished me to be present at this wonderful ceremony when I was barely nine years old. He placed me on a chair, that I might be able to follow it, and with his arms around me, explained the meaning of the holy rites.[97]

In 1878 tragedy came to the family once more. The youngest boy, Alyosha, died. Anna Grigorievna wrote:

He loved Alexey with a strange, almost morbid love, as if foreboding his early death. My husband's grief was intensified by the fact that the boy died of epilepsy inherited from his father. Outwardly Fyodor Michailovich was very resigned and bore this blow of fate manfully, but I dreaded that this outwardly-controlled sorrow which was all the time eating out his heart would ruin his health, which was already so poor.[98]

She encouraged him to visit the monastery Optina Pustyn. In June, Dostoevsky made a journey with the young philosopher, Vladimir Solovyev, to the famous monastery which was celebrated for the piousness of the elder Starets Ambrose. "At the monastery he talked with the elder who consoled him on the loss of his child in words which Dostoevsky recalled when writing the effective consolation of Zosima to the poor peasant woman bereaved by the death of her child. Indeed Optina Pustyn and Father Amvrosi provided special details for the monastic scenes and the characterization of Zosima in the novel." [99] That summer Dostoevsky began his last major novel, *The Brothers Karamazov*, whose hero was the young Alexey.

These last years were arduous ones, for along with the new work, Dostoevsky continued his *Diary*, and now began public readings for the benefit of student groups and literary institutions. He had also become a corresponding member of the Royal Academy of Sciences in 1878.

In the spring of 1880 he was invited to the Pushkin Memorial celebrations in Moscow. Before this famous literary event, Dostoevsky wrote valuable and explanatory letters to his publisher, N. A. Linbimov of *Russky Vestnik*, about *The Brothers Karamazov*. From the following excerpts one can see the main ideas of this vast work. On the book "Pro and Contra" in *The Brothers Karamazov*, he wrote: "Its idea, as you will see from the text I have sent you, is the presentation of extreme blasphemy and of the seeds of the idea of destruction at present in Russia among the young generation that has torn itself away from reality. . . ." Zossima will have the refutation; Ivan is the "synthesis of contemporary Russian anarchism. The denial not of God, but of the meaning of his creation. The whole of socialism sprang up and started with the denial of the meaning of historical actuality, and arrived at the program of destruction and anarchism." [100] Ivan will take an unassailable theme: the suffering of children. "In *The Devils* there were a number of characters, for which I was reproached, on the ground that they were fantastic; then afterwards, would you believe it, they all proved to be real; therefore they must have been truthfully divined. . . ." The events Ivan cites are all based on actuality; they "were published in newspapers and I can show where they happened. I did not invent them." [101] Dostoevsky continues:

The modern *denier,* the most vehement one, straightway supports the advice of the devil, and asserts that that is a surer way of bringing happiness to mankind than Christ is. For our Russian socialism, stupid but terrible (for the young are with it)—there is here a warning, and I think a forcible one. Bread, the tower of Babel (i.e. the future kingdom of socialism) and the completest overthrow of freedom of conscience—that is what the desperate denier and atheist arrives at. The difference only being that our socialists (and they are not only the underground nihilists—you are aware of that) are conscious Jesuits and liars, who will not confess that their ideal is the ideal of the violation of man's conscience and of the reduction of mankind to the level of a herd of cattle. But my socialist (Ivan Karamazov) is a sincere man who frankly confesses that he agrees with the "Grand Inquisitor's" view of mankind and that Christ's religion (as it were) has raised man much higher than man actually stands. The question is forced home: "Do you despise or respect mankind, you, its coming saviours?"

And they do all this in the name of the love of mankind, as if to say: "Christ's law is difficult and abstract, and for weak people intolerable"; and instead of the law of liberty and Enlightenment they bring to mankind the law of chains and of subjection by means of bread.[102]

The chapter on Zossima will be a story, not a sermon:

I will compel people to admit that a pure, ideal Christian is not an abstraction, but a vivid reality, possible, clearly near at hand, and that Christianity is the sole refuge of the Russian land from all its evils. I pray God that I may succeed, for the part will be a pathetic one. If only I can get sufficient inspiration: And the main theme is such, that it does not even occur to the mind of anyone of contemporary writers and poets, therefore it is quite original. For its sake the whole novel is being written.[103]

Zossima's section will be "one of the culminating points of the novel."

I have called that book "The Russian Monk," a bold and provocative title, for all the critics who do not like us will cry out: "Is the Russian Monk like that, how dared he put him on such a pedestal?"

But better if they do cry out, is it not so? (And I know that they will not be able to contain themselves.) I think I have not sinned against reality: it is true not only as an ideal, but it is true as a reality.

You will understand that a great deal in the precepts of my Zosima (or, rather, the manner of their expression) belongs to his character, that is, to the artistic presentation of his character. Although I myself hold the same opinions, which he expresses, yet if I expressed them personally *from my self*, I should express them in a different form and in a different style. But he *could not* speak in a different style, *nor express himself in a different spirit,* than the one which I have given him. Otherwise the imaginative character would not be created. Such for instance, are Zosima's views on *what is a monk,* or *on servants and masters,* or *on can one be the judge of another* and so on. I took the figure and character from among the old Russian monks and prelates. With profound humility he has boundless, naïve hopes of the future of Russia, of her moral and even political mission. St. Sergius, Bishops Peter and Alexey, have they not always regarded Russia in that light? [104]

To Ivan Aksakov in the summer of 1880, Dostoevsky wrote that he was working day and night to finish the "Karamazovs," which was personally dear to him:

I have put a great deal of my inmost self into it. I work, in general, very nervously, with pain and travail of soul. . . . And now I have to sum up all that I have pondered, gathered, set down, in the last three years. I must make this work good at all costs, or at least as good as *I* can. . . . You will hardly believe me: many a chapter, for which I had been making notes . . . after finally setting it down, I was obliged to reject, and write anew. Only separate passages which were directly inspired by enthusiasm, came off at first writing; all the rest was hard work. . . .[105]

On May 25, 1880, the Moscow writers and journalists held a banquet in Dostoevsky's honor. From June 6 to 7 festivities in Moscow were held in connection with the unveiling of the Pushkin Memorial. On June 8, Dostoevsky delivered his speech on Pushkin at the Meeting of The Society of Lovers of Russian Literature. This speech "electrified a distinguished audience and aroused the people to a recognition of him as a national literary hero." [106]

Dostoevsky's speech on Pushkin temporarily reconciled the opposing factions of Westernizers and Slavophiles. Anna Grigorievna defined correctly the significance of

Dostoevsky's letters to her during the Festivities. She has left us a vivid picture of the times and the views of the influential man:

Dostoevsky reveals the struggle of the two irreconcilable tendencies of the social ideas and ideals of that period, and he points out his part in it and the significance of his own utterance. We see, too, the active and impatient party spirit of his contemporaries. On May 28–29, 1880, he writes to his wife: "Remain here I must and I have decided to remain. . . . The chief point is that I am needed here not only by *Lovers of Russian Literature,* but by our whole party, by our whole idea, for which we have been fighting these thirty years. For the hostile party (Turgenev, Kovalevsky, and nearly the whole University) is quite determined to belittle Poushkin's significance as the representative of the Russian nation, and thereby to deny the very nation itself." And further, explaining why his presence is absolutely necessary: "Against them, on our side, we have on Ivan Sergueyevich Aksakov (Yuriev and the rest have no weight), but Ivan Aksakov has grown rather out of date and Moscow is rather bored by him. Myself, however, Moscow has not heard nor seen, and it is in me alone that the people are interested. My voice will have weight, and thus our side will triumph. All my life I have been fighting for this; I can't run away from the field of battle now. When Katkov, who on the whole, is not a Slavophil, says to me: "You mustn't go away, you can't go away," then, certainly, stay I must.[107]

Dostoevsky had worked long and carefully on his speech. The many variants and rough sketches of this discourse which have been preserved show that he wished to reveal the whole of himself.[108]

Ivan Aksakov's letter to his wife of June 14, 1880, stated:

. . . He read, read masterfully, such a superb original thing, comprehending the national question still more widely and deeply than my article, and not merely in the form of a logical exposition, but in real and living images, with the art of a novelist; the impression was indeed overwhelming. I have never seen anything like it. . . . Hitherto Turgenev has been the idol of the younger generation; . . . But Dostoevsky went straight and defiantly to the point: . . . he put his finger straight on Socialism; gave the young a whole sermon: "Humble thyself, proud man, cease to be a wanderer in foreign lands, seek the truth in thyself, not outward truth." . . . It was indeed remarkable how the young men, of whom there were perhaps a thousand in the hall, took that speech. . . .[109]

Students gave Dostoevsky a huge laurel wreath. Late the same night of the speech, he took it and went alone to Pushkin's monument. Raising the heavy wreath, he laid it at the feet of the beloved poet.[110]

With the Epilogue to *The Brothers Karamazov* Dostoevsky sent a letter to his editor in which he stated hopefully that he intended to live another twenty years and to go on writing. In his notebook he jotted down several projected works: to write a Russian *Candide,* a book on Christ, an epic on *The Commemoration of the Dead,* and his reminiscences. These hopes were not to be fulfilled.

At the beginning of 1881, the Dostoevskys were finally free from the debts which had burdened them for so long. His wife recorded that he had been well: "During the last three years his attacks of epilepsy had ceased to torment him, and his healthy and cheerful manner gave us all the hope that he would get through winter satisfactorily." [111] Dostoevsky worked on a new issue of *The Diary:* on January 25, copy went to the printer.

On the night of the twenty-fifth Dostoevsky burst an artery in one of his lungs, from overexertion in shifting his bookcase. This hemorrhage subsided, but the next day it was repeated. He lived quietly through the twenty-seventh, but on the morning of the twenty-eighth Dostoevsky knew he would die that day. He asked his wife to give him the New Testament, his copy which had been given to him by the wives of the Decembrists in 1854.

Anna Grigorievna recorded:

And all his life afterwards that book was always on his writing table. Very often, as he thought of something or doubted something, he would open the New Testament, and read the first lines on the opened left-hand page. This time, too, Fiodor wished to verify his doubts by means of the New Testament. He opened the holy book and asked me to read.

It opened on St. Matthew, Chapter III, 14.

"But John forbad him, saying, I have need to be baptised of thee, and comest thou to me? And Jesus answering said unto him, 'Suffer it to be so now: for thus it becometh us to fulfil all righteousness.' "

"Do you see, Anya? 'Suffer it to be so now,' it means that I am to die," my husband said, and closed the book.[112]

Dostoevsky took leave of his children, and requested the New Testament be given his son, Fedya. At 8:38 P.M. on January 28, 1881, Dostoevsky died. The January issue of *The Diary of a Writer* appeared on this day of his death.

On January 30, the Minister of Finance sent to Madame Dostoevsky a letter which stated that in gratitude for the services her husband had rendered to Russia, the family would have an annual pension of two thousand rubles conferred by His Majesty the Tsar.[113]

On January 31, the funeral took place at the Alexander-Nevsky Monastery:

The funeral procession presented a majestic spectacle: long rows of wreaths, carried on poles, numerous student choirs, and a huge crowd of many tens of thousands of people following the coffin. . . . All institutions, societies and associations, each on its own initiative, sent deputations with wreaths. All parties of all schools united in the common feeling of grief at the death of Dostoevsky, and in a sincere desire to honour his memory.[114]

Epilogue

The following selections are tributes friends have paid to Dostoevsky's life and work: Pobiedonoszev wrote to the Tsarevitch Alexander III:

. . . his death is a great loss to Russia too. In the circle of writers he—he alone almost—was an ardent preacher of the fundamental principles of religion, nationhood, love of the country. Our unhappy younger generation, gone astray like sheep without a shepherd, cherished a belief in him, and his influence was very great and beneficial. Many, unhappy young people, turned to him as to a confessor, personally and in writing. There is no one now to replace him.[115]

Count Leo Tolstoy wrote to Strakhov in the beginning of 1881:

I wish I had the power to say all that I think of Dostoevsky. When you inscribed your thoughts, you partly expressed mine. I never saw the man, had no sort of direct relations with him; but when he died, I suddenly realized that he had been to me the most precious, the dearest, and the most necessary of beings. It never even entered my head to compare myself with him. Everything that he wrote (I mean only the good, the true things) was such that the more he did like that, the more I rejoiced. Artistic accomplishment and intellect can arouse my envy; but a work from the heart—only joy. I always regarded him as my friend, and reckoned most confidently on seeing him at some time. And suddenly I read that he is dead. At first I was utterly confounded, and when later I realized how I had valued him, I began to weep—I am weeping even now. Only a few days before his death, I had read with emotion and delight his "Injury and Insult." [116]

And Dostoevsky's friend Ivan Aksakov wrote:

The death of Dostoevsky is a real chastisement from God. Now for the first time it is fully felt what value he had as a teacher of the younger generation. Even those who did not know *him* personally must perceive it. Those noble ideals which many a youth cherished unconsciously in his soul, found in him an upholder. For "injured and insulted" is, in very truth, only the religious and moral sense of the Russian intelligence. . . .[117]

Chapter Three

Dostoevsky and Contemporary Educational Problems

CONTEMPORARY PROBLEMS of education were of deep concern to Dostoevsky. The central focus of his thought, as will be seen, was ethical. In *The Diary of a Writer* Dostoevsky discussed and analyzed educational issues in relation to the ethos of the people: its ideals and aspirations. He looked upon education not only from the point of view of schools, curriculum or pedagogical process, but also included in education society's institutions, the courts, the press, and so on. "For education one shall strive unto one's life's end," Dostoevsky wrote to his son.[1]

THE AIM OF EDUCATION

"Not the form but the content is essential (even though the form, too, is beautiful). The content, however, is incontestable." [2] For Dostoevsky the ultimate aim of the education of man is the ripening of Christian moral character. Dostoevsky developed this theme in his article on "Best Men" in *The Diary*.[3] What is the ideal of the "best" man which should be the guide for the nation and its youth? Dostoevsky wrote: "Best men are they without whom no society and no nation can live and stand even in the face of the broadest equality of rights." [4] And this aim, that is, the forming of a man, is defined in the following way: ". . . the 'best man' is he who has not bowed before material temptation; who is incessantly seeking work for God's cause; who loves truth and, whenever the occasion calls for it, rises to serve it, forsaking his home and his family and sacrificing his life. . . . I mean to state specifically . . . that the image of 'the best man' . . . is radiating more brightly . . . its provider, guardian and bearer nowadays is precisely the common people." [5] Dostoevsky saw that among the common people the religious ideal still lived, and he maintained that the Christian image sustained their lives.[6] He observed that his definition was opposed to the contemporary one of the educated beau monde which held the enlightened man of science to be the ideal. But he further noted that "an educated man is not always honest . . . science does not guarantee valor in man." [7]

What is needed to become "a man," to achieve the realization of oneself? The principle of self-discipline is essential:

. . . it is possible to rationalize and to perceive a thing correctly and at once, but to become a man at once is impossible: one has to mould oneself into a man. Here discipline is required. But it is precisely this relentless self-discipline that our present-day thinkers reject; they say: "There is too much despotism; liberty is needed." However, this liberty leads the overwhelming majority to nothing but lackeyism before another man's thought, since people are awfully fond of things which are ready made. Moreover, thinkers are proclaiming general laws, i.e., such rules as will suddenly make everybody happy, without any refinement: let only these rules come into existence. Why even if this ideal were feasible, no rules, even the most obvious ones, could be put into practice with *un-finished* men. Now, it is in this relentless self-discipline and uninterrupted work on one's self that our citizen could reveal himself.[8]

Further, Dostoevsky concluded: ". . . to those pure in heart there is one advice: self-control and self-mastery before any first step. Before compelling others, fulfill it yourselves—herein is the whole mystery of the first step." [9]

What really matters in education, and he employs the concept broadly in this respect, is whether there is goodness, humaneness.[10] He maintained that in the people, although they were not "schooled," there was preserved a solid core of moral fiber. This should be respected and developed together with formal education in skills and cultural learning.[11] Thus, the aim of enlightening the people through education involves more than the teaching of skills, trades, and professions. For, Dostoevsky wrote, real teaching is enlightenment: "The enlightenment of the people—this . . . is our right and our duty—this is a right in the highest Christian sense: he who knows the good, the true word of life, must, is duty-bound, to convey it to him who knows not, to his brother groping in darkness—thus it is according to the Gospel. . . . Teaching is useful, and one has to learn. The people themselves even before us said, 'Knowledge is light, ignorance is darkness.' " [12] Enlightenment meant for Dostoevsky the acquisition of "large ideas, great culture and knowledge" outside one's special vocation.[13]

VIEWS ON PUBLIC EDUCATION

UNIVERSAL EDUCATION

Education in the sense of schooling which would provide knowledge of basic skills and general culture should be given to all the people, Dostoevsky maintained. He affirmed clearly the principle and aim of universal education:

I was never able to understand the thought that only one-tenth of the people should have the benefits of higher education, while the remaining nine-tenths should merely serve as material and means therefor; continuing to dwell in darkness. I do not wish to think, or even to live, otherwise than with the faith that all of the ninety millions of us Russians (or whatever number of them may be eventually born), will someday all be educated, humanized and happy. I know that universal education can harm none of us.[14]

The present need is education. This is the foremost public issue, Dostoevsky asserted. "The people are pure in heart; what they need is education—this is the most momentous thing! In this we should believe above all, and this we should learn to discern. . . ." [15] In his article "Visions and Reveries," Dostoevsky deplored the lack of a genuine public-spirited concern for the needs of Russia; one such need was, of course, education.[16] There should be greater appropriations for education itself; this should come from the state. There is no doubt in Dostoevsky's mind that education is the state's responsibility, but, in turn, the citizens constitute the state.[17]

THE ROLE OF THE TEACHER

Schools and funds for the institutional apparatus are not enough, of course: "With money, for example, you may build schools, but you would be unable forthwith to produce teachers. A teacher is a delicate proposition; a popular, national teacher is the product of centuries; he is maintained by tradition, by endless experience," [18] wrote Dostoevsky.

The mastery of specialized field, for example, pedagogy, is also insufficient. And a true pedagogue is more than a scientist. Men of independent thought are needed: "Men, men—this is the most pressing need. Men are dearer even than money. In no market, and no matter for what amount of money, can men be purchased . . . they are evolved by centuries; well, and centuries require time. . . ." [19] And, Dostoevsky concluded: "A man of ideas and of independent learning, a man independently versed in business, is capable of being moulded only by the long independent life of a nation, its century-long labours full of suffering; in short, he is produced by the country's historical life in its totality." [20]

While the new reforms of the sixties and seventies, under Alexander II, were broadening the structure of education among the people, Dostoevsky's confidence lay in the new, young teachers who now had the opportunity, as public servants in the true sense, to accomplish a great deal if they would take upon themselves the task of understanding and appreciating the ideals of the people; they could lead the people away from the vices of ignorance and debauchery.[21] This necessitated on the part of the teachers a willingness to live with the people and to share in their life, but not to go among the people and condescendingly "teach them." [22] His main criticism of the *narodniki* or populists was precisely their "condescending" attitude toward the Russian peasantry.

In nineteenth-century Russia the schools of the state, the church, and the private schools were joined by the central Ministry of Education. In referring to public education among the people, Dostoevsky probably had in mind the new *zemstvo* or community schools which were developing in the provinces, as well as the established city secondary institutions. "Public" meant, therefore, the state and locally supported peoples' institutions.

In raising the question, What is the foundation of public education? Dostoevsky again had in mind the new teachers who were "going to the people," the *narodniki* of the seventies. Their attitude was alien to the people whom they would enlighten. Therefore his answer to the problem was that, first, the people must respect the educated who would enlighten them.[23] There should be no schism between the people and the educated classes, and to the young teachers Dostoevsky wrote: ". . . by earning the respect of the people, you are already serving the cause of public education." [24]

SOCIAL INSTITUTIONS

In several articles Dostoevsky discussed various social institutions of the state: the juvenile home, orphanages, and the courts of justice. The last was especially important for education, for the legal reforms under Alexander II had introduced the jury trial system. This brought new civic responsibility upon the people without preparation. Dostoevsky wrote: "The tribunes of our new courts are unquestionably an ethical school for our society and our people. Indeed, the people learn in this school truth and morality; how, then, shall we remain indifferent to things which once in a while are uttered from those tribunes?" [25]

In an article entitled "The Milieu," written in 1873, Dostoevsky took up the problem of acquitting. The jurors were, he felt, twisting sentiment and misapplying compassion. The predominant note of the court seemed to be that to ruin anyone's fate was a pity. Here, Dostoevsky touched upon the moral problem of justice. He argued against wholesale acquittal, which rested upon the new doctrine of environment. The Christian position, he maintained, advocates mercy for the wrongdoer, but, nevertheless, "makes it a moral duty for man to struggle against environment, and draws a line of demarcation between where environment ends and duty begins." [26] The danger in the doctrine of environment was that it was undermining faith in the law, and further, it took away responsibility for one's own acts. For Dostoevsky, this was an educational issue as well as a politico-social one.[27]

Dostoevsky gave full support to the humanitarian state institutions like the orphanages and the juvenile homes. He urged further implementation in that direction. In his analyses he again emphasized the ethical side of the question, raising the problem of the spiritual development of children and youth. His examination of several educational methodological principles in connection with the juvenile home will be discussed under the chapter on youth.

PROBLEMS RELATED TO THE CURRICULUM

We now turn to several problems which relate to what is formally called curriculum. It must be said, however, that Dostoevsky was not mainly concerned with the school curriculum in subject matter; rather he went beyond this to the problem of general education versus specialized education, the problem of language and what it involved in its study, and the value of reading to the imagination of the student.

THE IMPORTANCE OF GENERAL EDUCATION

In formal, higher education, Dostoevsky held the view that a broad and general education should be encompassed preceding or in addition to specialization. He thus supported what many would call a liberal education, that is, acquaintance with broad knowledge and culture.[28] He deplored the situation in the universities where specialization had gained primacy, and true education with the breadth and scope of the humanities and sciences was lacking: ". . . the majority of our students—men and women—have no true education! They study only just enough to get paid appointments as soon as may be. . . ." [29]

THE MASTERY OF LANGUAGE

Dostoevsky was well aware of the classical reform in education initiated by D. A. Tolstoy in the seventies in Russia. In *The Diary* for 1876, he wrote: ". . . exactly five years ago we inaugurated the so-called classical reform of education. Mathematics and the two ancient languages—Latin and Greek—were recognized as the most effective means of mental, and even spiritual, development. It was not we who recognized and invented this: this is a fact, undeniable fact, empirically ascertained by the whole of Europe in the course of centuries. We merely adopted it." [30]

While Dostoevsky acknowledged that the two ancient languages of Greek and Latin were important, his main concern was the native Russian language, which had virtually been suppressed: "The question arises: if the Russian language is in neglect, how, by what means, through the medium of what material are our children going to master the forms of those two ancient tongues? Is it possible that the mere mechanics of instruction . . . of these two ancient languages constitute their developmental force?" [31] Even mechanics cannot be mastered at all "without a parallel most intense and profound instruction in the *living* language." [32] He concluded that "the whole morally developmental effect of these two ancient languages, these two most perfectly structuralized forms of human thought—which, in the course of centuries, have lifted the barbarian West to the highest level of civilization—this whole effect will, naturally, be missed by the new school precisely because of the decline in it of the Russian tongue." [33]

On the question of languages not only in the schools, but in private instruction by tutors, Dostoevsky vigorously advocated the native language. His argument goes to the root of the matter: What is the purpose for which the word was created?

Undeniably, the language is the form, the flesh, the membrane of the thought (I am not explaining what thought is), so to speak, the last and concluding word of organic evolution. Hence, it is clear that the wealthier the material—the forms provided for the thought which I adopt for its expression—the happier I shall be in life, the more distinct and intelligible I shall be to myself and to others, the more sovereign and victorious; the quicker I shall say to myself that which I wish to say, the deeper I shall express it and the deeper I myself shall comprehend that which I sought to express, the firmer and the calmer will my spirit be, and—it stands to reason—the wiser I shall be.[34]

What is the relation between the velocity of thought and human expression of thought?

. . . even though man is capable of thinking with the velocity of electricity, in fact he does not think so quickly, but, in an infinitely slower tempo, though infinitely more quickly than, for example, he speaks. Why is this so?—Because, nevertheless, of necessity, he thinks in some language. Verily, we may not be conscious of the fact that we are thinking in some particular language, yet this is so; and if we are not thinking in terms of words, that is, by uttering words, be it only mentally—nevertheless we think, so to speak, by "the elemental underlying power of that language" in which we choose to reason, if it be permitted to express it this way. Of course, the more flexibly, the more wealthily, the more multilaterally we master that language in which we choose to think, the more easily, the more multilaterally we shall express our thought in it.

Essentially, why do we learn European languages—French, for instance? First, simply to be able to read French and, secondly, to be able to converse with the French when we happen to come in contact with them—yet, under no circumstances, to converse with Russians and with one's self. For a loftier life, for depth of thought, a foreign language is insufficient precisely because it always will remain alien to us; for this purpose one's native tongue *is* required, with which—so to speak—one is born.[35]

The main problem of language in the Russian educated society went further than the Russian "school grammar" for Dostoevsky: "Russians—at least those belonging to the upper classes—have long ceased to be born with a live language; only subsequently do they acquire some kind of an artificial language, while they get to learn Russian virtually in school, by the grammar. Why, certainly, with eager desire and much diligence, one may, in the long run, re-educate oneself and, to a certain extent, learn the live Russian tongue, having been born with a dead one." [36] He humorously cites the example of a writer who became outstanding, who "had learned not only the Russian language, but even the Russian peasant and, in later days, he wrote novels dealing with peasant life." [37] The reference is to Pushkin who had to re-educate himself, and "he learned the popular language and the people's spirit *inter alia,* from his nurse Arina Rodionovna." [38]

Does it make any difference whether one learns French or Russian, since one has to have a *live* language? It is not the particular language but the native language which is important, Dostoevsky contends:

. . . to a Russian, the Russian tongue is nevertheless easier, despite the governesses and the mise-en-scene; and by all means, one has to take advantage of this case, while there is time. In order to master the Russian tongue in a more natural way, without specific strain, and not merely scientifically (of course by science I mean not only the school grammar), it is necessary, following the example of Arina Rodionovna, to borrow it from early childhood from Russian nurses without fearing that these might impart to the child various prejudices. . . .[39]

Youth must later on, of course, in school, memorize specimens of the Russian language, beginning with the most ancient epochs—annals, legends, and in the Church-Slavonic language, notwithstanding the limitations in the method of memorizing.[40] Dostoevsky also noted the lack of organized, structuralized forms in the Russian language, but nevertheless, "the spirit of our language is unquestionably multifaceted, wealthy, universal, and all-embracing, since even within its unorganized forms it has proved able to express the gems and treasures of European thought, and we feel these have been expressed correctly and with precision." [41]

Then, with the mastery of one's native tongue, and only after its mastery, is one in a position to master a foreign language. "We shall then imperceptibly appropriate from a foreign language several forms, alien to our tongue, and, also imperceptibly and involuntarily, we shall bring them in accord with the modalities of our thought, and we shall thereby broaden it." [42]

A year later, in 1877, Dostoevsky continued his argument about the native language, stating that the lack of independent thought and the imitation of the European mind lay "in the Russian language, i.e., the insufficiency of the Russian native tongue because of upbringing abroad, with foreign governesses and nurses." [43] For, in order to express the wealth of one's being, one must master a language, and that "there is such a mystery of nature, her law, by virtue of which man can have a perfect knowledge of that language only with which he is born, i.e., that which is spoken by the people to whom he belongs." [44]

One may know many languages and catch snatches of thoughts and sentiments of all nations, and make superficial valuations, a muddled concoction. But one should have a mastery of one language, and the native language is, of course, the most natural.[45] Dostoevsky emphasized the grave danger to character for the European-educated Russian of his time. Why such a danger to character? Because, in due time, thoughts, ideas and feelings arise and press upon one from within, demanding expression for themselves. Without "the rich ready forms of expression contracted since childhood," without the cultivation, fineness, the mastery of the nuances of one's native language, a person is dissatisfied.[46] Fragments of thoughts no longer satisfy, for life is experience accumulated in mind and heart, and demands elaborate expression.[47] This belief in the spiritual and psychological significance of language mastery as an aid to character development was important to Dostoevsky.

THE VALUE OF READING

In one of the letters to a parent, Dostoevsky was asked to recommend reading material for an adolescent daughter. Here one finds views, based on his own experience, about the problem of what to read.

First of all, reading itself nourishes the inborn capacity of imagination. Deprive a child of this and imagination "may die out or overdevelop itself." [48] Reading is valuable educationally, for moral sensitivity as well as for knowledge.[49]

Secondly, Dostoevsky listed authors and works which he thought significant. He included the works of Walter Scott and Dickens; they are suitable for youth from the age of twelve years. The literature of past centuries (*Don Quixote, Gil Blas,* etc.) is important. Of the Russian writers, he named Pushkin, Gogol, Turgenev, Leo Tolstoy, and Gontscharov; but of his own works Dostoevsky wrote: "I don't think that all of them are suitable for your daughter." [50] He considered the classics of Shakespeare, Schiller, and Goethe of great value, and "in general, historical works have immense educational value." [51] He listed the works of the Russian historians, Solovyev and Karamzin, as well as the American Prescott.[52]

Religious Education

On the subject of religious education and religious instruction, Dostoevsky actually has little to say, directly. He does affirm the idea of religious education itself, however.

First, religious education begins in the home; parents are responsible for the religious foundations of their children. In a letter to a parent, Dostoevsky advised: "Make the child acquainted with the Gospel, teach him to believe in God, and that in the most orthodox fashion. This is a *sine qua non;* otherwise you can't make a fine human being out of your child, but at best a sufferer, and at worst—a careless lethargic 'success,' which is still a more deplorable fate. You will never find anything better than the Saviour anywhere, believe me." [53]

He assumed that religious instruction was included in the general curriculum, along with the secular, cultural education, and the skills. He further held that religious instruction "should not be entrusted to anyone but priests." [54] However, lay teachers could relate stories and episodes from the history of the Church and from the Bible.[55]

Dostoevsky did not mention the issue of separation of

church and state, which probably means that he assumed the interrelationship of the two functions of these institutions. He is more concerned with the essence of religious learning. Pointing out that there is a difference between bureaucratic moralizing and real spiritual beauty in religious instruction, he wrote: "But it would be best if pupils were simply told episodes from the history of the Church without any special bureaucratic moral, temporarily confining the religious instruction to this alone. A series of pure, holy, beautiful pictures would exercise a potent influence upon their souls craving beautiful impressions." [56]

WOMEN'S EDUCATION

The question of women's higher education was one of the pressing social and educational problems of mid-nineteenth-century Europe and America.[57] The historian Kornilov wrote that in Russia "before 1863 women had forced themselves into the universities as 'free hearers,' or unclassified students; but the commission which discussed the statute of 1863 rejected the clause about admitting women into universities." [58] Nevertheless, women continued to attend the lectures which were open to both sexes. D. A. Tolstoy, as Minister of Education from 1866 to 1880, opposed higher education for women, but he yielded on the point of their "attending" lectures read by university professors. Women had been filling the universities of Switzerland, since they were deprived of higher education in the universities at home. In Switzerland they came into contact with the "upsetting" socialist and anarchistic views.[59]

Ushinskii had reformed the Smolny Institute for Noble Girls in the sixties, bringing about a high standard in women's education. Qualified women of the upper classes were now pressing for admittance into the universities in the late sixties and throughout the seventies.[60]

Dostoevsky was particularly concerned about the access to institutions of higher learning for women. It was this field of higher education to which he gave his attention. In *The Diary* for 1873, he wrote:

I have already stated that in her resides our only great hope, one of the pledges of our revival. The regeneration of the Russian woman during the last twenty years has proved unmistakable. The rise in her quests has been lofty, candid, and fearless. From the start it has commanded respect or, at least, made people think of it, despite several parasitic anomalies which have revealed themselves in this movement. At present, however, it is already possible to render an accounting and to draw an undaunted conclusion. The Russian woman chastely ignored all obstacles and all scoffs. She resolutely announced her desire to participate in the common cause and proceeded in this direction, not only disinterestedly but even self-denyingly. During these last decades the Russian man has become terribly addicted to the debauch of acquisition, cynicism and materialism. But the woman has remained much more faithful to the pure worship of the idea, to the duty of serving the idea. In her thirst for higher education she has revealed earnestness, patience, and has set an example of the greatest courage. *The Writer's Diary* has given me an opportunity of beholding the Russian woman at closer range. I have received several remarkable letters. They ask me, the incompetent, "what to do?" I value these questions, and I make up for any lack of competency in my answers with sincerity. I regret that I am unable, and have no right, to recount here many a thing.[61]

Dostoevsky did not eulogize uncritically the Russian woman. His honesty and realism also detected a fault in the contemporary woman:

I also perceive certain faults in the contemporary woman, and her principal fault—her extraordinary dependency upon several essentially masculine ideas; her inclination to accept them credulously and to believe in them without scrutiny. I am by no means speaking of all women; but this defect is also proof of excellent qualities of the heart; women value most a fresh feeling, a live word; but what they treasure even more is sincerity, and once they believe in sincerity, even if it be a false one, they are inspired by certain opinions—and this, at times, excessively. In the future, higher education could be of great help in this respect. By admitting, sincerely and fully, higher education for women, with all the rights granted by it, Russia once more would take a great and original stride in advance of all Europe in the great cause of the renaissance of mankind.[62]

In a later issue of *The Diary*, for 1876, Dostoevsky approached the problem of higher education for women in another way. He wrote of a student who had called on him and asked for his advice, whether she should go to serve in the Balkan war and care for the sick and wounded, or whether she should continue her education. Undaunted by his painting of a dark picture of war and suffering, the young woman was an example of the genre which Dostoevsky described as follows:

Here we have precisely the same straightforward honest but inexperienced young feminine character—with that proud chastity which does not fear and cannot be soiled even by contact with vice. Here is an urge for sacrifice, for work supposedly expected of her, and the conviction that it is necessary and that she must start herself, first without any excuses, all the good which she expects and demands from other people—a conviction which is sound and moral in the highest degree, but one which, alas, is inherent mostly in youthful purity and innocence. But the main point is—I repeat—that here there is only work, and not the slightest vainglory; not the slightest self-conceit, and self-infatuation with one's personal exploit, which—contrariwise—we often perceive in our contemporaneous young men, even among mere raw youths.[63]

This occasion raised in Dostoevsky's mind the question of higher education for women which was "a most urgent necessity, particularly in view of the serious quest of work in the present-day woman, quest of education, of participation in the common cause. I believe that the fathers and mothers of these daughters should be insisting on this themselves. . . ." [64] Only the highest science possesses sufficient seriousness for them: "Only science is capable of answering their questions, of strengthening their minds and, so to speak, of placing under its tutelage their seething thought." [65] For Dostoevsky, the strict discipline of the sciences required diligence, but this by no means excluded the deeper, spiritual side of man. Often life experiences themselves form part of education:

I believe that in a way this journey to the war zone may, perhaps, even prove useful to her: all the same, this is not a bookish world, not an abstract conviction, but an enormous forthcoming experience which God Himself, in His infinite goodness, has sent her. Here is a forthcoming lesson for her active life—an ensuing broadening of her thought and views; here is a future reminiscence, for her whole life, of something dear and beautiful, in which she had taken part and which will make her treasure life and not get tired of it without actually having lived.[66]

In advocating higher education for women, Dostoevsky gave his support to the liberal but minority voices which were pressing in Europe and in Russia for full equality of rights for women.[67]

The Foundation of Education for Citizenship

From *The Diary* it is clear that Dostoevsky was a national patriot, urging his countrymen to respect and to further the greatness of their nation. One of the central themes in Dostoevsky's journalistic writings and letters was his insistence that the educated classes cease their "imitation" of Europe; they should turn to their own heritage. In this respect, Dostoevsky was close to the Slavophiles.[68]

There are no questions raised in *The Diary* about the separation of church and state, or about the rights of the people to a free, compulsory, secular education. Rather the theocratic principle of the unity between church and state can be assumed, and as a corollary, the ideal of "sobornost," that is, a cohesive unity in community life.

Dostoevsky's approach to the problem of citizenship as a concern for the entire nation, including the younger generation, is developed from the ethical perspective; it is an educational problem as well as a politico-social one. He developed his thesis as follows: The problem of allegiance to one's native land involves attention to the historical reality in addition to the ideal for one's nation. Citizenship is a fundamental question for the education of youth. Dostoevsky wrote: "There is a seriousness in our youth, and I pray God only that it be directed more intelligently." [69]

The first question which arises for the citizen is whether there is or can be a different moral ideal for the individual and for the nation. In his view, Dostoevsky states: "Let that which is truth to man as an individual be also truth to the nation as a whole. Yes, of course, one may be temporarily put to a loss, one may be impoverished for the time being, deprived of markets; one's production may be curtailed and the cost of living may increase. But let the nation's organism remain morally healthy, and the nation will undoubtedly gain more, even materially." [70] He does not accept a moral relativism, and says in reference to Russia, . . . "we, as a political organism, have always believed in eternal morality, and not in a relative one, good but for a few days." [71] A duo-morality should not split a nation either:

. . . it is necessary that in political organisms the same Christ's truth be recognized as by any believer. Somewhere at least this truth must be preserved; some nation at least must radiate. Otherwise what would happen? Everything would be dimmed, distorted and would be drowned in cynicism. Otherwise you would be unable to restrain the morality of the individual citizens, too, and in this event how is the entire organism of the people going to live? Authority is needed. It is necessary that the sun shine.[72]

The Christian ideal for the nation in its political life should be the challenging one, and Dostoevsky hoped that his country would radiate this truth.[73] Further on he speaks of the "sustaining ideal" of a people in general:

Nations live by a great sentiment, a great all-unifying and all-illuminating thought; by cohesion of the people, and, finally, on condition that the people, involuntarily consider themselves to be in accord with their upper men. This generates national vigor. This is what nations live by, and not merely by stock-exchange speculations, and by concern about the rate of the ruble. The wealthier a nation is spiritually, the richer it is materially.[74]

What is important, then, is that "which the people believe as their truth; in what they conceive and perceive in it; what they recognize as their loftiest aspiration; what they love; what they are asking from God; what they worshipfully lament." [75] This can be meant for nations in general, but for Russia, Dostoevsky believed that Orthodoxy contained the "sustaining ideal": "And does not Orthodoxy comprise everything, indeed everything, which they [the people] are seeking? Isn't there in Orthodoxy alone both the truth and the salvation of the Russian people? . . ." [76] In Orthodoxy, in its purity, the Divine image of Christ has been preserved.[77] "And perhaps, the most momentous preordained destiny of the Russian people, within the destinies of mankind at large, consists in the preservation in their midst of the Divine image of Christ. . . ." [78]

Upon what is the organic unity of a people based? The strength of a great moral idea lies in the fact that

. . . it cements men into a most solid union; that it is not measured in terms of benefit but makes men aspire to the future, to eternal aims and absolute gladness. How will you unite men for the attainment of your civic aims if there is no foundation in the form of an initial great moral idea? But all moral ideas are identical: they are all based upon the principle of absolute individual self-betterment in the future, in an ideal which comprises all aspirations, all longings, and consequently, all our civic ideals emanate there-from. Just try to cement men into a civic society with the sole aim of "saving their skins"!—You will derive nothing but the moral formula: *"Chacun pour soi et Dieu pour tous."* With such a formula no civic institution can live long.[79]

Dostoevsky's phrase "initial great moral idea" simply means here the highest value, the primary and ultimate value which men hold to be truth for them. He does not say directly that it is Christian. However, as will be seen, the foundation of a people's highest value has, historically, its roots within and emanates from the religious consciousness of a people. He speaks of "social ideals" first:

. . . there are not social, civic ideals, as such, not originally tied to moral ideals, and existing independently in the form of a separate half, chipped off from the whole with your scientific knife, ideals which can be borrowed from without and successfully transplanted into any new spot in the form of a separate "institution." There are no such ideals, they never have existed, never can exist.

Besides, what is a social ideal? How is one to understand the term?—of course, its essence resides in the attempt of men to find a formula of social organization, faultless, if possible, and satisfying everybody. Isn't this so? But men do not know such a formula. Men have been looking for it during six thousand years of their historical existence, and they have failed to find it. The ant knows its ant-hill formula; the bee the formula of its beehive (even though they do not know them in a human way; they know them in their own way, and this is all they need). Man, however, does not know his formula.[80]

From whence, then, comes the ideal of civic organization in human society? Dostoevsky continues:

Trace it historically and you will forthwith perceive whence it is derived. You will see that it is solely the product of moral self-betterment of individual entities; it has its inception there. Thus it has been from time immemorial, and thus it always will be. In the origin of every people, of every nationality, the moral idea invariably preceded the origination of the nationality itself, *since the former created the latter*. The moral idea always emanated from mystical ideas, from the conviction that man is eternal, that he is not a mere earthly animal, but that he is tied to other worlds and eternity. Invariably and everywhere these beliefs assumed the form of religion, the form of a confession of the new idea. And just as soon as a new religion came into being, a new civic nationality came into existence. Look at the Hebrews and the Mohammedans: Jewish nationality came into being after the Mosaic Law, even its beginning can be traced to the law of Abraham, while the Mohammedan nationalities arose only after the Koran.[81]

And further:

To preserve the acquired spiritual treasure, men are forthwith attracted to each other, and only then do they zealously and anxiously, *"working beside each other, one for the other, one with another"* . . . begin to investigate how they should organize so as to preserve the treasure without losing any part of it; how to find such a *civic* formula of common existence as would help them to promote throughout the world the acquired moral treasure in its full glory.[82]

Dostoevsky states next that the civic or social ideals of a nation are integrally connected with the nation's moral ideals. When the spiritual-moral ideal weakens, the civic ideals begin to degenerate.[83]

And please observe that just as soon as after centuries and ages . . . the spiritual ideal of this or that nationality begins to loosen and weaken, the nationality begins to degenerate, together with its civic constitution, and the civic ideals which have moulded themselves within it become extinct. The civic forms of a people assume the character in which their religion is expressed. Therefore the civic ideals are always directly and organically tied to the moral ideals, and—what is most important—the former indisputably are derived only from the latter. Civic ideals never appear of their own accord because when they do appear they have as their only object the consummation of the moral aspirations of the given nationality, in the form and in so far as these moral aspirations have moulded themselves in that nationality.

On this ground "self-betterment in a religious sense" in the life of the peoples is the foundation of everything, since self-betterment is *the confession of the acquired religion,* whereas "civic ideals," devoid of this longing for self-betterment, never do appear, and never can come into being.

. . . Individual self-betterment is not only "the *beginning* of everything," but also its continuation and outcome. It—and it alone—embraces, creates and preserves the national organism. It is for the sake of self-betterment that the civic formula of a nation exists, since it came into being only for its preservation as an initially acquired treasure.[84]

It is not possible to maintain that social progress is dependent upon social *institutions* which mold in man, if not Christian, then civic virtues, Dostoevsky states, because when a "nationality loses the urge of individual self-betterment *in the spirit which procreated it,* gradually, all 'civic institutions' begin to disappear because there is nothing more to preserve." [85]

How can one divide Christian and civic virtues, he asks:

"If not Christian, then civic virtues!" Doesn't one see here the scientific knife dividing the indivisible, cutting a homogeneous live organism into two separate halves—the moral and the civic? You may say that "social institutions" and the dignity of the "citizen" may comprise a very great moral idea; that "the civic idea" in ripe and developed nations always replaces the initial religious idea which degenerates into the former and which it legitimately inherits. Quite so, this is being maintained by many people, but thus far we have never seen this fantasy realized. When in a nation the moral or religious idea wears itself out, there always comes the panicky, cowardly urge to unite for the sole purpose of "saving the skins": then no other civic unity exists. At present, for instance, the French bourgeoisie sticks together only for the purpose of "saving its skin" from the fourth estate which tries to break into its door.

This idea of "saving one's skin" is the lowest of all ideas uniting mankind, Dostoevsky maintains:

. . . This is the beginning of the end. People pretend to stick together, but at the same time they are on a sharp look-out for the first moment of danger, ready to disperse. And what,

in this case, can an "institution" as such, save? If there be
brethren, there will be brotherhood. But if there are no
brethren no "institution" will ever produce brotherhood.
What is the sense of establishing an "institution" and inscrib-
ing on it: *Liberté, Égalité, Fraternité!* Nothing will be
achieved by an "institution," so that it will become necessary,
quite inevitably, to add to these three "constituent" words,
three new ones: "où la mort," "fraternité où la mort," and
brethren in order to achieve brotherhood through "the civic
institution." [86]

Dostoevsky repudiates a civic policy of self-interest. The
social and political expression of a nation must be united
organically with the religious and moral foundations. A
severance between the two is "the beginning of the end."

Chapter Four

Dostoevsky and
Character Education

DURING THE LAST TEN YEARS of his life, Dostoevsky was visited by many students who frequently came to
him for advice concerning their education. Their questions
dealt with the furthering of their studies, or choice of profession. But, most significantly, they came for guidance in
finding the purpose of their lives.[1] Dostoevsky's extant correspondence contains letters received from both students
and parents. The letters cover a variety of educational
problems: the question of general or specialized education,
religious upbringing and instruction, works to be read by
the adolescent, responsibility in contemporary social and
political events of the nation, professional work, *et al.*[2]
  The theme of youth recurs in Dostoevsky's *Diary of a
Writer.* Several educational issues and their contemporaneous situations, problems which were of vital concern for
youth, are carefully and critically examined by Dostoevsky.
Three works in addition to *The Diary* are of special significance to the psychological study of character: "The Little
Hero," a short story; *Netochka Nezvanovna,* an unfinished
novel; and *The Raw Youth.* These three works are studies
of the adolescent. By education Dostoevsky meant the nurture of character rather than a pedagogical "study of the
learning process."

THE IMPACT OF SOCIETY UPON THE CHARACTER OF YOUTH

The influence of the ideological atmosphere or *Zeitgeist* upon the young generation may constitute social and political problems of culture, but, for Dostoevsky, this influence is also a primary educational problem; it relates to the moral foundation of character. His critique and analysis is, of course, in reference to the Russian society of his time, but the principles are applicable to the influence of society upon youth in general. In this respect he belongs to the tradition of educational thinkers like Plato, Comenius, and Pestalozzi, who recognized the importance of the role of society in the influence upon the character of youth.

The phenomenon of the young nihilist revolutionary, bent upon destructive activities in society, was one issue which Dostoevsky analyzed. The problem is introduced by the following passage:

Some of my critics have observed that in my last novel *The Possessed* I have made use of the plot of the notorious Nechaiev case; but they hastened to add that . . . I took the phenomenon and merely sought to explain the possibility of its occurrence in our society as a social phenomenon . . . all this is quite correct . . . I have read in *The Russian World* the following curious lines: "It seems to us that the Nechaiev case could have demonstrated the fact that our student youth does not participate in such follies. An idiotic fanatic of the Nechaiev pattern manages to recruit proselytes only among idlers, defectives—and not at all among the youths attending to their studies." And further: ". . . all the more so as only a few days ago the Minister of Public Education had declared (in Kiev) that after the inspection of the educational institutions in seven districts he could state that '*in recent years the youth has adopted an infinitely more serious attitude toward the problem of learning and has been studying far more diligently.' " [3]*

This one illustration from the many in the press raised a very important issue, Dostoevsky thought. Were the critics trying to shield the college youth or flatter them? True, some youth are fond of flattery, though by no means the entire younger generation. Furthermore, "led-astray" youth are not composed of idle defectives. Yes, there may be among youth some disconsolate creatures

with a thirst for intrigue of a most complex origin and for power, with a passionate and pathologically premature urge to reveal their personalities, but why should they be called "idiots"?—On the contrary, even real monsters among them may be highly developed, most crafty and even educated people. Or you may think, perhaps, that knowledge, "training," little bits of school information (picked up even in universities) finally mould a youth's soul to the extent that, upon receipt of his diploma, he immediately acquires an irrevocable talisman enabling him once and forever to learn the truth, to avoid temptations, passions and vices? [4]

The significant point raised by Dostoevsky is that the formation of character involves much more than formal education. The moral factor in the nurture of character is at the center of the educational process.[5]

The followers of these radical youths, and one cannot separate the isolated case from the generic whole, are not simple defectives; they had indeed learned something, Dostoevsky points out. They had learned the revolutionary socialist idea of reforming society:

. . . in my novel *The Possessed* I made the attempt to depict the manifold and heterogeneous motives which may prompt even the purest of heart and the most naïve people to take part in the perpetration of so monstrous a villainy. The horror lies precisely in the fact that in our midst . . . the most villainous act may be committed by one who is not a villain at all! This, however, happens not only in our midst but throughout the whole world; it has been so from time immemorial, during transitional epochs, at times of violent commotion in people's lives—doubts, negations, scepticism, and vacillation regarding the fundamental social convictions. But in our midst this is more possible than anywhere else, and precisely in our day; this is the most pathological and saddest trait of our present time—the possibility of considering oneself not as a villain, and sometimes almost not being one, while perpetrating a patent and incontestable villainy— therein is our present-day calamity! [6]

Dostoevsky continues by pointing out that the suppression of independent thought, the aping of Europeanism, and the disparagement of one's native land has infected the younger generation.[7] The European "teachers"—the Mills, Darwins, Strausses—"sometimes consider the moral obligations of modern man in a most astonishing manner." [8] Dostoevsky refers here to the contemporary radical Westernizers in Russian thought, particularly the influence of Chernyshevsky, Dobroliubov, Bakunin, Mihailovski, et al, who had accepted the European philosophies of utilitarianism, positivism, and radical socialism. These men who represent the educated society have become a compelling influence upon the younger generation. While their ideas seem to be lofty and noble, these "teachers," if given the opportunity to destroy the old society and build it up anew, would create chaos and blindness.[9] The dilemma facing youth is the uprootedness from their own, that is, Russia's heritage.[10]

In a lengthy letter to a group of Moscow university students who had appealed to him because they were concerned about their social and moral responsibilities in one

of the student outbursts of the late seventies, Dostoevsky
had a good deal to say to them about the uprootedness of
contemporary youth. He did not blame them for the outbursts, for they "were children of this very society. . . ." [11]
However, the dilemma of the youth rested upon the fact
that "the younger generation lives in dreams, follows foreign teaching, cares to know nothing that concerns Russia,
aspires, rather to instruct the fatherland. Consequently
. . . the younger generation becomes prey to one or another of those political parties which influence it wholly
from the outside, which care not for its interests, but use
it. . . ." [12] And what do the students do? They flee abroad
and talk about the "Universal man," thus severing all
bonds which still connect them with the Russian people.[13]
As these students were of the *narodniki* intelligentsia, Dostoevsky explained to them why they, who loved humanity
and would liberate the people, were repudiated by the
Russian people themselves:

. . . Instead of living the life of the people, these young men,
who understand the people in no wise, and profoundly scorn
its every fundamental principle—for example, its religion—go
to the people *not* to learn to know it, but condescendingly to
instruct and patronize it: a thoroughly aristocratic game! The
people call them "young gentlemen," and rightly. It is really
very strange; all over the world, the democrats have ever been
on the side of the people; with us alone have the democratic
intellectuals leagued themselves with the aristocrats against
the people; they go among the people "to do it good," while
scorning all its customs and ideals. Such scorn cannot possibly
lead to love! [14]

Again Dostoevsky points out the basic significance of one's
moral attitude toward others.

Concluding his letter to the students, Dostoevsky restated that they were in no wise to blame for the outbursts,

but that they had a grave responsibility in healing the breach between the upper classes and the people. In order to do this "one must first of all learn not to scorn the people; . . . in the second place, one must believe in God, which is impossible for Russian Europeans. . . ." [15]

THE RE-EDUCATION OF "INSULTED AND INJURED" YOUTH

In *The Diary* Dostoevsky called attention especially to the "insulted and injured" children and youth.[16] These would be the "juvenile delinquents" today. The problem then as now was how to re-educate these youth and to bring them back into society as responsible citizens. The occasion of visiting one such juvenile home for delinquent boys provided the opportunity for him to state his views. He described a day in the colony where about fifty boys, ages seven to seventeen, lived in a family setup. The momentous problem was to eradicate the dreadful impressions that had been made upon their souls. The director of the home informed Dostoevsky of one means of reform: "work; an altogether different way of living, and fairness in our dealings with them. Finally—the hope that after three years their old predelictions and habits will be forgotten of their own accord, by the mere lapse of time." [17]

Another method of reform was the institution of autonomous justice. Dostoevsky's thought on this was as follows:

Essentially, this autonomous court is, of course, a good thing, but it smacks of something bookish. There are many proud children—proud in a good sense—who may feel insulted by this self-governing authority of boys and delinquents such as themselves; and thus they may misunderstand this authority. There may happen to be some individuals much more talented and clever than the rest of the "family," and the judgment of their milieu may thwart their ambition and instill hate into them. And the milieu is practically always the average, the mediocre. Besides, do the boys themselves, when passing judgment, properly understand their business? On the contrary, is it not possible that among them, too, there might develop children's groups of some rivalling boys, stronger, more alert than the others, who always and unfailingly appear among children in all schools, and who give tone to the rest and lead the others as by a rope?— After all, these are only children—not adults.[18]

The private and personal attention and care of one of the youths, undertaken by the director of the colony, and which brought about the transformation of the boy, gave Dostoevsky the opportunity of noting what he held to be a key educational principle. He suggests indirectly that the underlying power of love and trust in an inviolable personal confidence can redeem a distorted and injured life.

Another observation to which he calls the reader's attention was the instructor's participation with the boys in the performance of work.[19] "This is the most perfect understanding of one's vocation and of one's human dignity," he wrote. This again stresses the inner attitude of respect towards others and fosters the ideas of co-operation and mutual dignity.

The significance of this account lies not only in the questions raised by Dostoevsky about the methods of autonomous justice and work, but in the emphasis upon the moral attitude. The instances of personal care, time, and effort which Dostoevsky describes contain significant psychological and educational principles in human relations.

IDEALS OF YOUTH

What really counts in the life of a youth is "purity of heart, the thirst for sacrifice and glorious exploits which gleam in him so brightly." [20] In his article "A Few Words About Youth," Dostoevsky saw in contemporary families no such sublime aims for life. Not only "do they [the families] not give the slightest thought to the idea of immortality[21] but much too frequently a satirical attitude is adopted toward it—and this in the presence of children from their early childhood, and perhaps with an express didactic purpose." [22] It is clear that if there are no ideals within, youth will seek them without, on its own resources:

This problem is all too important at this moment. . . . Our youth is so placed that absolutely nowhere does it find advice as to the loftiest meaning of life. From our brainy people, and, generally, from its leaders, youth—I repeat—can borrow merely a rather satirical view, but nothing *positive*, i.e., in what to believe, what should be respected and adored, what should be sought; and yet all this is so needed, so indispensable to youth; there is, always has been, craving for this in all ages and everywhere.[23]

He concludes by stating that the contemporary family and the school have both become indifferent to the vital religious and moral questions of life. Thus, quite naturally, the important and interesting problems shifted to the interest and absorption in the "practical." [24] Dostoevsky again focuses our attention upon the development of moral character of the highest quality which is based upon religious foundations, and he relates this to the social life in the family and in the community.

PSYCHOLOGICAL OBSERVATIONS ON CHILDREN AND YOUTH

Dostoevsky's observations of childhood and adolescence can be studied in *The Diary* and in many of his fictional works. His contributions to the science of psychology have been recognized by European pioneers in this field.[25]

In the article entitled "An Anecdote from Children's Lives" Dostoevsky recounted an event which involved a rash action of an adolescent girl.[26] The opportunity afforded him the chance to draw his readers' attention to this "curious age of adolescence" which results in sudden awakenings of dreams and fantasies. The resolute action of the contemporary youth upon these fantasies, that is, their lack of restraint posed a special problem. Formerly a sense of duty, of obligation towards parents and principles, and convictions restrained action. Now, however, there was a "looseness." Even more important was the psychological phenomenon of the split personality, that is, two dissimilar halves which awaken in the adolescent and constitute a critical danger in their lives. This phenomenon of the "split" in personality should be studied by pedagogues.[27] In Dostoevsky's words: "[adolescence] is an age which still retains the most touching infantile innocence and immaturity, on the one hand—and, on the other, which has already acquired an avidly quick faculty of apperceiving and readily familiarizing itself with such ideas and conceptions as . . . this age cannot even conceive." [28]

In another article he made further significant observations on child psychology. First, on detecting the mediocre and the talented: "It stands to reason that the most unrestrained and cheerful are those who in the future will belong to mediocrity and be without talent: this is a general rule; mediocrity is always unrestrained; be it among children or among parents. More gifted and segregated children are always more reserved, and if they are joyous, it is invariably with a knack at leadership and bossing." [29] Secondly, Dostoevsky called the tendency to make things easy for children "soft pedagogy." He touched on the areas of study and play: "It is a pity that nowadays everything is being made easy for children, not merely study, acquisition of all knowledge, but even plays and toys. Just as soon as a child begins to lisp its first words, forthwith people begin to relieve it. At present pedagogy is altogether dedicated to the task of relieving. At times easement does not signify progress but, on the contrary, constitutes a deviation." [30] Studies and play must suit the age, of course, but this is different from the encouragement of children and youth in their own initiative and ingenuity. The "difficult" in itself is sometimes the challenging and lasting motivation. This brings us to the third point—that of accomplishing something by one's own effort:

Two or three thoughts, two or three impressions, deeply felt in childhood as a result of one's own effort (or, if you please, also as a result of suffering) will enable a child to penetrate life much more deeply than the easiest school which frequently produces something that is neither this nor that, neither good nor bad—something that even in depravity is not depraved, and in virtue not virtuous.[31]

Closely related to this is the importance of childhood experiences: "The strongest and most influential recollections are those produced in childhood . . . unquestionably, those memories and impressions—possibly the strongest and most sacred ones—will be carried into life . . . by present-day children." [32]

In one of the letters, Dostoevsky discussed the fancy of children:

. . . fancy is an inborn capacity of human beings; in a child, it outweighs all others, and should most undoubtedly be nourished. For if we give a child's imagination no nourishment, it may easily die out, or, on the other hand, may over-develop itself from its own sheer force, which is no less desirable. For such an abnormal overdevelopment prematurely exhausts the child's mental powers. And impressions of the beautiful, moreover, are precisely in childhood of the greatest importance.[33]

Thus, Dostoevsky introduced in Russia a new psychological and educational approach to the child and to the youth for both teachers and parents.[34]

One can study Dostoevsky's psychological insights in the full length novels. They provide rich material for the psychologist.[35] *The Diary* was in many respects Dostoevsky's means of recording his observations and analyses of children and youth. His findings were incorporated into the major work, *The Raw Youth,* and in his last novel, *The Brothers Karamazov.* A serious and systematic study of childhood nature and youthful adolescent nature as understood by Dostoevsky has yet to be undertaken. The attempt here is to open up and to indicate the materials which are pertinent to a more intensive study.

Two shorter and earlier works of Dostoevsky, both written in the forties, trace the period from childhood through adolescence. The first work is a story, "The Little Hero," which unfolds the inner psychological and spiritual awakening of an eleven-year-old boy who comes to the threshold of adolescence. The second work is an unfinished novel, *Netochka Nezvanovna,* which is a study of childhood and adolescence to the threshold of adulthood. In both works the child is seen as a fully structuralized personality: Dostoevsky views the human being as a unique, unitive personality, in contrast, one can say, to the genetic, biological interpretation of human nature (of G. Stanley Hall, for example). Dostoevsky's view of the human soul is spiritual and psychological.

The theme of *The Raw Youth* is the relationship between father and son, a simple but universal problem. The

German critic Meier-Graefe has written that ". . . it is only after arduous reading that the educational trend becomes apparent. . . . It is another of Dostoevsky's studies of childhood by a mind which had matured since "The Little Hero." He adds further: "The psychological relationship is only gradually revealed. The current theory of an Oedipus-complex could, if necessary, be completely refuted, for the reason that everything in the work seems to point to it." [36]

Arkady, the hero of the work, is the product of the contemporary "accidental family" of Dostoevsky's time. [37] The youth is full of promise, vital and quick in temperament, idealistic and searching for meaning to his life. Dostoevsky gradually unfolds the inner spiritual growth of the "raw youth" who comes to the threshold of adulthood. The scenes between father and son reveal the process of genuine human relationships, which take time to ripen. They finally are truly father and son.

These studies of adolescence, *Netochka Nezvanovna* and *The Raw Youth*, would be a valuable aid to teachers for the psychological understanding of youth from ages twelve to twenty; I am convinced of this from many years of teaching experience. The above-mentioned works seem to confirm the textbook theoretical presentations, and illustrate in a dramatic way the psychological processes of adolescence.

Meier-Graefe is one of the few critics who has discerned the significance of Dostoevsky's insight and grasp of childhood and adolescent natures, not only for literature, but for pedagogy:

Dostoevsky introduced the child into literature. Previously it had been granted only a supernumerary role with its stereotyped smile reminiscent of the *putti* of Donatello and Della

Robbia, merely a pleasant ornament. Dostoevsky gave the little person his atmosphere, which was not limited to dolls and fairy-tales, and indicated his place in the world of adults. He dispelled the traditional notion and revealed countless living types, as well as versatility in the type. Dostoevsky's children live through their eyes; their sight is keener than that of adults, they visualize in the picturesque and simple reliefs of the Primitives. Their co-ordination is neither the result of psychological experience nor directed by any sense of personal interest. The child's restricted field of selection forces on it a more definite decision and disposes it to heroism. Dostoevsky's child is far less young than the primitive being who does not need learning as a guide to thought and action.[38]

He continues: "Objectivity was at bottom the most essential token of his love." True, Dostoevsky comprehended the incalculable qualities of the child. His children have the quality "which distinguishes the human being from plants and are children in spite of it, are in fact children for that very reason. . . . His last and most significant work does not for nothing conclude with a chorale of youth to the future. He is lost who loses his childhood. The world without childhood succumbs." [39]

Dostoevsky anticipated both psychoanalysis and psychiatry.[40] He was directly interested in the psychic phenomena of the mind and soul and how to redeem the sick soul; his concern was the religious-ethical and educative one. He was not interested in illnesses or the pathological per se. This is the meaning of his own statement: "They call me a realist and a psychologist. I am not. I am a realist in the higher sense, that is, I depict all the depths of the human soul." [41]

The purpose here, however, is not to enter upon a presentation or analysis of Dostoevsky's general psychological insights. This field can be studied in many competent texts.[42] However, his studies of the young remain valuable for the educator, verifying textbook expositions by way of image and dramatic situation.

THE ROLE OF THE FAMILY IN THE FORMATION OF CHARACTER

Dostoevsky's analysis and critique of the family, as well as his positive ideal of the family are treated in several articles in his *Diary*. First, his critique:

To my way of thinking, the casualness of the contemporary Russian family consists of the loss by the modern fathers of every general idea about their families, an idea general to all fathers, tying them all together, which they themselves believe in, and which they would teach their children to believe in, conveying to them this faith for their lives. . . . A general idea binding society and the family is the beginning of order, i.e., moral order.[43]

Moral order, Dostoevsky continues, is subject to change, progression, correction, but it is order. And where you have no general belief binding and holding people together, what do you have? Cynicism and relativity: "First wholesale, sweeping renunciation of the past (renunciation and nothing positive); second, attempts to say something positive, yet neither general nor binding; but everyone in his own way—attempts parcelled into units and individuals, devoid of experience, practice, even without full faith in them on the part of their inventors. . . . Finally, an indolent attitude toward work." [44] Never has the Russian family been "shaken so loose, more disintegrated, more unsorted, and more uninformed." [45] There was, formerly, character completeness, although not all families were wholesome, Dostoevsky declares. Nowadays there is *casualness*. While externals are taken care of, that is, food, clothing, shelter, formal education, still there is no father because "the lad enters life alone because his heart has not lived, it is not bound with youth's past, with family or childhood." [46] What is the picture of family upbringing in the contemporary times? Dostoevsky's answer is:

Our young men belonging to the educated classes, brought up in the fold of their families, where, as a rule, one encounters dissatisfaction, impatience, coarse ignorance (despite the fact that these are educated classes), and in which, almost everywhere, for genuine education is substituted impudent negation of other people's opinions; where material motives prevail over the loftiest idea; where children are brought up without foundation, without natural truth, with disrespect for, and indifference to, their native land and with a scoffing contempt for the people, which has been spreading so fast, particularly in recent times—is it from here, this well-spring, that our young men will draw the truth and faultlessness of their convictions during the initial stage of their lives? [47]

Furthermore, in the majority of the poor families, children will carry bad memories from the cheating and cruelty they see. Despite the cruelest surroundings of childhood, only a great faith is capable of "generating *the beautiful* in children's memories." [48] This faith is lacking, says Dostoevsky, and "man should not step out of childhood into life without the embryos of something positive and beautiful; without these a generation should not be permitted to start on its life journey." [49]

Dostoevsky's positive ideal of the family was that is it a holy unit, a living organism of active and incessant labors of love:

. . . only when these creatures penetrate our souls and take hold of our hearts when we, having begotten them, are watching *over* them ever since their childhood, never parting with them from the time of their first smile, and thereafter continuing spiritually to be mutually drawn closer to each other, day after day, hour after hour, throughout our whole lives. This is family; this is sanctity!

The family is *created*, and is not given to us ready-made; and here no obligations are made to order, but they all result one from another. Only then is this unit solid; only then— holy. And the family is created by the incessant labor of love.[50]

Thus, sanctities are founded upon faith in the ideals of family life: "We love our sanctities but only because they are, in fact, holy. We support them not only to defend *l'ordre* by using them. Our sanctities are founded not upon their utility but upon our faith in them. . . . We love the sanctity of the family when it is in reality holy, and not because the state is solidly founded upon it." [51]

Two public court trials of families who had maltreated their children (The Kronberg Case of 1876 and The Djunkovsky Case of 1877) were studied and analyzed by Dostoevsky. The educational implications for the whole society which were involved in the issues and in the decisions are discussed by him. The latter case illustrated the casual or "accidental family" which Dostoevsky elaborated in *The Raw Youth*. His psychological insight into young children in these cases is extremely revealing. For example, he drew attention to the importance of children's unconscious trust, the play of fancy in childhood nature, and the assertion of will.[52]

Dostoevsky illustrated his ideas about the nurture of children in the form of an imaginary judge's discourse. His appeal was to the court of conscience. He pointed out that patience and zeal are required in love, and that it is a natural and civic duty as well as a labor of love to bring up children. Always in the correction of a child, to torture or to humiliate another being is bad psychology because "even within a child, the smallest child, there is structuralized human dignity." [53] Dostoevsky's view of the human soul is that it is an independent entity, a spiritual whole. Next he speaks of the role of the teacher: a teacher instructs and is a guide, a friend to children and youth, but no parent. The idea that parents turn over their parental responsibility to the teacher is an erroneous one, for children require "constant, uninterrupted contact" with their parents' souls. Spiritually, parents should be objects of love, of genuine respect and beautiful imitation." [54] The labors of love, incessant training, explaining, admonition (for discipline there must be as well), reasoning when this dawns in the lives of youth, and patience are the principle points stressed by Dostoevsky. "Even love is a labor, even in love one has to learn." [55] He concludes with the following:

If parents are kind, if their love for their children is zealous and fervent, children will forgive many a comical and ugly thing, and they will not unconditionally condemn them even for some of their altogether bad deeds; on the contrary, their hearts will unfailingly find extenuating circumstances. . . . Seek love, and store love in your hearts. Love is so omnipotent that it even regenerates ourselves. It is only with love, and not with our natural authority over our children that we buy their hearts. . . . Should we cease to love children, whom then would we love? And what would become of us?— Recall that it was only for the sake of children, for the sake of their little golden-haired heads, that our Saviour promised to curtail "the times and the seasons." [56]

SUMMARY

From the foregoing material, it can be seen that Dostoevsky's main emphasis is on the ethical aspect of education in the sense of upbringing, nurture for character. The impact of the *Zeitgeist* of society and the atmosphere in the life of the family are the most formative and developmental factors from which youth learns the fundamental ideals and values for life.

Dostoevsky's psychological observations and discoveries about the nature of the young are now familiar to us, but, for his own historical times, he was well in advance of the science of psychology which has now validated and verified many of his intuitions, insights, and observations. It might be helpful to cite significant statements here. René Fueloep-Miller wrote: "Recent progress in the science of psychiatry has given us a deeper understanding of the anomalies of the psyche. Psychoanalytic expressions have become part of everyday speech. . . . We cannot help seeing that Dostoevsky anticipated many of the discoveries which psychoanalysis, psychiatry, and character analysis have only recently made after prolonged clinical observation, investigation, research and psychological tests." [57] Dostoevsky started from the religious and metaphysical realities of psychic phenomena, not from that of positivistic psychology; his intention was to reveal the primal contradictions of the mind and soul of man. His knowledge was obtained not only from observation, but also from his own experience and suffering.[58] To cite but two examples of Dostoevsky's pioneer work in the general field of psychology, there is first the phenomenon and interpretation of the dream. Sigmund Freud wrote: "The interpretation of dreams is in reality the *via regia*, the royal road to knowledge of the psyche." [59] Dostoevsky had already set out upon this road in *Crime and Punishment*. To the preface of Raskolnikov's dream, Dostoevsky wrote: "In a morbid condition of the brain dreams often have a singular actuality, vividness, and extraordinary semblance of reality." [60] About Dostoevsky's analysis of the dream, Alfred Adler stated that "Dostoevsky's view on the dream and his dream analyses have not been surpassed to this day, and his idea that no one thinks and acts without a goal and without an ultimate climax, is in accord with the modern findings of psychology." [61] For reference to this latter statement of Adler and its verification, I refer the reader to Dostoevsky's story "The Village of Stepanchikovo" and the novel *The Raw Youth*.[62] Estimates of Dostoevsky's contributions have been made and confirmed by analysts of the caliber of Freud and Adler, whom we have quoted, and by Steckel and Rank as well.[63]

Chapter Five

Dostoevsky's Philosophy and Literary Art

DOSTOEVSKY CRITICISM

DOSTOEVSKY HAS BEEN CALLED the "cruel talent" by Nikolai Mikhailovski,[1] and a "realist with a difference; the apostle of the 'religion of human suffering,'" by Vogüé.[2] In answer to Gide's statement that Dostoevsky deserved "serious attention" for he was "a great writer who was *real* because he was concerned with man's conscience and the desire for absolute truth," the English critic Gosse wrote that one must free oneself from the "magic" of this "epileptic monster whose genius has led us astray."[3] To Middleton Murry's praise of Dostoevsky's psychological and philosophical insights, D. H. Lawrence answered that Dostoevsky was impure, perverse, an evil genius and a marvelous seer who was false to the truth of his own Grand Inquisitor.[4] In post World War I France, Praz called Dostoevsky the "imp of the perverse" who went further than the Marquis de Sade,[5] but at the same time, the American critic Malcolm Cowley spoke for his whole generation, and said that Dostoevsky was too close to their own tragic experiences of life.[6] Another French critic of the post World War I period, Faure, wrote: " 'If there is any Christianity anywhere . . . it is only since Jesus, in St. Francis of Assisi and in Dostoevsky.' But Dostoevsky's Christian charity has been so enlarged that indulgence swallows up the usual distinctions between virtue and vice, and only love remains, dominant and omnipresent." [7]

In the post World War II period of Dostoevsky criticism in the West, one finds the summary statement of C. M. Woodhouse: "Today the young generation now finds that the world which Dostoevsky was describing is the world which we are living in." [8] And Thomas Mann wrote about *The Notes From Underground* by Dostoevsky:

. . . those heresies are the truth: the dark side of truth, away from the sun, which no one dares to neglect who is interested in the truth, the whole truth, truth about man. The tortured paradoxes which Dostoevsky's "hero" hurls at his positivistic adversaries, antihuman as they sound, are spoken in the name of and out of love for humanity: on behalf of a new, deeper, and unrhetorical humanity that has passed through all the hells of suffering and of understanding.[9]

The early critical studies of Dostoevsky in Russia range from the interpretation of Dostoevsky as a social reformer and humanitarian (Belinsky), Dostoevsky as a psychological anatomist (A. Maikov), to the *raznochinets* appraisal of the "champion of the downtrodden" by Dobroliubov.[10] In the 1870's the *narodniki*, through the voice of Mikhailovski, condemned Dostoevsky for the "libel" of *The Possessed*, and thus grew the legend of Dostoevsky's "cruel talent." From the 1880's into the twentieth century two factions gradually gathered their forces: the "modernists" or decadents who were later called the symbolists and the impressionists, and the Marxists. Of the former, Merezhkovsky hailed Dostoevsky as a prophet; Shestov and Rozanov called him the great religious mystic; and the poet Ivanov detected the symphonic polyphony of voices in Dostoevsky's architectonics. Ivanov's thesis was the *sobornost* of Dostoevsky. The early Marxist critics (Solov'yov, Plekhanov, Vcresayev, Kranikhfel'd) worked out his ideology.

Later Marxists (Lunacharski, Gorki, Pereverzev, *et al*) adhered to the political interpretation.[11]

The main bulk of work in Soviet scholarship on Dostoevsky has favored biographical research, ideological analyses, and the editing and publication of letters and manuscripts. The freedom of thought during the NEP period saw valuable studies on Dostoevsky by the formalists, the most penetrating study of which is the work of M. M. Bakhtin, *Problems of Dostoyevski's Writing* (1929).[12] In the thirties, Gorki's influence predominated, and the party doctrine of "socialist realism" was enunciated. Gorki held an ambivalent attitude towards Dostoevsky. On the one hand, Dostoevsky was the voice of conscience and of the protest of the oppressed,[13] but Gorki decried the characteristics of Dostoevsky which championed "the complete autonomy of the personal element, the need for harmony, the recognition of some supraterrestrial, superhuman will. . . ."[14] While he acknowledged Dostoevsky's genius, Gorki followed the interpretation of the "cruel talent;" he called the positive heroes, Prince Muishkin and Alyosha, "half-dead fatalists."[15]

During World War II, the Soviets hailed Dostoevsky's patriotism, but in the late forties and early fifties—the Zdhanov period—Dostoevsky scholars were silenced. Later the Soviet critic, Zaslavski, wrote: "Dostoevsky is an outstanding Russian writer, a master of artistic image and word. But at the same time he is one of the most passionate opponents of socialism, revolution, and democracy."[16] And Yermilov dismissed the main tenet of Dostoevsky's philosophy that all are guilty for all as "trite, sanctimoniously witless crotchet of lifeless Christian morality."[17] Only since 1956, the seventy-fifth anniversary of Dostoevsky's death, has serious study of him been resumed, his works republished and dramatized. Criticism at present rests upon Lenin's appraisal, and the chief bête noire is Dostoevsky's *Notes From Underground*.[18]

Returning again to Dostoevsky criticism in Europe, one must keep in mind that it is necessary to have some knowledge of the intellectual background of ideas which the critics brought to bear in their interpretation of him. The intellectual climate from the 1880's in Europe and in Russia was predisposed to scientific realism and inclined toward naturalism. The philosophies of positivism, agnosticism, and utilitarianism postulated that the reality of the physical world was ultimate and indubitable. For C. Darwin, H. Spencer, J. S. Mill, and Auguste Comte, the supernatural was excluded. Certitude rested on "proof" which was a matter of logical deduction from the accumulated empirical facts, and "insight" and "intuition" had no place.

Empiricism was carried over into art and literary criticism as "realism" and "naturalism." Some of the questions now asked by the aesthetic utilitarian critics were: did Dostoevsky truthfully depict the Russian people, customs, institutions; was he ethically ennobling; was he "socially useful." [19]

From 1890 to World War I, the critical reaction to scientific realism and naturalism by idealism and mysticism shifted Dostoevsky criticism.[20] Shestov, Merezhkovsky, Middleton Murry, Janko Lavrin, and O. Spengler were all critics of this new trend, which was anti-rationalist and personalistic. Dostoevsky was now hailed as a prophet; his characters were "everybody seen by a genius." And Dostoevsky expressed the spiritual experience of humanity. According to idealism, "reality" in art now presented philosophic truth. There also emerged the Marxist interpretation of Dostoevsky, as has been pointed out, and the psychoanalytic studies (Freud, Adler, Yarmolinsky, *et al*) entered the field. Dostoevsky was praised or blamed in the area of aesthetic preference and philosophic convictions. Important studies of the philosophical nature of Dostoevsky emerge from the thirties of the present century in the works of N. Berdyaev, M. Graefe, N. Zernov, and L. A. Zander. The combined spiritual-life biographical work of K. Mochulskii, *Dostoevsky: Zhizn' i Tvorchistvo* (Life and Work), and the thorough study of his philosophy, *Die Philosophie Dostojewskis,* by Reinhard Lauth, are the two most significant recent scholarly works.

The studies by Muchnic, Hemmings, and Seduro all show the fluctuations in Dostoevsy criticism as attributable to the visible movements of historical currents of thought. Thus, Dostoevsky criticism is not a matter of recording his "admirers and detractors," but involves studying what the intellectual legacy and conviction of the critic is and comparing a given interpretation with, at least in attempt, an objective and independent study of Dostoevsky himself. Of course, one is necessarily confronted with examining one's own convictions which are involved in any study.

In the present work, the author is aware that the elements of involvement and detachment are both present. One necessarily brings to bear personal judgment which is based on the accumulated sum of critical perceptions from the critics and cited in this work are ones which have seemed to the author important to an understanding of Dostoevsky.

DOSTOEVSKY'S METHOD OF CRITICISM
AND HIS METHODOLOGY

Dostoevsky's criticism of the current thought of his age is not itself of a scientific or philosophical character. He was able, however, to discern the essence, the fundamental principles of nineteenth-century thought, and many have called him the "prophet and seer of our times." [21] The scene for the novels of Dostoevsky is set by the protagonist in *The Notes From Underground*. He is a man of the 1860's in Russia, but he is also our contemporary, and, man in general. Man's condition *in general* is one of a fallen state; in his existence he is alienated from God. The man from underground is the first tragic hero of Dostoevsky. He is trapped in the workings of his own self-consciousness; but asserting his own "caprice," his independent will and his personality leads to a split within himself. The destiny of the underground man is to find his way back to God or to try to assume the place of God himself in his own self-assertion, self-will and solipsism. He exists in isolation and division, both socially and within himself. But in spite of everything, he still remains a whole personality, even within his doubleness. We are thus introduced to the problem of man's freedom. And it is this essence of man, that is, man's freedom to do good or evil, which is the focal point to which Dostoevsky draws our attention. In this same work, *The Notes*, Dostoevsky's protagonist also criticizes the philosophical positions of positivism, rationalism, and utilitarianism which were held by the Westernizers of the sixties in Russia (Chernyshevsky, Dobroliubov). In the major works which succeeded the above-mentioned work, *The Idiot, The Possessed, Crime and Punishment, et al*—Dostoevsky clarified and deepened his analyses and critique of the predominant ideologies of the age. As L. A. Zander has written: "His characters are seekers in the realm of thought, striving to solve various problems by the dialectical methods of conceptual thinking. . . ." [22] They apply pragmatically their "ideas" wherever they may lead. In this respect Dostoevsky's work "might be compared to a plan with a number of streets and alleys marked on it, named after the endless variety of human theories, errors and enthusiasms: the street of atheistic idealism, the street of anarchist ethics, the alley of 'Geneva ideas' and so on. . . ." [23] Therefore, one finds in some of Dostoevsky's works both a radical attack on faith in God (Raskolnikov, Stavrogin, Kirillov, Ivan Karamazov) and the conviction that existence has a meaning on the basic religious and moral premises (Sonia, Tikhon, Muishkin, Zossima, Alyosha). Dostoevsky needed atheism to purify his Christianity. He was a man of two worlds and knew them both.

Underlying all Dostoevsky's work, which is presented in artistic form—*Dictung*—there is a logical unity, integrating the religious, philosophical, ethical, and psychological levels. Dostoevsky's dialectic is one of antinomies; it is not a dialectic of thesis, antithesis, synthesis. He could express contradictions simultaneously, true to the realities which exist in life, without doing violence—that is, without pressing things into an a priori system.

This does not mean that in Dostoevsky there is no system. He has an organic system tested in and coming out of the reality of life in practice. He wanted to explore his own psychological, philosophical, and religious insights without changing them to fit some previously established system. His insights and experiences led him to conclusions and convictions which form a definite world-outlook. In the deepest sense, Dostoevsky is realistic, not superficially optimistic or pessimistic, but dramatic and tragic. The destructive and the constructive: both ways are possible for man. However, Dostoevsky does show a way out of tragedy.

In the different and contradictory elements and ideas of his characters, Dostoevsky allowed the characters their own attitudes toward life; he followed each of them through his or her own unique development. The critics Leonid Grossman, Otto Kaus, V. L. Komarovich, and M. M. Bakhtin rightly detected the uniqueness of Dostoevsky's style which is "polyphonic." Every voice or opinion is endowed with traits of a living being, and is indivisible from the human personality of a specific character; there is a "multiplicity of discrete consciousnesses" in Dostoevsky's works.[24] Dostoevsky did not equate the real nature of man with only the physical, external activities. His characters begin inwardly from themselves, and his works are, as E. Vivas has pointed out: ". . . a dramatic organization of life which includes characters most of whom are deeply interested in ideas."[25] Rather than imposing an organization of life upon his characters, Dostoevsky caught the "contemporaneous flux," to use his own term, of men and events.

Dostoevsky saw the importance of ideas men hold and have held. Ideas tend to realize themselves in life, in reality. " 'Reality should be represented as it is' they [the artists] say, whereas there is no such reality," wrote Dostoevsky, and "never has been because, to man, the substance of things is inaccessible, while he apperceives nature as it reflects itself in his idea after having passed through his senses. This is why one should give more leeway to the idea without fearing the ideal."[26] One can say that Dostoevsky's characters develop a certain tendency (idea) inherent in their being, attitudes, and views, and that the idea develops according to its own inner logic. On the historical level, one can see the operation of ideas: the prevailing ideas of a time, the atmosphere or *Zeitgeist* tend to realize themselves in social and political life. Life is dynamic; there is no standing still. Further, the personal element or personality and the *Zeitgeist* continually intersect.[27]

In this respect Dostoevsky's insights are deep. He was able to penetrate into human personality and the social structure, and to predict, or warn of, future developments. *The Possessed* is a warning of the impending revolution coming upon Russia; in *Crime and Punishment,* the philosophy of the "superman" of Nietzsche, and the consequences to which it would lead, was worked out long before Nietzsche or the powers of Nazism.[28] Dostoevsky consistently followed ideas and their tendencies to their ultimate conclusions, or to their blind alleys. In all his work he speaks out of a genuine compassion and sympathy with the destiny of man and his suffering; upon this point all critics are agreed, but not all, of course, see him as a "prophet."

The dialectic of Dostoevsky, as previously noted, is antinomic. It is another kind than that of Hegel, based on a logical, mechanical method which leads to a deterministic scheme and approach when and if applied consistently to human life and thought (Hegel, Marx). The dialectic of Dostoevsky is an essential outgrowth of human life itself, of the contradictions involved in life. Dialectic may be based on the conscious or unconscious association of contrast in regards to the contradictions inherent in and involved in human life itself. While Dostoevsky did not theoretically formulate his dialectic in an abstract treatise, it can be seen and analyzed from his works, for example, in the scenes from *Crime and Punishment* where the protagonist, Raskolnikov, receives a letter from his mother. Later he comes by chance upon a street girl whom he has tried to save, but, at the same time that he does so, he lashes out against society which permits this, and yet, rationalizes the situation away.[29] Antinomies in human life produce dialectical processes.

A logical dialectical method can be used in order to

lead the human mind and its understanding to the point of its logical limitations, and to open the possibility of a further apprehension, intuitively grasped. This method of Dostoevsky presupposes another principle guiding such logical dialectical method while applying it to human understanding. This "principle" for Dostoevsky is the religious one.[30] For example, a negative principle has to come to the fore first, before it can live itself out and a positive principle can take its place. Again, in *Crime and Punishment,* the protagonist asserts the proposition that for the superior man "all is permitted." He acts upon this thesis, and comes to see that "all is not permitted." It is not his logic or reason which persuades him, but something else. This "something else" is the relationship of love with another human being. In the character of Sonia, Dostoevsky has drawn the Christian ideal of "love, and then do as you please," or "all is permitted which Christian love permits" as opposed to the ethic of the autonomous man.

In Dostoevsky, the antinomic dialectic does not result in synthesis. Antinomies neither "evolve" nor "resolve" into one another. There can result only transformation—the displacement of one by the other—and this happens in real life and simultaneously. Dostoevsky's spokesman on this point is the underground man:

Tell me this: why does it happen that at the very, yes, at the very moments when I am most capable of feeling every refinement of all that is "good and beautiful," as they used to say at one time, it would, as though of design, happen to me not only to feel but to do such ugly things, such that. . . . Well, in short, actions that all, perhaps, commit; but which as though purposely, occurred to me at the very time when I was most conscious that they ought not to be committed.[31]

The transformation does not, however, happen to the

underground man. The section which would have led to this was deleted by the censors from the manuscript.[32] In *The Notes* Dostoevsky explored spiritually and psychologically the range of human nature and adjustment. One is born into one's environment, cultural tradition; it is imposed upon one. The logical mind of man tries to adjust to the circumstances, of course. But he meets in himself opposites which are against mathematical logic, which tends, justly, to eliminate contradictions. This is the underground man's dilemma. The question raised by Dostoevsky is whether the contradictions which arise in man are of *logical* origin. His answer is no. Contradictions cannot be overcome by the application of the laws of mathematical logic. They can only be resolved on the metaphysical, the religious plane. How? Through love: because one loves *in spite of contradictions,* and love liberates, frees one from the tyranny of environment and circumstance. *Crime and Punishment,* the work which followed *The Notes,* pivots on this premise. In *Crime and Punishment* the adjustment is one on the organic, essential plane of life and is not a mechanical one. The projecting of love, the gift of being able to love is the life force.[33]

Zenkovsky stated that Dostoevsky's thought "moved wholly in the framework of *antinomies:* his positive views were matched by sharp and decisive negations." [34] What Zenkovsky calls the key to Dostoevsky's "Christian naturalism" is "faith in the goodness of man and human nature." [35] He stated:

During the last years Dostoevsky wrote (in the *Diary* for 1877): "Man's greatest beauty . . . and greatest purity are turned to no account, are of no use to mankind . . . solely because there has not been genius enough to direct the wealth of these gifts." These words clearly express one pole of Dostoevsky's basic historiosophical antinomy—a faith in "nature" and its hidden "sanctity," but also a recognition that there is not enough "ability" to "direct" this hidden wealth into fruitful action.[36]

The term "Christian naturalism" of Zenkovsky is, to me, a contradiction in terms.[37] His expression "faith in the goodness of man and human nature (akin to Rousseau), applied to Dostoevsky, can be misleading. However, Zenkovsky further stated: ". . . let us point out that his thought did not hold to the position of Christian naturalism, but came close, with extraordinary profundity, to the opposing thesis of the inner *ambiguity* of human nature, and the ambiguity of beauty—approaching a doctrine of the tragic quality of the 'natural' freedom which leads man to crime." [38] Dostoevsky's thought moved in antinomies until the end of his life: "specifically, a Christian naturalism, on the one hand, and a lack of confidence in 'nature' on the other, continued to coexist in him without reaching a culminating or integral synthesis." [39]

The question which comes to mind is whether Dostoevsky *sought* synthesis. The "event" in *Crime and Punishment* which brings reconciliation to Raskolnikov is not "synthesis." Nor is Alyosha's experience in the garden the evening after Zossima's death a synthesis. The vision of Dostoevsky expressed in image and in thought reveals transformation and transfiguration and not logical synthesis. Zander noted that the phrase "transition to another plane of being" in ontology means a miracle—and this is what the two events mentioned above signified. In logic this is "one of the most dangerous fallacies. . . . That which, from the religious point of view, is desirable above all things is not permissible in the realm of self-contained and self-sufficient thought." [40] The events bringing reconciliation to Raskolnikov and the "differentness in Alyosha for his whole life" meant that human nature illuminated and flooded with and by Divine Grace is only then within the good, and is the bearer of the good.[41]

Dostoevsky as an artist and as a man was not concerned with art for art's sake or society's sake, but he was concerned with helping man on a religious, ethical, and spiritual basis. He saw man as a being created in the divine image. Thus, there is no separation of beauty and spirit, art and faith in Dostoevsky, "since for him there is the constant, often relentless realization that behind all things is a spiritual law, that in the struggle between belief and disbelief lies the key to man's happiness, that the moral and metaphysical, not the physical reality of life is the important issue." [42]

THE RELIGIOUS THEME

In his notebook of 1880 Dostoevsky wrote: "It was not as a child that I learnt to believe in Christ and confess his faith. My Hosanna has burst forth from a huge furnace of doubt." [43] Dostoevsky is essentially a religious philosopher, and "in Dostoevsky . . . we see philosophic activity growing out of the womb of the religious consciousness." [44] It is, therefore, correct to say that the theoretical structure of his thought is united with and informed by the religious perspective of Orthodox Christianity. The adequate terminology to express this would be to say that Dostoevsky's philosophy is a religious philosophy. His metaphysics is grounded in the God of Christianity.

In Dostoevsky's philosophy both the theocentric and anthropocentric positions meet; that is, Dostoevsky's religious perspective of theocentricity regards God as active in human life and in history (in contrast to the deistic religious perspective which acknowledges the principle of God, but one which is not actively participating in human life or history). In stating that Dostoevsky's perspective is also anthropocentric is meant that through the living God of Christianity, he is drawn closer to man and is vitally concerned with man's life and destiny. This can be called the Christocentric perspective, for it is the image and ideal of Christ, his life, and way which Dostoevsky acknowledged. The life and teachings of the Elder Zossima in *The Brothers Karamazov* give a very clear statement of Dostoevsky's Christocentricity and his understanding of Christianity.[45]

To state that Dostoevsky is also an existential thinker means that he depicted his analysis of what it means to exist, his study of man's predicament. Since the terms existential and existentialism are often confusing in their usage, it is important here to define them. Paul Tillich has made a succinct statement in this respect. Existential refers to a human attitude, and existentialist refers to a philosophical school. "The opposite of existential is detached; the opposite of existentialist is essentialist. In existential thinking, the object is involved. In non-existential thinking, the object is detached. By its very nature, theology is existential; by its very nature, science is non-existential. Philosophy unites elements of both. . . ." [46]

Dostoevsky saw that each man and all men were involved in the total commitment to humanity. He expressed this in one of his letters in this way: ". . . the sons of men have *not* the right to turn away from anything that happens on the earth and ignore it; no, on the highest moral ground they have not." [47] Zossima spoke these words: "Make yourself responsible for all men's sins, that is the truth, you know . . . for as soon as you sincerely make yourself responsible for everything and for all men, you will see at once that it is really so, and that you are to blame for everyone and for all things. But throwing your own indolence and impotence on others you will end by sharing the pride of Satan and murmuring against God." [48] And in *The Diary of a Writer,* Dostoevsky detected the falsity of a theoretical love for humanity: "To love the universal man necessarily means to despise, and, at times, to hate the real man standing at your side." [49] One finds oneself participating with the characters in the novels of Dostoevsky; this is the sense of existential involvement.

Dostoevsky's artistic works present a description, a parabolic-poetic representation of his religious experience and of his knowledge of life. His journalistic writings and his correspondence also contain direct statements of his religious and philosophic ideas and convictions. As he lived through a time which was predominantly concerned with science and with scientific truth, he set out to show that man cannot live without religion, that there were areas in life which remain outside the scientific grasp and which demand fulfillment in man's life. As Eleseo Vivas stated: ". . . while positive science and naturalistic philosophy were straining to reduce man to purely naturalistic terms and to deny his metaphysical dimension in empiric terms, Dostoevski was rediscovering that dimension in empiric terms which gave the lie to the modernists by reinvoking ancient truths whose old formulation had ceased to be convincing." [50] Vivas means here that Dostoevsky gives more than a phenomenological description of psychological processes; Dostoevsky restated the religious and metaphysical truths which had ceased to be meaningful in their old forms to modern man.

Dostoevsky saw the shift from theocentrism to anthropocentrism in man's perspective which had been taking place since the Renaissance. Humanism had led to the glorification of man's intellect, and rationalism to the glorification of scientism and naturalism. Man despiritualized and depersonalized himself, and became the tool of his own dialectic of power; Raskolnikov and the Grand Inquisitor are both exemplars. The gap between the two worlds of spirit and matter, of time and eternity had become almost unbridgeable. Dostoevsky was convinced that in negating Christ and Christian ideals, contemporary civilization was in a confusion of thought and action, and held in the vise of the dialectic of power, a will to power, which was leading man to unmitigated arrogance, irresponsibility, despair, and even suicide. Thus, Dostoevsky wrote: "Why, Europe is on the eve of a general and dreadful collapse. The ant-hill which has been long in the process of construction without the Church and Christ (since the Church, having dimmed its ideal, long ago and everywhere reincarnated itself in the state), with a moral principle shaken loose from its foundation, with everything general and absolute lost—this anti-hill, I say, is utterly undermined. The fourth estate is coming, it knocks at the door, and breaks into it, and if it is not opened to it, it will break the door. The fourth estate cares nothing for the former ideals; it rejects every existing law. It will make no compromises. . . . Do I rejoice?—I merely foresee that the balance has been struck." [51] He feared that a total war within Western civilization would break out "in which everybody will be involved" and "in the course of the current century." [52] It is in this light that Berdyaev could write of Dostoevsky:

[He] unveiled a new spiritual world. He restored to man the spiritual depth of which he had been bereft when it was removed to the inaccessible heights of a transcendent plane. Man had been left with only his bodily envelope and the lesser faculties of his soul; he could no longer see the dimension of depth. The Orthodox Church began this deprivation when she relegated spiritual life to another and transcendent world and created a religion for the soul that was homesick for the spiritual life it had lost. This process could only lead to positivism, gnosticism, and materialism, that is, to the utter despiritualization of man and his universe. The transcendent world itself was pushed back into the unknowable and all the ways leading to it were closed, till at last its very existence was denied.[53]

Another Dostoevesky scholar, V. Ivanov, compared Dostoevsky to Dante in respect to their religious emphasis: "Dostoevsky seeks to rescue those whose roots in religion have been severed. . . . both alike are teachers of the Faith; both peer down into the deepest chasms of evil; both accompany the sinful and redemption-seeking soul along the difficult paths of its ascent; both perceive the blessedness of the divine harmony."[54]

Thus, two worlds intersect in Dostoevsky's religious philosophy: the natural and the supernatural. The problems of the human spirit which constitute philosophy are religious problems as well as philosophical ones for Dostoevsky.[55] Both religion and philosophy deal with ultimates. Each is an attitude toward fundamental reality. For Dostoevsky, the source of values and the relationship of values to reality is rooted in theistic Christianity. Dostoevsky's metaphysics and ethical theory are derived from his religious orientation and not vice versa.

The Ethical Theme

The foreground of Dostoevsky's world is ethical, the life or death combat as men come to grips with and struggle with problems and predicaments involving good and evil. Man is split between the absolute and the relative, between good and evil—beauty and ugliness. Dmitri in *The Brothers Karamazov* gives expression to this contradition in man: "I can't endure the thought that a man of lofty mind and heart begins with the ideal of Sodom." In man as man "the boundaries meet and all contradictions exist side by side." In the mind of man "God and the devil are fighting . . . and the battlefield is the heart of man." [56]

The ethical is rooted in the nature and activity of the eternal. Dostoevsky wrote:

Every single organism exists on earth but to live—not to annihilate itself. Science has made this clear, and has laid down very precise laws upon which to ground the axiom. Humanity as a whole is, of course, no less than an organism. And that organism has, naturally, its own conditions of existence, its own laws. Human reason comprehends those laws. Now suppose that there is no God, and no personal immortality (personal immortality and God are one and the same —an identical idea). Tell me then: Why am I to live decently and do good, if I die irrevocably here below? If there is no immortality, I need but live out my appointed day and let the rest go hang. And if that's really so (and if I am clever enough not to let myself be caught by the standing laws), why should I not kill, rob, steal, or at any rate live at the expense of others? For I shall die, and all the rest will die and utterly vanish! By this road, one would reach the conclusion that the human organism alone is not subject to the universal law, that it lives but to destroy itself—not to keep itself alive. For what sort of society is one whose members are mutually hostile? Only utter confusion can come of such a thing as that.[57]

To illustrate further, Dostoevsky criticized, for example, the contemporary European philosophies of his age (J. S. Mill, C. Darwin, D. Strauss) as ethical relativism, for they grounded morality either in "social environment" or in "intellect." For Dostoevsky, the ground of the moral structure is in the eternal or divine, that is, the ultimate ground of being and hence, all values, is in God. He thus warned that while the teachings of the philosophies of his age seemed "lofty and noble," nevertheless "if all these modern, sublime teachers be given ample opportunity to destroy the old society and build up anew, there would result such a darkness, such chaos, something so coarse, so blind, so inhuman, that the entire edifice would crumble away to the accompaniment of the maledictions of mankind, even before it would finally have been constructed. The human mind, once having rejected Christ, may attain extraordinary results. This is an axiom." [58]

What is the source of "the good?" The source of the good is in mystery, that is, in the eternal living God. Zander's view is correct, that, for Dostoevsky, ". . . the metaphysical 'abode' of the good is not so much the human soul as the super-personal and all-embracing principle in which man and the whole world remain in complete harmony and unity with their Creator. The good thus transcends the limit of the purely human mind and is directly connected with ontology and mysticism—those primary sources of Dostoevsky's thought." [59] Dostoevsky expressed the mystical foundation of morality in the words of Zossima:

God took seeds from other worlds and sowed them on this earth, and His garden grew up and everything came up that could come up, but what grows, lives and is alive only through the feeling of its contact with other mysterious worlds. If that feeling grows weak or is destroyed in you, the heavenly growth will die away in you. Then you will be indifferent to life and even grow to hate it. That's what I think.[60]

Dostoevsky's ethic is an ethic of freedom and love. Janko Lavrin, a British authority on Dostoevsky, has correctly stated: "While the ethical theme was of central concern, Dostoevsky was not after morality, but the intensity and fullness of life. . . . The problem of good and evil which crops up on the plane of the spirit is something much more formidable than the sterile moral book-keeping of the puritans. And it was on this plane only that Dostoevsky tackled it." [61] Alyosha agrees with Ivan that one must love life "regardless of logic, as you say. It must be regardless of logic, and it's only then one will understand the meaning of it." [62] It is this instinctively creative life principle which is the ground of everything in man, and it is based upon the act of will and faith, not upon intellectual cognition. Ivan's suffering and madness is the result of trying to base the good precisely upon intellectual cognition, and it is significant that through Ivan one finds the most painful problem for the moral consciousness of man—the problem of innocent suffering. Ivan renders these words: "If all must suffer to pay for the central harmony, what have children to do with it, tell me, please? It's beyond all comprehension why they should suffer, and why they should pay for the harmony. . . ." [63] The innocent suffering, the tears of one child is too high a price for harmony, he concludes, for "it's beyond our means to pay so much. . . ." [64]

The problem of the good and the "ground" of the good is worked out by Dostoevsky, first, in the secularized consciousness of man (Goliadkin, the man from underground); what is revealed is a moral relativism which brings with it the "split" in personality. Second, Dostoevsky works out the split in the religious consciousness where the struggle of good against evil begins (Dmitri Karamazov). It is *within* the religious consciousness that the struggle of good and evil takes place; the first steps toward a way out is the recognition of wrongness or sinfulness. As a matter of fact, almost all Dostoevsky's characters are aware of their "wrong position," even though they often do not "find the way out" (Stavrogin in *The Possessed*). It is this that brings tragedy unredeemed.

Crime, for example, is suffering; it is pitiful. The criminal should be pitied.[65] But crime is an infringement on ethical, moral, and religious life and, therefore, it can be redeemed only through the ethical, moral, and religious way, that is, through repentance, change of heart, and ex-piation (suffering) to redemption.[66] It does not mean that the criminal is justified in his deed outwardly and can run freely, "be acquitted." The confessions of the rebellious characters in Dostoevsky's works are not of deeds, but of evil thoughts and temptations. Deeds there are also, but the central struggle is *within the man,* his sin. "Lead us not into temptation." Purity of heart is for Dostoevsky the ultimate, not merely a clean conscience. Purity of heart is something positive; it is the force by which the sin is cleansed, wiped out. Who can claim a clean conscience?

Dostoevsky's ethic differs from the categories of Kant's ethic in that he realized no single law could be applied a priori to all. Life is not law, but love, that is, the Christian ethic which depends on the direction of the will, the orientation of intention in an act, drawing its strength from and living by faith through Christ.[67]

Kant's moral philosophy maintains that for the moral consciousness of man, the existence of God, as the highest ethical value, is in the last resort a postulate of reason, or the universality of reason. By virtue of this all rational beings can and must be guided by its maxims if they want to live in harmony. To the contrary, for Dostoevsky, this "reasonableness" of the existence of God for the moral consciousness of man is not satisfactory; the noumenal reality (God) must be cognized directly or intuitively, a living bond in relationship with man and not a mere postulate.[68] Zander stated it in the following way:

> Kant says: we must think of God as existing, because our reason teaches us that not all things are lawful. Dostoevsky says: if God is, there is virtue; if there is no God, all things

are lawful;[69] but since we cannot find out whether the judgment "all things are lawful" is objectively true or false, our faith cannot depend upon our moral consciousness. Faith in God cannot, indeed, depend upon anything at all: it is the final and basic intuition of the mind, it is an immediate and objective *datum* with which all spiritual life begins and ends: "I am Alpha and Omega, the beginning and the end, the first and the last" (Rev. xxii.13).[70]

The *good* or "virtue" is in the creativity of <u>active love</u>. Zossima is given these words by Dostoevsky:

. . . love in action is a harsh and dreadful thing compared with love in dreams. Love in dreams is greedy for immediate action, rapidly performed and in the sight of all. Men will give their lives if only the ordeal does not last long but is soon over, with all looking on and applauding as though on the stage. But active love is labour and fortitude, and for some people, too, a complete science. . . . Kiss the earth and love it, with an unceasing, consuming love. Love all men, love everything. Seek that rapture and ecstasy. Water the earth with the tears of your joy and love those tears. Don't be ashamed of that ecstasy, prize it, for it is a gift of God and a great one; . . .[71]

The rebel heroes of Dostoevsky—Raskolnikov, Stavrogin, Ivan Karamazov, Kirillov, *et al*—are the embodiments of the dilemma of being confined within their own egos. They cannot love. Their ethics is the rationalistic ethic of the autonomous man. The negative heroes—the supermen— are all possessed by ideas or "an idea." They assert that there is no God, there is no eternal life, and "everything is allowed." For Dostoevsky, the crisis of contemporary man involved not alone the moral valuation but the religious problem as well. Religion and morality are interdependent.

In calling Dostoevsky the "cruel talent," Mikhailovski

was repelled by the cruelty and lust of the rebellious heroes, and he came close to identifying the proclivity of "cruelty and torture" with Dostoevsky himself. Not a few critics have been drawn to the negative philosophy carried by the "great rebels." Their power and strength has fascinated, like Milton's Satan in *Paradise Lost,* and has occupied the time of the critics rather than the sublime figures: Sonia, Prince Muishkin, Zossima and Alyosha. The latter are "pale" and "ineffectual" beside the "colossal atheists." Gogol is right: "How sad it is not to see good in goodness."

The *kind* of goodness in Dostoevsky is not that which some like or prefer. For example, Belinsky and Dobroliubov and the Marxists have interpreted Dostoevsky as a socialist reformer who championed the "insulted and injured." And D. H. Lawrence thought that Dostoevsky should have sided with the Grand Inquisitor and, therefore, Ivan, in a "benevolence over" the majority of mankind, which, in a final analysis, is an abiding contempt for mankind. However, Dostoevsky can not successfully be made to fit the various preconceived theories of the critics, whether aesthetic utilitarianism (J. M. Murry) or socialist humanitarianism (Belinsky). It is precisely the Christian religious ground which gives us the key to Dostoevsky's meaning of goodness. This is what many deplore, as for instance, D. H. Lawrence, Yermilov, Gorki, *et al.* In his article, "The Spiritual Art of Dostoevsky," George A. Panichas has briefly outlined the various critical interpretations of Dostoevsky's faith in the conception of the "good" which is Christ, and has found that most critics have failed "to comprehend and appreciate Dostoevsky's Christian Orthodoxy which assigns primary importance to the belief that man, created in God's image, relies upon the indwelling Deity to lead mankind from sin to righteousness." [72] And the critics can not understand "why Christ should sit down and eat with publicans and sinners—a vivid picture of the indwelling Logos in communion with humanity stricken with a sense of its transgression and guilt." [73]

If one approaches Dostoevsky dispassionately, one must also seriously and thoroughly study the positive philosophy in the sublime characters, that is, the "good" through Sonia, Muishkin, Zossima, Alyosha, *et al.* The positive, creative heroes of Dostoevsky are possessed of life and deed. They assert that there is God, there is the will to live, and that the love for life and eternal life and the union with all creatures is the meaning of life. It is Dostoevsky's *kind* of goodness with which this study is basically concerned. As we know, this exists in and through the image of man which is Christ, the God-man.

What are the guiding principles of the characters who embody the "good" in Dostoevsky? The answer to this question is of utmost importance if we are to understand Dostoevsky's significance as an educator. I have chosen the character of Alyosha and his relationships with youth as a case in point. First, the principle of personal recognition and acceptance of another for "his own sake" not for one's own sake is evident.[74] Part of the "art" of Alyosha's genius for getting along with everybody and especially with youth is that he helps others become conscious of their own resources and potentials *within themselves*. Real and true beauty and "live" life, creative life, is to be found in well-doing and good feeling existentially. Alyosha says to the boys in the scene after the funeral of their friend, Ilusha:

Even if we are occupied with most important things, if we attain to honour or fall into great misfortune—still let us remember how good it was once here, when we were all together, united by a good and kind feeling which made us, for the time we were loving that poor boy, better perhaps than we are. . . . You must know that there is nothing higher and stronger and more wholesome and good for life in the future than some good memory, especially a memory of childhood, of home. People talk to you a great deal about your education, but some good sacred memory, preserved from childhood, is perhaps the best education. If a man carries many such memories with him into life, he is safe to the end of his days, and if one has only one good memory left in one's heart, even that may sometime be the means of saving us.[75]

Alyosha concludes:

Goodness & childhood NV

. . . Let us be, first and above all, kind, then honest, and let us never forget each other! . . . You are dear to me . . . the good boy, the dear boy, precious to us forever! Let us never forget him. . . .

Ah, children, ah, dear friends, don't be afraid of life! How good life is when one does something good and just! [76]

The second principle is that of "*we* in participation one with another" which is emphasized in and through Alyosha. One can call it a sense of security or the feeling of belonging, but by whatever name, together with the conscious recognition of another *alongside* oneself, and as a *subject* like oneself, it is essential towards lifting the self out of a self-centered world or solipsism.[77] Alyosha's art in human relations also involves a spontaneous interest, the attention in listening, and the trust in and courage given over to another to allow self-expression to thoughts and feelings which may even be absurd, fantastic, often fragile —but which *must be respected*. Far more important than the bizarre ideas of another is the structure of the personality, of a human being. For example, in the scene with the young, fourteen-year-old Kolya, Alyosha seriously and sympathetically listens patiently to the difficulties of this young mind (Kolya rushes headlong into an exposition and defense of the "latest" and "new" ideas of the atheist and socialist theories which he has read about. He is well aware himself that he "muddles" the whole thing.) Instead of rebuking or moralizing, Alyosha is ready *when asked* to meet the awakened challenge of the youth with another point of view.[78] Thus, what he does is to open up Kolya's further intellectual searchings rather than to put him on the defensive, which might stifle the spiritual and mental gropings of this youth.

What Alyosha *is himself* and what his way with others involves is the awakening of youth's intuitive impulses and the bringing to consciousness potentials of good and evil within the self, and helping to strengthen the will for the good and the beautiful, which alone can overcome the evil. The goal in learning which Alyosha emphasizes is a vision of life to be integrated with real life experience. and embodied in Alyosha himself, potential in the youth surrounding him, the vision of Christ is real and present.

It is not for nothing that Dostoevsky ended his last and greatest work, *The Brothers Karamazov,* by surrounding his hero, Alyosha, with twelve youths. And the conclusion of *The Brothers* is this:

"Karamazov," cried Kolya, "can it be true what's taught us in religion, that we shall all rise again from the dead and shall live and see each other again, all, Ilusha, too?"

"Certainly we shall all rise again, certainly we shall see each other and shall tell each other with joy and gladness all that has happened!" Alyosha answered, half laughing, half enthusiastic.

"Ah, how splendid it will be!" broke from Kolya.[79]

The Origin, Meaning and
Significance of Ideas

It is true that Dostoevsky's characters are supremely interested in ideas. Some individuals like Raskolnikov and Kirillov become possessed by an idea. Upon what is Dostoevsky intent? He traces not only the nucleus of the birth of an idea in man, "of an emotionally colored outlook in its inception as a conscious or unconscious series of inner attitudes and decisions of man, but also the consequences of ideas in their tendencies to become fully materialized and realized in life itself." [80] For example, Dostoevsky is against "any light heartedness in thinking whether there is God or not, and the consequences in denying the loftiest idea[81] of human existence, which he showed to be destructive for man." [82] Zenkovsky has stated, as aforementioned, that, for Dostoevsky, all problems of human existence are religious problems. Therefore, Ivan can say: What the Russian youth talks about are the "eternal questions, of the existence of God and immortality. And those who do not believe in God talk of socialism or anarchism, of the transformation of all humanity on a new pattern, . . . they're the same questions turned inside out. . . ." [83]

Ideas take root in human existence; they enter the dynamism of life. In so doing ideas are subjective, and authentic ultimate objectivity in reality is impossible.

Following the duo-philosophies of Dostoevsky's different characters, one vicariously lives through their "proofs" in life. It is not enough to claim an idea as a truth; this must be lived to be proven. At the negative pole with the deniers of the ideas of God, immortality, morality, and life's meaning one finds the strongly convinced atheists:

Raskolnikov, Svidrigailov, Stavrogin, Kirillov, *et al.* At the positive pole there are the believers: Sonia, Muishkin, Zossima, Alyosha, *et al.* The truth of an idea, then, according to Dostoevsky, has to show itself as positive, life-giving in its application and practice.

It is possible to take the various juxtaposed ideologies of Dostoevsky's characters and to construct a systematic, monologic unity, that is, a composite of author and characters, and many critics have done this (for example, Rozanov, Merezhkovsky, Shestov). One can also analyze the characters as "objects" of the author, along the line of the socio-psychological realistic novel (Belinsky, Dobroliubov). However, in so analyzing in a monistic way, critics fail to resolve the antinomies, and reach the conclusion that in Dostoevsky himself they are not "resolved" (Carr, Berdyaev, Zenkovsky). V. Ivanov first discovered a new approach to Dostoevsky's art when he grasped that each "I" character is a "subject" in itself and not an "object" for the author. And Leonid Grossman in his work, *Dostoyevski's Style,* also understood that every "voice" is endowed with characteristics of a living being. M. M. Bakhtin stated that in Dostoevsky's architectonics, ideas play the central role, *as the very thing portrayed,* not as principles guiding the portrayal or as conclusions. In other words:

These ideas are only those of Raskol'nikov, Ivan or Alyosha Karamazov, Prince Myshkin, Stavrogin, or the Grand Inquisitor, determining their perception of the world, and by no means the principles of the writer in the construction of the novels. Their monologic structure, therefore, in no way determines the construction of the novel as a whole. Dostoyevski's novels are not philosophically tendentious and single-stressed in the obvious sense, for the ideas of the characters do not form the architectonics of the novels.[84]

According to Bakhtin, the over-all arching structure is "the supraverbal, supravocal, supra-accentual unity of the polyphonic novel." [85] And, further:

The ideas in man are not the heroes of his novels; the hero is man himself in man, whom the idea—instead of the usual environment and circumstances of fiction—reveals and expresses. The consciousnesses, struggle with them, are sharply aware of their opponents. They are internally dialogic, polemical and always open to the consciousness of another. As artist, Dostoyevski here "rises to an objective vision of the life of consciousnesses and the forms in which they coexist in life," —his own sociology of consciousnesses.[86]

The ideas of the characters make it possible for their consciousness to define itself and to assert its independence. The characters are bearers of their own valid ideas, and Dostoevsky does not encroach upon them. Each idea or thought of a character derives from the total personality. As Bakhtin again stated: "The author himself does not think in isolated thoughts, but in points of view, in terms of the voices of his characters, in which the whole man is heard, 'his entire world-view from alpha to omega.' " [87] In juxtaposing various ideologies, Dostoevsky's world is one of

consciousnesses illuminating one another, a world of concomitant formulations of the meaning of man. Among them he seeks the loftiest formulation, the one most deserving of faith, and he perceives it not as his own true thought, but as another true man and his word. In the image of the ideal man or in the image of Christ there is offered to him a solution to his ideological searches. This image or this loftiest voice is to crown the world of voices, organize, and subject it. It was the image of man, with his voice that is not the author's voice, which was the final ideological criterion for Dostoyevski—

not to remain true to his own convictions and not the truth
of his own convictions taken in the abstract, but to remain true
to the faith-commanding image of man.[88]

Bakhtin goes so far as to say that Dostoevsky's own view
is only one view among other views. However, Dostoevsky
is behind his entire work, and his conscious aim and purpose can be stated as formulating a new Christian theodicy.
The Christian image is not a theoretical idea, but a concrete, historic, and existential image of man. The very
independence of all the characters *must be,* because Dostoevsky's Christian world-view is grounded in freedom itself. There is the value judgment of Dostoevsky, of course,
for the ideologies of the self-willed characters lead to destructiveness and the loss of freedom. What Dostoevsky
follows is the free choice which the characters make in
their lives; these choices lead to juxtaposed ideologies, the
"negative" choices of which can only be overcome by the
road to Calvary.

THE ROLE OF REASON

The place of *reason* is especially important in any discussion of Dostoevsky's philosophy. Too often he is
thought to be against reason, but this is not true. When
it is said that Dostoevsky enthrones irrationalism in his
protagonist in *Notes From Underground* what is meant
is that Dostoevsky detected the essence of man's freedom.
Freedom is, in itself, not "rational" but something different, other than rational. The proclamation of the underground man is the assertion of his "essence" which is in
the metaphysical or spiritual plane: "What man wants is
simply independent choice, whatever that independence
may cost and wherever it may lead." [89] The underground

man insists that "the whole work of man really seems to consist in nothing but proving to himself every minute that he is a man and not a piano key." [90]

The protagonist of *The Notes* further observes the following about reason:

. . . reason is an excellent thing, there's no disputing that, but reason is nothing but reason and satisfies only the rational side of man's nature, while will is a manifestation of the whole life, that is, of the whole human life including reason and all the impulses. And although our life, in this manifestation of it, is often worthless, yet it is life and not simply extracting square roots. Here I, for instance, quite naturally want to live, in order to satisfy all my capacities for life, and not simply my capacity for reasoning, that is, not simply one twentieth of my capacity for life.[91]

Dostoevsky is not putting the either/or of rationalism as the value superior to irrationality or vice versa. But he questions whether rationalism itself and by itself is the sufficient bulwark against the negative forces which rise out of the freedom of man.[92] Dostoevsky's criticism of the naturalistic philosophies (utilitarianism, positivism), all forms of rationalism, indeed—contemporary humanism— reveals the insufficiency of reason by itself understood as the guiding principle to the "good," the solution of man's dilemmas. He likewise points to the dangers of an irrationalism which is understood as the abandonment of the previous capacity to reason. In *Crime and Punishment*, Raskolnikov embodies paradoxically both rationalism (his theory of the "superman") and irrationalism (his delirium). In *The Possessed* through Shigalev and Peter Verhovensky the dimensions reach out into the societal whole. The underground man's observation also shows the simultaneous contradictions within man of these two forces, the rational-irrational in actual life: "Man has such a predilection for systems and abstract deductions that he is ready to distort the truth intentionally, he is ready to deny the evidence of his senses only to justify his logic." [93]

The source of both good and evil resides not in reason but in something beyond or other than reason. Dostoevsky's concept is the "heart"; in this he is in agreement with Pascal, Dickens, and Hawthorne. These thinkers are all, of course, rooted in the biblical tradition. As Herman Dooyeweerd has restated: The real center of man is "the religious center of our existence which in Holy Scripture is called our *heart,* the spiritual root of all the temporal manifestation of our life." [94] In a letter to his brother in 1838, Dostoevsky wrote:

To *know* more, one must *feel* less, and vice versa. . . . Nature, the soul, love, and God, one recognizes through the heart, and not through the reason. Were we spirits, we could dwell in that region of ideas over which our souls hover, seeking the solution. But we are earth-born beings, and can only guess at the Idea—not grasp it by all sides at once. The guide for our intelligences through the temporary illusion into the innermost centre of the soul is called *Reason.* Now, Reason is a material capacity, while the soul or spirit lives on the thoughts which are whispered by the heart. Thought is born in the soul. *Reason is a tool,* a machine, which is driven by the spiritual fire. When human reason (which would demand a chapter for itself) penetrates into the domain of knowledge, it works independently of the feeling, and consequently of the heart. But when our aim is the understanding of love or of nature, we march towards the very citadel of the heart.[95]

The primary category out of which both good and evil issue is freedom, and what is important is the *direction* of a man's will. "Good will and bad will are decided *beyond Reason,* beyond the function of the brain; they are decided in the *hearts* of men." [96] This is what is meant in Dostoevsky's image of God and the devil fighting in man, and the battleground being the heart of man. The rebellion of the underground man is in the name of man's basic sense of freedom, of the will of man against the rule of reason. He refuses to be a number or a "stop on an organ." And while the tragic dilemma of the underground man is not resolved, the plea in this pivotal work of Dostoevsky is on the side of man, man's human dignity as a free, responsible being.

Dostoevsky advocated neither rationalism nor irrationalism. He saw that man's rational capacity or faculty and man's irrational impulses are both given phenomena of life; they belong to human nature. Dostoevsky lucidly followed the proposition that the supremacy of reason is the only preventive and normative element and power in man, and showed its breakdown (the underground man, Raskolnikov, Stavrogin, Kirillov). Likewise he showed that an irrationalism based on the naturalistic position, that is, the supremacy of the "natural" man which subjugates reason to his natural drives and impulses leads man to destruction (Svidrigailov, Stavrogin, Old Karamazov).

There is, of course, a positive and a negative irrationality. Both God and the devil, to use Dostoevsky's images, are "irrational." The positive irrational allows for and strives to reach the good, God. The negative irrational allows for, consciously or unconsciously, the devil, and insists that everything is allowable.[97] There is also a positive and a negative rationality. Reason is a God-given gift to man, and it is used in the service of man's freedom, positively or negatively. But reason is not the only gift to man. Man has also his senses and his heart. Without his reason, man would hardly have been conscious of his existence, of the universe, and without his heart, man would hardly have *content* in his life. In both *knowing* and *loving* God and his fellow creatures is the fullest life, according to

Dostoevsky, and he himself utilized his power of consciousness and of reason to the utmost.

MAN AND FREEDOM

The ethical theme is integral with man. As Zenkovsky noted, Dostoevsky's conception of man is "internally pervaded by an *ethical* category. He not only describes the struggle of good and evil in man; he seeks it." [98] For Dostoevsky, "the theme of man and his destiny is in the first place the theme of freedom," wrote Berdyaev.[99] And Dostoevsky's deep and abiding compassion towards man as a living being is revealed in his own words from *The House of The Dead:*

And how much youth lay uselessly buried within those walls, what mighty powers were wasted here in vain! After all, one must tell the whole truth; those men were exceptional men. Perhaps they were the most gifted, the strongest of our people. But their mighty energies were vainly wasted, wasted abnormally, unjustly, hopelessly. And who is to blame, whose fault was it? That's just it, who was to blame? [100]

The answer to the questions "whose fault?" and "who is to blame?" involves, as Dostoevsky found, the problem of freedom, man's freedom. All his creative works are concerned with the experiment of human liberty.

We often associate freedom with the "political" life, that is, rights and privileges. However, these "rights" and particular liberties may coincide with freedom, but they are not freedom. The essence of freedom is metaphysical; it is spiritual, as personality is spiritual. Dostoevsky's *content* of freedom as spirit accounts for interpretations of him which have held him to be a "conservative" or even "reactionary" in the political sense. Incidentally, the Marxists could never forgive him for being against the "revolution."

Freedom is "the axis around which and out of which everything else turns or evolves. If human freedom is taken in the amoral metaphysical sense, it is limited. In Dostoevsky, human freedom can be judged and seen only from the religious point of view when it ceases to be a limitation because, ethically speaking, man becomes really free only when he becomes purified and strengthened by the Divine Spirit (Agape)." [101]

Thus, the problem of freedom has no meaning at all if this is a chaotic, purposeless world in which man is a mere "manipulated" and irresponsible creature. If the following view of man is valid, then, indeed, freedom itself is an "illusion."

It took more than the undeniable but negative fact of the gradual attenuation and decay of the importance once attached to the soul as seat of knowledge to effect an adequate elimination. The new movement of science had to achieve, on the ground of its own methods and conclusions, a positive conquest of those aspects of natural fact that deal with life and human history before complete elimination could occur. Only during the last hundred years (less than that in fact) have the sciences of biology, cultural anthropology, and history, especially of "origins," reached a stage of development which places man and his works squarely within nature.[102]

Dostoevsky's underground man asks the following questions of us:

Do you really think and believe that man will learn when he gets rid of certain old bad habits, and when common sense and science have completely re-educated human nature and turned it in a normal direction (to live) as reason and science dictate? (Then man will) cease from *intentional* error and science itself will teach man (though to my mind it's a superfluous luxury) that he never has had any caprice or will of his own, and that he himself is of the nature of a piano-key or

the stop of an organ, and that there are, besides, things called
the laws of nature; so that everything he does is not done by
his willing it, but is done of itself, by the laws of nature? [103]

And then the protagonist of *The Notes* states:

Even if man were nothing but a piano key, even if this were
proved to him by natural science and mathematics, even then
he would not become reasonable, but would purposely do
something perverse out of simple ingratitude, simply to gain
his point. And if he does not find means, he will contrive destruction and chaos, will contrive suffering of all sorts, only
to gain his point. . . .

. . . mathematical certainty is, after all, something insuffer-
able. Twice two makes four seems to me simply a piece of
insolence. Twice two makes four is a pert coxcomb who stands
with arms akimbo barring your path and spitting. I admit
that twice two makes four is an excellent thing, but if we are
to give everything its due, twice two makes five is sometimes
a very charming thing too.[104]

The underground man concludes:

I, for instance, would not be in the least surprised if all of
a sudden, *a propos* of nothing, in the midst of general pros-
perity a gentleman with an ignoble, or rather with a reactionary and ironical countenance were to arise and putting his
arms akimbo, say to us all: "I say, gentlemen, hadn't we better
kick over the whole show and scatter rationalism to the winds,
simply to send these logarithms to the devil, and to enable us
to live once more at our own sweet foolish will!" [105]

The traditional interpretation of Dostoevsky as the
"cruel talent" can be understood only in the sense that
Dostoevsky would not relieve man of the burden and the
responsibility involved in the gift of freedom. Man's essential human dignity lies in his freedom and not in man's
rational faculty (humanism) or in the "laws of nature"
(naturalism). It is in the name of freedom that Dostoevsky

detected that man will rebel against "necessity"; in fact, man is ready to suffer any misery, even madness, provided he can feel free, that is, act according to his own "foolish will." The critique of positivism and rationalism in *Notes From Underground* pivots on the problem of freedom. But rebellion is not the only theme. There is also the quest of the protagonist for final and absolute freedom. Dostoevsky merely hints at this in *The Notes:* "Where are the primary causes on which I am to build? Where are my foundations? Where am I to get them from?" [106] And he ends by saying, ". . . I know myself that it is not the underground that is better, but something different, quite different, for which I am thirsting, but *which I cannot find!*" [107]

There are two kinds of freedom: initial and final.[108] The initial freedom is man's free choice, his independent "caprice." Man has the freedom to choose the good, which presupposes the choice also of evil. The second, final freedom is within the heart of the good itself, that is, freedom in and with God. One can state this, as Berdyaev does, in biblical terms: the first freedom is that of Adam, and the final freedom is that of the second "Adam" or Christ. Another way of looking at Dostoevsky's two types of freedom is as follows. There is first the outward, external, political freedom, involving the "rights and privileges" of the societal whole, and, second, the inward, spiritual freedom or freedom of consciousness and self-awareness. Hierarchically, for Dostoevsky, spiritual freedom precedes any other freedom.[109]

It was clear already in Hegel that freedom did not exist outside morality or the moral law, and more especially the Christian system of values. But, one asks, what is the firm and true base of morality? Does it have any roots in the sum total of reality in our life? In order to be empirically

true, can the foundation of morality reside in a convention-
ally accepted formulae or even in a logically formulated
categorical imperative of moral conduct (Kant)? Are not
these only *logical* conclusions of our *mind* of something
else evident and existing as a phenomenon of human life?
If moral values are only the formulations of our reason
without penetrating to their source in life itself and without *personal response* to and a *feeling* for their real source
in life, then man's sense of freedom rebels against them.[110]
This is the dialectic worked out by Dostoevsky in *The
Notes* and in *Crime and Punishment,* and in fact, all his
subsequent novels develop the complexity of this dialectic
of freedom. The conclusion which Dostoevsky reaches is
that true freedom is only in love, the Christian Agape.
This is implicit in the Epilogue of *Crime and Punishment,*
that is, in Raskolnikov's "renewal," and explicit in the
garden scene where Alyosha's "visitation" takes place.[111]

The dialectic of freedom by Dostoevsky presupposes the
free choosing of the good or evil. The latter entails suffering, what is called man's sense of "sin" or guilt which is the
estrangement from the good. Evil leads finally to the loss
of freedom and consequential evil necessity (Raskolnikov,
Stavrogin). However, to deny evil "in the name of the
good," even for the happiness of mankind (The Grand
Inquisitor), and in compelling man to be good, the good becomes good necessity and is not good. Goodness resides in
freedom and not in necessity. And this is the meaning behind the words of The Grand Inquisitor which he re-
quotes from his "prisoner": "You shall know the truth and
the truth shall make you free." Only in the free acceptance
of Truth can man really have the final freedom. Ivan's
Inquisitor is firmly convinced that the majority of mankind cannot bear this "free" gift. In opening up the problem of freedom, Dostoevsky pursued it from every possible

angle, and he saw across man's history and destiny the tragic principle in life. There is tragedy and suffering in human life because there is freedom.

The tragic heroes of Dostoevsky all live lives in which man's freedom deteriorates to self-will and defiant self-affirmation. Dostoevsky showed that arbitrary, autonomous freedom ends up in a deadening, self-defeating, evil necessity. Spiritually and psychologically this takes place within human nature, striking the conscience of man; it is not a "divining rod" from a transcendent divinity.

True freedom, the final freedom, is possible only in and with God; freedom and love are one. Dostoevsky sees the achievement by man of true freedom as possible only in God and His moral law, the living and essential core of which is love. Again Zossima's words take on their full meaning:

. . . have no fear of men's sin. Love a man even in his sin, for that is the semblance of Divine Love, and is the highest love on earth, Love all God's creation, the whole and every grain of sand in it. Love every leaf, every ray of light. Love the animals, love the plants, love everything. If you love everything, you will perceive the divine mystery in things. Once you perceive it, you will begin to comprehend it better every day. And you will come at last to love the whole world with an all embracing love.[112]

Living, creative love is God's love, and its achievement by man and its incarnation is the meaning of Christ. Further, love in the human being is the sphere where man meets God and God meets man. It is the greatest mystery of human life, and this is basically what man lives for, thirsts for, strives for. Love is the token of the possibility of man's spiritual resurrection into a new being, a new Adam, and into eternal life.[113] The conclusion of Dostoevsky is that true liberty and true equality are possible only in Christ, in following the God-made-man.

EVIL AND SUFFERING

Berdyaev wrote that Dostoevsky's conception of evil is "so original that many people do not grasp it properly."[114] One naturally asks, then, how did Dostoevsky conceive evil and the solution to the problem of evil?

Without freedom, evil is unexplainable, according to Dostoevsky. Freedom, and the primary idea that freedom is irrational, allows the possibility of and fact of evil, as well as the good; for without freedom, there would be no goodness either. If one rejects freedom on the ground that evil can be brought forth, this makes evil twice as bad, because constrained evil means also constrained, compulsive good which is good "necessity" and not free goodness. Christianity rests upon the free and unconstrained choice of the good, and therefore *risks* the possibility of evil. This fact Dostoevsky understood thoroughly, and "The Legend of the Grand Inquisitor" of Ivan Karamazov is the consumation of Dostoevsky's dialectic of freedom and evil.

Freedom which is arbitrary degenerates into self-will, which in turn leads to evil and thence to crime. What is allowable to man, then? Is there a limit to man's freedom or is everything allowable? These are the questions which some of his protagonists put to themselves, and live through.

In Dostoevsky's works, one finds that crime has an important place. What is the nature of crime? It is in *Crime and Punishment*[115] that the question of crime and its meaning is elucidated by Dostoevsky through the logical and living consequences of his hero's thesis that "everything is allowable," and that no authority is higher than man himself. This is Raskolnikov's theory: *"Men are in general divided by a law of nature into two categories, inferior or ordinary, that is to say, material that serves only to reproduce its kind, and men who have the gift or the talent to utter a new word."* [116] The men in the ordinary category are law-abiding. "It is their duty to be controlled." The second category all transgress the law; they are destroyers or disposed to destruction according to their capacities. It is the *new word* which is the ideal for man, that is, "the destruction of the present for the sake of the better" that governs such men, men like Lycurgus, Solon, Mahomet, Napoleon.[117] "I maintain," continues Raskolnikov, "that if the discoveries of Kepler and Newton could not have been made known except by sacrificing the lives of one, a dozen, a hundred or more men, Newton would have had the right, would indeed have been duty bound . . . to *eliminate* the dozen or the hundred for the sake of making his discoveries known to the whole of humanity. . . ." [118] Of course, he adds, "If one is forced for the sake of his idea to step over a corpse or wade through blood, he can . . . find within himself, in his conscience, a sanction for wading through blood—that depends on the idea and its dimensions, note that." [119]

The "idea" of Raskolnikov necessitated the act of the murder of an old woman. He chose the pawnbroker because she was worthless to society anyway. His "idea" was to find out if he had the daring to do *anything,* as he confessed to Sonia later:

. . . I wanted *to have the daring* . . . I wanted to murder without casuistry, to murder for my own sake, for myself alone . . . I didn't do the murder to gain wealth and power and to become a benefactor of mankind. Nonsense! I simply did it;

I did the murder to find out then and quickly . . . whether I can step over barriers or now. . . .[120]

Dostoevsky saw through the explanation of evil as solely attributable to bad or unfortunate social environment,[121] and he denounced the humanitarian-positivist theory[122] because it deprived man of his essential human dignity, that is, man as a free and, therefore, responsible being. He did not, of course, deny the relative influence of the impact of environment upon man,[123] but he went beyond the historico-sociological explanation to the depth of human nature which is the realm of consciousness or spirit of man, where liberty *is*. Man is not a passive "reflection" of irresponsible and impersonal forces; man is not a "stop on an organ" or a "number," but a free, responsible creature. Responsible to whom? Responsible to himself, to God, to his fellow men. And if there is no God, then there is no "man," or, man is God. Man is created in the image and likeness of God, "a little lower than the angels," or he is nothing, or, man is God. Man, God, freedom, good, evil, suffering, eternal life—all these "ideas" are bound inextricably together. Raskolnikov and the man from underground both go beyond all the "reasonable" theories; none of them can claim the total allegiance of the protagonists.

Evil results from arbitrary freedom, and leads to crime. Crime itself exists only in the light of the criterion of the divine or good; conscience alone can make the value judgment. And conscience lies within a man, not in external "law."

There is a complex range in the dialectic of evil in Dostoevsky's works, from the underground man through Luzhin, Rakitin, Shigalev, *et al*, to the extreme consequences seen in a Raskolnikov, Stavrogin, Kirillov, Peter Verhovensky, and finally the Grand Inquisitor of Ivan. The symbol of the web of evil, which in its roots is metaphysical, is psychologically the "devil" (Ivan's hallucination), and in religious terms, the antichrist (The Grand Inquisitor). Dostoevsky detected the subtlety of evil which parades in the name of the good itself. For example, the socialist utopian ideal for mankind's happiness *seems* just and good, but as one follows the actual development in the historical life presaged in *The Possessed,* the reversal occurs. Any human being who falls away from the committed group is sacrificed; the "idea" takes precedence over a "living being" (Shatov's murder by Peter Verhovensky's cell group). This is further complicated in actual life by the fact that among the members of the cell group were actually "respectable, good" men who were by no means intent upon criminal deeds, but who found themselves hopelessly involved. The presentation of the Russian Revolution in Boris Pasternak's *Dr. Zhivago* supports Dostoevsky's insights in many ways.[124]

In "The Legend of the Grand Inquisitor," the monologic argument of the Cardinal is in the name of "love of mankind," and for the "happiness" of mankind. The crux of mankind's unhappiness and suffering is the "burden" of freedom which Christ "risked" in his love for man. Mankind is "average"; only the "elect" of "spiritual aristocrats" are capable of Christ's way, and the Inquisitor thinks this is inhuman. He and his followers are now bent upon "correcting" Christ's work. Man wants miracle, mystery, and authority, the three temptations which Christ refused in the wilderness. The majority of mankind are weak little children who need to be cared for, and who cannot take the terrible gift of freedom. The antichrist is by no means coarse or harsh; he is the "benevolent" man. His ideal is the compulsory organization of mankind for its own good.

The "devil" of Ivan is no figure with "horns and fire."

He is an accommodating gentleman, and a rather shabby one, who loves mankind, too. In his own words:

"My dear friend, above all things I want to behave like a gentleman and to be recognized as such," the visitor began in an access of deprecating and simplehearted pride, typical of a poor relation. "I am poor, but . . . I won't say very honest, but . . . it's an axiom generally accepted in society that I am a fallen angel. I certainly can't conceive how I can ever have been an angel. If I ever was, it must have been so long ago that there's no harm in forgetting it. Now I only prize the reputation of being a gentlemanly person and live as I can, trying to make myself agreeable. I love men genuinely, I've been greatly calumniated! . . . You see, like you, I suffer from the fantastic and so I love the realism of earth. Here, with you, everything is circumscribed, here all is formulated and geometrical, while we have nothing but indeterminate questions! I wander about here dreaming. I like dreaming. Besides, on earth I become superstitious. I adopt all your habits here: I've grown fond of going to the public baths, would you believe it? And I go and steam myself with merchants and priests. What I dream of is becoming incarnate once for all and irrevocably in the form of some merchant's wife weighing eighteen stone, and of believing all she believes. My ideal is to go to church and offer a candle in simplehearted faith, upon my word it is. . . ." [125]

In the relative sense, the devil is real, as real as Ivan's hallucination. In the absolute sense, the devil symbolizes nothingness, all the emptiness and void of life (Svidrigailov, Smerdyakov).[126]

One might properly ask, what about the "average" man, the ordinary people in Dostoevsky? The dramas of Dostoevsky include not alone the extraordinary, but all shades of ordinary people, some of whom are essentially goodwilled in spontaneous ways (Marmelyadov), and others who are conniving and self-willed (Luzhin, Rakitin). All the "average" are rather muddled, inconsistent, knowing neither themselves nor why they are as they are. They do not think much, or, if they do, get all twisted up. Nevertheless, every person (the Lebiadkins, Epanchins, the old usuress) is of intrinsic worth, because in every soul one must consider the divine image. Dostoevsky's art allows every individual an essential and existential role. This digression is important because it is easy to categorize the extraordinary figures and to dismiss them as "extreme" cases having nothing or little to do with the rest of humanity. But they have "everything" to do with all of humanity; the great protagonists live in extremes, and they infect those around them, for good or ill. The potentials are in every man, potentials for good or evil, and often both are found in man and simultaneously, too.

The nature of evil, then, is the alienation from the divine; it is metaphysical, and arises out of freedom. Man is responsible for evil, and evil is the tragic road man treads *because* of freedom. In life itself, man learns the destructiveness, the nothingness of evil, but in accepting suffering he can atone for it and redeem.[127] For Dostoevsky, "The torments of a man's conscience are more frightening than the severities of a whole code of law, and he [man] looks at his legal punishment as a relief from his moral torture."[128] Furthermore, "There is no criminal more unfortunate than he who no longer even considers himself a criminal: he is an animal, a beast." In killing his own conscience he is "doubly unfortunate, but also twice as criminal."[129]

One is now led to the correlative idea in Dostoevsky which is bound up with evil. This is the problem of suffering. Suffering can regenerate and redeem man. The meaning of the cross itself is the acceptance of suffering. In all Dostoevsky's novels man goes through the spiritual process: freedom, evil, redemption. The positive heroes successfully meet the "test of freedom" and come out victors, but they by no means escape suffering (Sonia, for example). Suffering by no means *always* redeems. Svidrigailov "suffers" and remains in his hell. The underground man "suffers" and does not know a way out. "What are my foundations?" he cries, and he drives himself to the brink of faith or a complete nihilism. Ivan suffers terribly; he cannot accept a world in which there will be some future "harmony" based upon the innocent suffering of children who have been victims of sadistic cruelties. The terrible sufferings of the innocent bothered Dostoevsky all his life. He asked as did Dmitri: "Why are there these fathers of families ruined by a fire? Why are there all these poor people, this crying baby? Why the barren *steppe*? Why don't they all hug and kiss and sing gaily together? Why are they grey with wretchedness? Why don't they feed the baby?" [130] Dostoevsky knew full well, however, that suffering must be the consequence for one who misused his freedom. In this sense he is relentless: he is no romantic sentimentalist. Suffering is a sign of "a greater dignity, the mark of a free creature" for him. It is a result of evil, "but evil is not worn down by suffering alone. Dostoievsky's heroes pass through hell and they reach the outer gates of paradise—which are less easily seen than hell." [131]

LIFE AND LOVE

In the last letter to his brother, after the stay of execution in 1849, Dostoevsky wrote the following: "Life is Life everywhere, life is in us and not in the world that surrounds us. . . ." [132]

The zest for life, the love of life, is the exuberant note throughout Dostoevsky's works, and, together with the theme of freedom, the keynote in his philosophic thought. The underground man passionately wants "to satisfy all [his] capacities for life, not simply [his] capacity for reasoning." [133] Ivan Karamazov, atheist, idealist and skeptic, declares to Alyosha:

I have a longing for life, and I go on living in spite of logic. Though I may not believe in the order of the universe, yet I love the sticky little leaves as they open in spring. I love the blue sky, I love some people, whom one loves you know sometimes without knowing why. I love the sticky leaves in spring, the blue sky—that's all it is.[134]

And Alyosha's reply is: ". . . You said that so well and I am awfully glad that you have such a longing for life. I think every one should love life above everything in the world." [135]

What Dostoevsky shows is that in each man, greater than the logic of his "idea" is the life that is in him. Life is greater, the most profound thing of all, the greatest mystery. When a man pursues the autonomous ethic, however, sooner or later life itself is lost. A Svidrigailov, a Kirillov, commit suicide; Ivan ends in psychic illness. In testing his idea of the super-individual who is completely a law unto himself, and therefore, "beyond morality," Raskolnikov kills the insignificant, harmful usuress. But his discovery is that he has killed *himself* as well, that is, the life in him.[136] He, too, experienced delirium and illness after his deed.

In life's complicated dialectic, the threads of which Dostoevsky lets unravel, is gradually revealed the fact that life, love, the temporal and the eternal, God, are all intertwined together. And at the opposite pole, the denial of God and the assertions of man's absolute godlike autonomy, the ethic of beyond good and evil or "everything is allowed," end in madness, suicide, destructive revolution —in a word—in death, which is not only on the natural level but in the metaphysical realm as well.

Love is integral with freedom. Here is the "irrational" good. "In the matter of love," wrote Dostoevsky in *The Diary of a Writer,* "constraint resembles a uniform, fidelity to the letter. The conviction that one has complied with the letter leads to haughtiness, formalism, and indolence. One has to do only that which one's heart dictates: if it orders a man to give away his fortune—let him give it away; if it orders him to go and work for all men—let him go and work." [137] And, he concluded, ". . . only your resolution to do everything for the sake of active love, everything within the limits of your possibility, everything which you sincerely consider possible for yourself—is obligatory and important." [138] Dostoevsky's ethic of the good, which is love, rests within the structure of freedom. The *structure* of life inheres in freedom, rooted in both the temporal and the eternal. Dostoevsky discerned the moral structure ingrained in the texture of life, but he did not moralize in the tendentious way, as, for example, did Leo Tolstoy.

The "dictates" of love are within a man's heart and conscience, and not without. Dostoevsky, indeed, loved life, and Ippolit in *The Idiot* enunciates these words: " 'It is life, life that matters, life alone—the continuous and everlasting process of discovering it—and not the discovery itself!' " [139] But Dostoevsky's meaning of life is not living "to the hilt" a self-indulging or self-assertive life; nor is it the sovereignty of man's intellect. The acceptance of and love of life means a total involvement in life, and, therefore, the mutual responsibility of everyone.[140] Here there is no "opposition" to God's creation, nor to his creatures. Prince Muishkin exclaims:

You know, I can't understand how one can pass by a tree and not be happy at the sight of it! To talk to a man and not be happy in loving him? Oh, it's only that I'm not able to put it into words, but—but think how many beautiful things there are at every step, things even the most wretched man cannot but find beautiful! Look at a child, look at God's sunset, look at the grass, how it grows, look at the eyes that gaze at you and love you. . . .[141]

The infinite compassion of Dostoevsky for man and his wonder of the universe, his zest for and abundance of life, fill the pages of his works. The carriers of "abundant" life —the self-sacrificing servants of God among Dostoevsky's creative characters: Sonia, Prince Muishkin, Tikhon, Zossima, Alyosha, move in a world of vice, crime, evil, and suffering; but their faith in and compassion for man never diminishes, or leaves them. Their saving message, which Zossima speaks, is: "Brothers, have no fear of men's sin. Love a man even in his sin. . . ."[142] As George A. Panichas lucidly stated: "Perhaps, then, one of the greatest contributions of Dostoevsky as a spiritual artist is his conception of the primary requirement of Christian belief: *the will to humility* as opposed to *the will to power*."[143]

In Dostoevsky, "The Christian verities of love, honor, pity, compassion, and sacrifice, are of absolute durability, and will not only purify but also redeem."[144] "Beauty will save the world!" cried Prince Muishkin in *The Idiot*. He echoes Dostoevsky's ultimate belief. And there is only one sublime and beautiful figure of man and for man—Christ.

Chapter Six

The Implications of Dostoevsky's Thought for a Philosophy of Education

DOSTOEVSKY'S EDUCATIONAL IDEAS, as we have seen, cannot be separated from his philosophy, for they are related to his religious, metaphysical, and ethical premises. Dostoevsky's analyses of different educational problems are chiefly developed in the light of the ethos of a people, their aspirations and their aims, the Russian nation particularly. All cultural institutions are of necessity educational.

Dostoevsky held that the essence of education, or rather the center of the educational process, lay in the nurture of moral character. He maintained that the real question in genuine education for man is whether there is goodness, humaneness, magnanimity of soul. Real education is enlightenment of the human spirit, not "trades, techniques, mathematics," although these have their places.[1] Dostoevsky's definition of the ideal of "best man" is "he who has not bowed before material temptation; who is incessantly seeking work for God's cause; who loves truth and, whenever the occasion calls for it, rises to serve it, forsaking his home and his family and sacrificing his life."[2] This is, of course, the Christian ideal.

A primary pedagogical principle which Dostoevsky emphasized was self-discipline, "uninterrupted work on one-self." Education for character must begin with the conscious effort by a man himself. The moral self-betterment of individual persons is also tied to the social aspect of life or the civic sense, for to preserve the spiritual ideal of a people, "men . . . zealously and anxiously, 'working beside each other, one for the other, one with another' . . . begin to investigate how they should organize socially so as to preserve the treasure." [3]

Dostoevsky discussed at length issues of public education which involved questions of financial appropriations, schools, and teachers. His first main point in this field probed below the specific issues to the question of the foundation of public education itself. It lay in the attitude of respect of the people towards those who would educate them and vice versa. "The more the people *personally* respect educated man, the more surely will public education be achieved. . . ." [4]

Other problems relating to education which Dostoevsky analyzed were social institutions like the orphanages, the juvenile homes, the law courts, women's higher education, religious education, universal education, and the field of language. In each of the specific problems, Dostoevsky brought to the forefront the moral implication as it related to human character.

Dostoevsky also expressed his views on the roles of society and the family in the education of youth. It was his conviction that the educational process involved the moral concern for character, as has been stated in the beginning of the present chapter. Both the uprootedness of youth and the disintegration of the family in the Russia of his time lay in the loss of the moral ideal and in the ridiculing of all that formerly had been held to be sacred. [5]

Several educational and psychological principles were

stressed by Dostoevsky: personal time and effort on the part of the adult towards the child or youth is essential; the controlling attitude of concern for another *for his own sake* rather than for self-interest; and the principle of accomplishing something by one's own effort. Dostoevsky likewise called attention to and analyzed many subtle and complex psychological principles concerning young children and the adolescent. His unfinished novel, *Netochka Nezvanovna,* the full-length work *The Raw Youth,* a short story, "The Little Hero," and the youth sections in *The Brothers Karamazov* give us significant insights in this respect. However, it was not the pedagogical side of the learning process itself which primarily interested Dostoevsky, although he called the attention of pedagogues to this field of today's "educational psychology." Rather the directions and the consequences of something learned was Dostoevsky's foremost interest, because this involved the whole soul of a man, his whole life and destiny. As George C. Strem has written, Dostoevsky was "preoccupied with the spiritual problems of man, his temptations, his moral growth, his redemption." [6]

In this work of the main aspects of Dostoevsky's philosophy, the first implication of his ideas for the education of man, which is of fundamental importance, is that Dostoevsky reopens for contemporary man's consideration the metaphysical dimension of life. Vivas, Berdyaev, Zernov, and Zenkovsky each stressed the point that Dostoevsky rediscovered in empiric terms the metaphysical dimension of life; that he converted all problems of the human spirit into religious problems.

In our own day, a Christian thinker, J. Donald Butler, supports this consideration of metaphysics: ". . . to build a philosophy of education will not only involve a formulation of educational objectives, or even a theory of value, but will lay upon us the responsibility of making explicit a theory of reality, more technically a metaphysic." [7]

An American educator, Frederick Eby, has succinctly summarized the philosophic climate of the present time. This can aid us in comprehending and contrasting the position of Dostoevsky.

The nineteenth century brought an end to the construction of comprehensive systems of philosophy founded upon metaphysics. The conception has generally prevailed that ultimate reality is unknowable, and the human mind must content itself with a knowledge of the contingent, temporal, changeable, and relative—in a word, with the phenomenal. The fact is, the mind of man is limited in its capability and it is not only impossible to transcend experience but unprofitable to do so. The effort to deduce knowledge from general principles results only in stark failure . . . , the most constructive minds threw themselves into the detailed pursuit of the natural sciences with an avidity never approached. . . . Man is predominately a creature of action . . . reflection . . . should not become morbid in the pursuit of ultimate reality. Philosophy, it has been generally accepted, is the study of the methods of learning from experience.

. . . Educational leaders generally adopted the scientific methodology and the philosophy and history of education were subordinated to psychology, administration, curriculum and methods. Experimentalism was the guiding philosophy, so far as there was any. However, as the years advanced, protests against this program of naturalism have become increasingly powerful. [8]

In general, the philosophy of naturalism (the earlier naturalistic realism as well as the later refined forms of pragmatism, experimentalism, instrumentalism, reconstructionism) considers man as the same in kind although different in degree within physical nature. The influence of the natural sciences, particularly Darwin's theory of evolution in biology, has been one of the main factors in the spread of naturalism. One of the naturalist thinkers, Yervant H. Krikorian, in his article "A Naturalist View of Mind," has written ". . . a basic belief that is characteristic of naturalism . . . is that nature is the whole of reality. . . . Differences in nature are nothing but differences in complexity of structure." [9] Naturalism denies, he continues, that there is any spiritual, metaphysical order superior to external nature which would be above the mechanism and laws of the material world.[10] Another naturalist, John H. Randall, Jr., says that

. . . [today] the fundamental importance of evolutionary thought, like that of those earlier naturalisms, lies primarily in its methodological significance: there . . . [is] no sharp difference in intellectual methods in treating man and the other aspects of Nature of which he [is] a part. . . . Now naturalism . . . can be defined negatively as the refusal to take "nature" or "the natural" as a term of distinction . . . it is opposed to all dualisms between Nature and another realm of being—to the Greek opposition between Nature and Art, to the Medieval contrast of the Natural and Supernatural, to the empiricist antithesis of Nature and Experience, to the idealist distinction between Natural and Transcendental, to the fundamental dualism pervading modern thought between Nature and Man. For present day naturalists "Nature" serves as the all-inclusive category, corresponding to the role played by "Being" in Greek thought, or by "Reality" for the idealists. . . . [For naturalism] eternity is no attribute of authentic Being, but a quality of vision, and divinity belongs, not to what is existent, but to what man discerns in imagination. Thus naturalism finds itself in thoroughgoing opposition to all forms of thought which assert the existence of a supernatural or transcendental Realm of Being and make knowledge of that realm of fundamental importance to human living. There is no "realm" to which the methods for dealing with Nature can not be extended.[11]

A Christian thinker, Paul Ramsey, summarizes the natural-istic position: "Methodologically predisposed to the task of erecting a 'physical' science of man, psychological and social sciences frequently speak as if, once their systems have been completed and a few more discoveries laid end to end, a complete account of human thought and human behavior can be given in terms of a closed system of natural laws which men are bound to observe like stars in their courses." [12]

Dostoevsky's view is theistic. This implies that educa-tion and life itself are incomplete without man becoming related to God and oriented toward eternal life as well as in his human relationships. In Dostoevsky's philosophy both the theocentric and anthropocentric positions meet. Reality embraces the natural and the supernatural.

The central theme of Dostoevsky's religious-philosophi-cal and psychological reflections about man is ethical. He holds that the moral life of man is dependent upon man's living awareness of God. Thus, utilitarian ethics, moral rationalism, and the autonomous ethics of naturalism are repudiated. This second point, the primacy of the ethical, would turn about the approach to educational philosophy. Once again consideration of metaphysics or the investiga-tion of the nature of reality and the origin of ethical values would predominate over interest in pedagogical method-ology. Dostoevsky's analyses point in this direction, for they must be viewed in the light of religious and meta-physical premises. Dostoevsky would not dispute the fact that life is growth, change, experience, a process. But to what end, he would ask. The crux of life and all educa-tion is this latter point: towards what qualitative ideal is a man or a people dedicated?

Dostoevsky's analysis of man proceeds in the realm of spirit, that is, consciousness. Man is not only a creature of nature, but even more significant, a being endowed with consciousness, awareness—and further, *self-awareness*. Here lies the realm of freedom which is in a sense, the "nucleus" of man. For out of man's freedom, which results in concrete self-acts in thought and deed, arise the moral issues of human life. Man finds that freedom is both a precious gift and a tremendous burden. The dialectic of good and evil arises out of the impulses of man's freedom and is set in motion by his own acts, his own will. As Strem noted: "The conflict in Dostoevsky's works arises from the struggle which complex human beings have to sustain as they come to grips with the basic moral laws of human destiny. With extraordinary passion and rare vigor the author demonstrates this truth." [13] Dostoevsky further sees man as a unity, a whole personality, a being potentially within the image of God. The precious mystic sense of man is precisely his awareness of and relationship with God (Zossima). For Dostoevsky the most perfectly revealed image, ideal and human reality, is Christ. Dostoevsky is concerned about man's relation to God, not only about man per se: "The Gospel . . . this is the *sine qua non:* you will never find anything better than the saviour anywhere. . . ." [14]

A further problem is raised about man's quest for knowledge, for truth. J. Donald Butler has stated that "epistemology, or knowledge theory is the decisive crux of philosophical thought because it examines the means by which we come to know our alleged truths, and thereby helps us to test them." [15] He further posits the question:

May there not be as legitimate a pattern of logic found in the relation between the human self and its world? May not proof be that which is tested by selfhood being in the fullest living and working relation with the world or not-self, rather than that which passes the test of the laws of deduction or induction, or a logic of symbols? Such a logic has not been attempted as yet, but it might prove very enlightening. . . . And it might more clearly approximate the patterns of revelation, as found in religion, than the patterns of proof common to science.[16]

It is suggested here that this logic of the relationship of selfhood to the world of not-self is contained within Dostoevsky's work and thought. The key lies precisely in the concept *relationship*. Relationship is not a void but an involving situation: oneself to oneself; oneself to other selves, the world; oneself to the eternal. This threefold structure is to be found developed in its intricacy and in the full context of Dostoevsky's philosophy. The "new logic" of Dostoevsky can be called antinomic dialectic. To cite one illustration: the work *Crime and Punishment,* for one thing, posits the question of the supremacy and autonomy of human reason. The "idea" of the protagonist, Raskolnikov, carried through, placed him precisely outside all relationships. (And it was no accident when he said that he had killed himself and not the old woman.) Raskolnikov discovered finally *in himself* and *through vital human relationships* that there was more to the human being than "reason," that man was not autonomous-unto-himself alone. While reason, intellect, is of great worth, it is always in some kind of relationship. Reason is an instrument either of pride or obedience; it is always in the service of a man's spiritual orientation, positively or negatively.[17] Herman Dooyeweerd's recent work, *In the Twilight of Western Thought,*[18] critically examines the "dogma" of the autonomy of philosophical thought, *i.e.,* the supremacy and autonomy of human reason; his analysis sustains Dostoevsky's insight.

Crime and Punishment, and indeed, all Dostoevsky's works, contain his social ethic of relationship which is formulated in the realistic adjustment to the concrete elements in any given situation of neighbor need. It is not achieved by deduction or from a revealed, intuitively grasped absolute natural law. Dostoevsky's ethics of love and freedom approaches the task of social relations among men with an indefinite and liberating norm, that of the attitude of other-than-self concern, rather than an extension of the laws of nature to the totality of human life. Dostoevsky concluded that only an element of concern for the other person *for his own sake* could create genuine community among men. Rather than *what* is the good, *whose good* is the primary ethical question for Dostoevsky. The sustaining element is love, Christian love, which endures all things (Sonia, Zossima, Muishkin, Alyosha). It is this love which values both each personality as an end in itself and all persons in community. The absence of this concrete valuing of people for their own sakes in human relationships has been leading contemporary civilization to the brink of the abyss (*The Possessed*). The essence of Dostoevsky's ethics is one of love and compassion, rooted in the religious awareness and reality of life.

In conclusion, Dostoevsky's contribution toward building a philosophy of education would bring to the forefront the serious study of and reflection upon the metaphysical dimension of reality which includes religion. In ethics he reformulates the Christian view, and ethics is brought back to religious sources. Moral awareness in character is placed at the center of the educational process.

Perhaps these basic principles renewed and emphasized by Dostoevsky are not unique in the history of Christian thought itself, but what is original with Dostoevsky is the lucidity and force of his dialectic. He compels us to reexamine and to rethink our basic philosophic premises and convictions. The intricacy and subtlety of his psychological analyses has enabled psychology to advance, and is attested by men like Freud, Adler, Rank and Steckel. In this mid-twentieth century, reconsideration of and a re-evaluation of the religious and metaphysical dimensions of philosophy is taking place. For those in the field of philosophy of education, Dostoevsky can be an inspiring, challenging, and compelling thinker.

Notes

CHAPTER ONE

1   Alexander Kornilov, *Modern Russian History* (New York, 1952), II, 89–95.
2   George Vernadsky, *A History of Russia* (New Haven, 1944), pp. 194–195.
3   Daniel B. Leary, *Education and Autocracy in Russia* (Buffalo, 1919), pp. 50–51.
4   In 1861, the emancipation finally came about. Many enlightened, thinking men worked to abolish this social institution. However, when it did take place, the radical group of the intelligentsia were no longer satisfied with "reforms"; they wanted "revolution."
5   Kornilov, *op. cit.*, I, 111–113.
6   *Ibid.*, pp. 187–189. See also William H. E. Johnson, *Russia's Educational Heritage* (Pittsburgh, 1950), pp. 78–86.
7   Kornilov, *op. cit.*, p. 189.
8   Johnson, *op. cit.*, pp. 79–81. The catechism and other religious writings were placed foremost in the curriculum of the schools.
9   Leary, *op. cit.*, p. 54.
10   *Ibid.*, p. 56.
11   On December 14, 1825, in St. Petersburg, a radical group of army officers under Pestel attempted to set up a republican form of government with Pestel as leader. See Kornilov, *op. cit.*, pp. 196–208 for details.
12   Kornilov, *op. cit.*, p. 236.
13   *Ibid.*
14   Leary, *op. cit.*, p. 63.
15   Kornilov, *op. cit.*, pp. 279–280.
16   *Ibid.*, p. 280.
17   *Ibid.*, pp. 299–301.

18   V. V. Zenkovsky, *A History of Russian Philosophy* (New York, 1953), I, 320.

19   *Ibid.*, p. 321.

20   *Ibid.*

21   Kornilov, *op. cit.*, II, 6–10.

22   *Ibid.*, pp. 11–33.

23   *Ibid.*, p. 62.

24   *Ibid.*, pp. 80–82. The culmination of the revolutionary outbursts ended with the attempt upon the life of the Tsar himself, in 1866.

25   *Ibid.*, p. 164.

26   *Ibid.*, pp. 163–175.

27   *Ibid.*

28   Nicholas Berdyaev, *The Russian Idea* (New York, 1948), p. 33.

29   *Ibid.*, p. 32.

30   Zenkovsky, *op. cit.*, p. 133.

31   Kornilov, *op. cit.*, pp. 284–285.

32   *Ibid.*, pp. 286–287. See also Zenkovsky, *op. cit.*, pp. 148–170.

33   Berdyaev, *The Origin of Russian Communism* (London, 1948), p. 26.

34   *Ibid.*, pp. 26–27. See also Kornilov, *op. cit.*, pp. 285–287.

35   Berdyaev, *op. cit.*, pp. 19–20. See also Herbert E. Bowman's article "Intelligentsia in Nineteenth Century Russia," *The Slavic and East European Journal* (Spring, 1957), 15:5–21.

36   Berdyaev, *op. cit.*, p. 20.

37   *Ibid.*

38   Zenkovsky, *op. cit.*, pp. 237–238.

39   Berdyaev, *op. cit.*, p. 37.

40   *Ibid.*, pp. 41–42.

41   *Ibid.*

42   *Ibid.*, pp. 39–40.

43   V. Belinsky, *Selected Philosophical Works* (Moscow, 1948), p. xvii: "Belinsky was the initiator of the revolutionary democratic movement in Russia . . . the pioneer of utopian socialism and revolutionary democracy in Russia . . . ." is the Soviet comment. During his lifetime, Belinsky was a great influence on the younger generation who felt that they owed Belinsky "their salvation." This was recorded by the Slavophile Ivan Aksakov. Kornilov, *op. cit.*, p. 303.

44   Berdyaev, *op. cit.*, pp. 34–35.

45   Bowman, *op. cit.*, p. 12.

46   Berdyaev, *op. cit.*, pp. 45–46.

47   *Ibid.*, p. 46.

48   Kornilov, *op. cit.*, pp. 213–214. Dostoevsky analyzed the "Nechaiev" type in his *Possessed*. See also Turgenev's *Fathers and Sons* for the nihilist type in the sixties.

49   Zenkovsky, *op. cit.*, pp. 348–374.

50   Berdyaev, *op. cit.*, p. 70.

51   *Ibid.*

52   *Ibid.*

53   *Ibid.*, pp. 70–71.

54   *Ibid.*, p. 71. See also Berdyaev's *The Russian Idea*, pp. 101–102, 111 ff.

55   Kornilov, *op. cit.*, p. 213.

56   *Ibid.*

57   Berdyaev, *The Origins of Russian Communism*, p. 62.

58   *Ibid.*, p. 63.

59   *Ibid.*, p. 64.

60   Kornilov, *op. cit.*, p. 223.

61   *Ibid.*, p. 223–224.

62   *Ibid.*, p. 292.

63   Berdyaev, *The Russian Idea*, pp. 48–49.

64   Zenkovsky, *op. cit.*, p. 204.

65   *Ibid.*, pp. 203–204.

66   *Ibid.*, p. 236.

67   *Ibid.*, p. 237.

68   *Ibid.*, pp. 237–238.

69   Marc Slonim, *The Epic of Russian Literature* (New York, 1950), p. 148.

70   Zenkovsky, *op. cit.*, pp. 237–238.

71   Johnson, *op. cit.*, p. 228.

72   *Ibid.*, p. 231.

73   Zenkovsky, *op. cit.*, p. 377.

74   A. P. Medvedkov, *Kratkii istoriya russkoi pedagogiki* (St. Petersburg, 1913), pp. 75–76.

75   *Ibid.*, p. 76.

76   Alexandra Tolstoy, *Tolstoy, A Life of My Father* (New York, 1953), Chs. 18, 20, 23, 24.

77   *Ibid.*

78   *Ibid.*, p. 135.

79 Johnson, *op. cit.*, p. 235. See also Charles-Baudouin, *Tolstoi: the Teacher*, tr. by Fred Rothwell (London, 1923).

80 *Ibid.*, p. 241.

81 *Ibid.*, p. 240.

82 *Ibid.*

83 *Ibid.*

84 Medvedkov, *op. cit.*, p. 91.

85 *Ibid.*, pp. 91–92. See also Johnson, *op. cit.*, p. 242.

86 Johnson, *op. cit.*, p. 241.

87 Medvedkov, *op. cit.*, p. 105.

88 Johnson, *op. cit.*, pp. 242–243.

89 *Ibid.*

90 *Ibid.*, p. 244. See also Medvedkov, *op. cit.*, p. 107.

91 Johnson, *op. cit.*, pp. 244–248.

92 *Ibid.*, p. 248. Two important followers of Ushinskii in the field of peoples' education were Staunin and Rachinskii. See Medvedkov, *op. cit.*, pp. 109–158.

CHAPTER TWO

1 *Diary of a Writer* (New York, 1949), II, 752.

2 *Ibid.*, I, 284–285.

3 *Ibid.*, pp. 207–210.

4 *Ibid.*, II, 752–753.

5 *Ibid.*, I, 184–186.

6 *Ibid.*, II, 753.

7 Ethel Colburn Mayne, *Letters of Fyodor Michailovitch Dostoevsky to his Family and Friends*, London, 1914, chronological table after V. Tchechichin, p. xi.

8 *Diary of a Writer*, I, 152.

9 Edward H. Carr, *Dostoevsky 1821–1881: A New Biography* (London, 1949), p. 14.

10 Zenta Maurina, *A Prophet of the Soul: Fyodor Dostoievsky*, tr. by C. P. Finlayson from Latvian (London, n. d.), p. 37.

11 *Ibid.*, p. 38.

12 The estate was a property 150 versts from Moscow, 1350 acres of land, comprising the villages of Darovoe and Chermashny.

13 Carr, *op. cit.*, p. 15.

14 Mayne, *op. cit.*, p. 254.

15 Eugene Soloviev, *Dostoevsky, His Life and Literary Activity*, tr. by C. J. Hogarth (London, 1916), pp. 42–43.

16 *Ibid.,* p. 43.
17 Carr, *op. cit.,* p. 17.
18 Maurina, *op. cit.,* p. 42.
19 *Idem.*
20 Carr, *op. cit.,* p. 18.
21 Mayne, *op. cit.,* p. 3. Letter of August 9, 1838.
22 *Ibid.,* pp. 3–4.
23 *Ibid.,* pp. 6–9.
24 *Idem.*
25 *Ibid.,* p. 9. After the death of his wife, Michail Andreyevitch
    was not to be consoled. He became a cruel master and finally
    his peasants murdered him.
26 Carr, *op. cit.,* pp. 24–25.
27 Henri Troyat, *Firebrand: The Life of Dostoevsky,* tr. by Nor-
    bett Gutemann from French (New York, 1946), p. 42.
28 Mayne, *op. cit.,* pp. 261–262.
29 Carr, *op. cit.,* p. 27. See also Mayne, *op. cit.,* pp. 10–16.
30 Mayne, *op. cit.,* pp. 16–17. Letter of September 30, 1844.
31 *Ibid.,* p. 22. Dostoevsky had also translated Balzac's *Eugénie
    Grandet;* Mihail worked on Schiller. Most of their dreams for
    publishing fell through for lack of capital.
32 *Ibid.,* p. 23.
33 William Hubben, *Four Prophets of Our Destiny* (New York,
    1952), p. 46.
34 F. M. Dostoevsky, *Insulted and Injured,* tr. by Constance Gar-
    nett, Macmillan edition, p. 65.
35 Carr, *op. cit.,* pp. 28–29. See also "Reminiscences of Grigoro-
    vich" in Mayne.
36 Nicholas Zernov, *Three Russian Prophets: Khomiakov, Dos-
    toevsky, Soloviev* (London, 1944), p. 84. The novel's publica-
    tion was held up because the censor had to pass it.
37 Mayne, *op. cit.,* pp. 26–27.
38 *Ibid.,* p. 30.
39 *Ibid.,* p. 33.
40 *Ibid.,* p. 36.
41 *Idem.* Belinsky could not go further than an appreciation of
    Dostoevsky's *humanism.* The poor hearts of the novel *Poor
    Folk* he understood, but "Goliadkin" in *The Double* utterly
    perplexed him. Dostoevsky's idea of the split personality was
    beyond Belinsky and most of the others. In 1847, V. Maikov,

the brother to Dostoevsky's closest friend, the poet Apollon Maikov, did recognize his distinctive gift: "Mr. Dostoevski's writings stabilize the reign of the aesthetic principles which Gogol introduced in our literature, demonstrating that even a very great talent cannot take a different road without violating the laws of art. Nevertheless, the creative method of Mr. Dostoevski is original in the highest degree, and he is the last one who may be called an imitator of Gogol. If you were to apply this term to him you would be obliged to call Gogol an imitator of Homer and Shakespeare. In this sense all true artists imitate one another, because beauty is always and everywhere subject to the same laws. . . ." And he concludes: "Both Gogol and Mr. Dostoevski portray actual society. But Gogol is primarily a social writer, and Mr. Dostoevski primarily a psychological writer. For one, the individual is significant as representative of a certain society or a certain circle; for the other, society is interesting insofar as it influences the personality of the individual." Maikov praised *The Double,* and advised Dostoevsky not to give attention to the critics. See V. Seduro, *Dostoevski in Russian Literary Criticism, 1846–1956* (New York, 1957), pp. 11–13.

42 *Ibid.,* p. 37.

43 Mayne, *op. cit.,* p. 8.

44 *Ibid.,* pp. 41–42.

45 *Ibid.,* pp. 45–46.

46 Nicholas I was alarmed at the revolutionary situation in Europe during the late forties. He took care that another Decembrist uprising would be forestalled. Belinsky was to be arrested also, but he was on his deathbed. See Ch. 4 of Carr for complete details.

47 Mayne, *op. cit.,* pp. 46–49. Andrei was mistaken for Mihail and held two weeks in prison. Mihail was held for four months. Dostoevsky himself underwent five or six cross-examinations. The only work he completed in the Fortress was his short story "The Little Hero" which was published after his release from prison.

48 *Ibid.,* p. 49.

49 *Idem.*

50 *Ibid.,* pp. 51–52.

51 *Ibid.,* p. 53.

52 *Idem.*

53 *The Diary of a Writer,* I, 9. "His comrade in chains on the way to Siberia, a Polish fellow prisoner, Jastrzembski, thus expressed himself about Dostoevsky: 'It was Dostoevsky's friendly and helpful conversations that saved me from despair . . . his sensitiveness, his delicacy of feeling, his playful sallies—all this exercised a calming influence upon me. . . .' The two men parted in tears at Tobolsk." Hubben, *op. cit.,* pp. 47–48.

54 Mayne, *op. cit.,* pp. 55–58.

55 *Ibid.,* pp. 59–67.

56 *Ibid.,* pp. 69–71.

57 *Ibid.,* p. 71.

58 *Ibid.,* p. 72.

59 *Ibid.,* pp. 289–320. Vrangel had been present as a young student at the ceremony of the execution in the Semyonovsky Square on December 22, 1849.

60 *Ibid.,* p. 308. *The House of the Dead* was published upon Dostoevsky's return to Petersburg.

61 *Ibid.,* p. 75. Letter of June, 1855.

62 *Ibid.,* p. 81. Letter of October, 1855.

63 *Idem.*

64 *Ibid.,* p. 82.

65 Carr, *op. cit.,* p. 95.

66 Robert L. Jackson, *Dostoevsky's Underground Man in Russian Literature* (The Hague, 1958), pp. 23–24. Dostoevsky called the exhibition a kind of biblical picture, and said that much "unremitting spiritual resistance and negation" would be necessary to avoid accepting this for one's ideal. See also the *Winter Notes.*

67 Mayne, *op. cit.,* pp. 109–110.

68 Zernov, *op. cit.,* p. 85.

69 Koteliansky, S. S., tr., *Dostoevsky Portrayed by His Wife, The Diary and Reminiscences* (London, 1926), pp. 20–21.

70 *Ibid.,* p. 29.

71 Carr, *op. cit.,* p. 173.

72 Mayne, *op. cit.,* pp. 129–130. This letter contains Dostoevsky's views on the congress.

73 *Ibid.,* pp. 142–143. Dostoevsky dedicated the work to his niece.

74 *Ibid.,* pp. 157–158.

75 *Ibid.,* p. 171.

76   *Ibid.*, p. 185.

77   *Ibid.*, p. 192.

78   Koteliansky, *op. cit.*, pp. 138–139.

79   S. S. Koteliansky, *Dostoevsky: Letters and Reminiscences* (New York, 1923), pp. 100–101.

80   Koteliansky, *op. cit.*, p. 103.

81   G. Abraham, *Dostoevsky* (London, 1936), p. 117. See also Koteliansky, *op. cit.*, pp. 109–144 for details from Madame Dostoevsky's reminiscences.

82   Koteliansky, *op. cit.*, pp. 149–151.

83   *The Diary*, I, p. 160.

84   E. J. Simmons, *Dostoevski, The Making of a Novelist* (New York, 1940), p. 319.

85   *Ibid.*, p. 320.

86   *Ibid.*, pp. 319–320.

87   Mayne, *op. cit.*, p. 225.

88   *Ibid.*, p. 226.

89   *Idem.*

90   *Ibid.*, pp. 233–235.

91   Aimée Dostoevsky, *Fyodor Dostoevsky, A Study* (London, 1912), pp. 183–185.

92   *Ibid.*, p. 189.

93   *Ibid.*, p. 191.

94   *Ibid.*, p. 195.

95   *Ibid.*, p. 201.

96   *Ibid.*, pp. 205–206.

97   *Idem.*

98   Maurina, *op. cit.*, pp. 100–101.

99   Simmons, *op. cit.*, p. 343.

100 "Letters: Dostoevsky, New Ones," *The Virginia Quarterly* (July–October, 1926), pp. 375–384, 546–556.

101 *Idem.*

102 *Idem.*

103 *Idem.*

104 *Idem.*

105 Mayne, *op. cit.*, pp. 256–257.

106 Simmons, *op. cit.*, p. 385.

107 Koteliansky, *op. cit.*, pp. 158–159.

108 Maurina, *op. cit.*, p. 104.

109 Koteliansky, *op. cit.*, pp. 161–162.

110   Maurina, *op. cit.,* pp. 105–106.
111   Reminiscences, *op. cit.,* p. 182.
112   Koteliansky, *op. cit.,* p. 187.
113   *Ibid.,* p. 192.
114   *Ibid.,* p. 193.
115   Koteliansky and Murry, *op. cit.,* p. 264.
116   Mayne, *op. cit.,* p. 337.
117   *Ibid.,* p. 334.

CHAPTER THREE

1   Ethel Colburn Mayne, *Letters of Fyodor Michailovitch Dostoevsky to His Family and Friends* (London, 1914), p. 134.
2   F. M. Dostoevsky, *The Dairy of a Writer,* p. 490.
3   *Ibid.,* pp. 480 ff.
4   *Ibid.,* p. 490.
5   *Ibid.*
6   *Ibid.,* pp. 286–293.
7   *Ibid.,* p. 483.
8   *Ibid.,* pp. 604–605.
9   *Ibid.,* p. 624.
10   *Ibid.,* p. 283
11   *Ibid.,* pp. 286–293.
12   *Ibid.,* p. 573.
13   *Ibid.,* pp. 571, 670; see also Mayne, *op. cit.,* pp. 230–231.
14   *The Diary,* p. 189.
15   *Ibid.,* p. 724.
16   *Ibid.,* p. 101.
17   *Ibid.,* pp. 101–102.
18   *Ibid.,* p. 103.
19   *Ibid.*
20   *Ibid.*
21   *Ibid.,* pp. 106–107.
22   *Ibid.,* p. 750.
23   Mayne, *op. cit.,* pp. 241–243, 286 ff.
24   *The Diary,* p. 750.
25   *Ibid.,* p. 329. Dostoevsky attended many trials and followed court proceedings during this period.
26   *Ibid.,* p. 13.
27   *Ibid.,* pp. 9–15.
28   Mayne, *op. cit.,* pp. 229–231.

29 *The Diary,* p. 231.

30 *Ibid.,* p. 401.

31 *Ibid.*

32 *Ibid.*

33 *Ibid.,* p. 402.

34 *Ibid.,* p. 400.

35 *Ibid.,* p. 399.

36 *Ibid.*

37 *Ibid.*

38 *Ibid.,* pp. 399–400.

39 *Ibid.,* p. 400.

40 *Ibid.,* p. 401. Dostoevsky also noted the lack of organized, structuralized forms in the Russian language, but nevertheless, "the spirit of our language is unquestionably multifaceted, wealthy, universal and all-embracing, since even within its organized forms it has proved able to express the gems and treasures of European thought, and we feel these have been expressed correctly and with precision."

41 *Ibid.,* p. 401.

42 *Ibid.,* p. 716.

43 *Ibid.*

44 *Ibid.,* p. 717.

45 *Ibid.*

46 *Ibid.*

47 Mayne, *op. cit.,* pp. 233–235.

48 *Ibid.*

49 *Ibid.,* pp. 254–255.

50 *Ibid.*

51 *Ibid.,* p. 255.

52 *Ibid.*

53 *Ibid.,* p. 236.

54 *The Diary,* p. 179.

55 *Ibid.*

56 *Ibid.,* p. 180.

57 See Thomas Woody, *History of Women's Education in the United States* (New York, 1929).

58 A. Kornilov, *Modern Russian History* (New York, 1952) II, 170.

59 *Ibid.,* p. 171.

60 Madame Konradi, editor of the progressive journal *Nedelia* (*The Weekly*) advocated the opening of the universities to

women throughout the sixties and in the seventies. See Daniel B. Leary, *Education and Autocracy in Russia* (Buffalo, 1919), p. 78.

61 *The Diary*, pp. 340–341.
62 *Ibid.*, p. 341.
63 *Ibid.*, p. 368.
64 *Ibid.*
65 *Ibid.*, p. 369.
66 *Ibid.*
67 *Ibid.*, p. 846. Dostoevsky also advocated the social and political equality for women: "Can we continue to deny [women] . . . full equality of rights with the male in the fields of education, professions, tenure of office . . . in connection with the re-generation and elevation of our society!"
68 *Ibid.*, pp. 724 ff. See also Ch. I of this work on the Slavophiles.
69 *Ibid.*, p. 703.
70 *Ibid.*, p. 608.
71 *Ibid.*
72 *Ibid.*, p. 609.
73 *Ibid.*
74 *Ibid.*
75 *Ibid.*, p. 843.
76 *Ibid.*, p. 63.
77 *Ibid.*
78 *Ibid.* Dostoevsky places the political problem within the context of the religious-ethical viewpoint. For his specific religious convictions, see Mayne, *op. cit.*, pp. 249–250, 233–234, 70–72. Also the teachings of Zossima give a clear exposition of Dostoevsky's Christianity.
79 *Ibid.*, p. 1000.
80 *Ibid.*
81 *Ibid.*, pp. 1000–1001.
82 *Ibid.*, p. 1001.
83 Convinced of this thesis, Dostoevsky looked upon the events in Europe of the second half of the nineteenth century with apprehension: ". . . Europe is on the eve of a general and dreadful collapse. The ant-hill which has long been in the process of construction without the Church and Christ . . . with a moral principle shaken loose from its foundation . . . [Europe] is utterly undermined. The fourth estate is coming,

it knocks at the door, and breaks into it, and if it is not opened it will break the door. . . . I merely foresee that the balance has been struck." The abnormality of Europe's political situation "must lead to a colossal, final, partitioning, political war in which everybody will be involved. . . ." *Ibid.*, p. 1003. Significantly Dostoevsky held that ". . . England and the United States [are] the only two remaining states in which political unity is solid and original," but "the moral and political condition of Europe has been undermined virtually everywhere." *Ibid.*, p. 283.

84 *Ibid.*, p. 1001.
85 *Ibid.*, p. 1002.
86 *Ibid.*

CHAPTER FOUR

1 Aimée Dostoevsky, *Fyodor Dostoyevsky* (London, 1921), pp. 183–185. See also E. Mayne, *The Letters of Fyodor Michailovitch Dostoevsky to His Family and Friends* (London, 1941), pp. 183–185, 225, 238.
2 Mayne, *op. cit.*, pp. 229–231, 235–239, 239–246, 253–255.
3 *The Diary of a Writer*, I., 142–143.
4 *Ibid.*, p. 145.
5 *Ibid.*
6 *Ibid.*, p. 149.
7 *Ibid.*, p. 150.
8 *Ibid.* Dostoevsky does not specify which particular works of Mill, Strauss, or Darwin are meant.
9 *Ibid.*
10 *Ibid.*
11 Mayne, *op. cit.*, p. 241.
12 *Ibid.*, pp. 241–242.
13 *Ibid.*
14 *Ibid.*, p. 246.
15 *Ibid.*
16 *The Diary of a Writer*, p. 166.
17 *Ibid.*, p. 175.
18 *Ibid.*, p. 176.
19 *Ibid.*, p. 181.
20 *Ibid.*, p. 201.

21 For a study of Dostoevsky's view on immortality, see pp. 540 ff. in *The Diary of a Writer*.
22 *Ibid.*, p. 543.
23 *Ibid.*, p. 544.
24 *Ibid.*
25 René Fueloep-Miller, *Fyodor Dostoevsky: Insight, Faith and Prophecy* (New York, 1950), Ch. VI. See also conclusion of this chapter.
26 *The Diary of a Writer*, pp. 544 ff.
27 *Ibid.*, p. 552.
28 *Ibid.*
29 Article entitled "Christmas Tree at the Artist's Club," *Ibid.*, p. 162.
30 *Ibid.*
31 *Ibid.*
32 *Ibid.*, p. 753.
33 Mayne, *op. cit.*, pp. 253–254.
34 See Frederick Eby, *The Development of Modern Education* (New York, 1952), pp. 601–602, for the history of educational psychological studies.
35 René Fueloep-Miller, *op. cit.*, Ch. VI.
36 J. Meier-Graefe, *Dostoevsky: The Man and His Work*, tr. by Herbert H. Marks (New York, 1928), pp. 236–237.
37 See the following section on "The Role of the Family in the Formation of Character."
38 Meier-Graefe, *op. cit.*, p. 77.
39 Ibid.
40 Freud was born in 1856, and was still a student when Dostoevsky's major novels had been written. The year Dostoevsky died (1881), Freud obtained his medical degree. Actually the science of psychiatry was introduced in the sixties in Paris by Charcot. Freud studied under him.
41 Mayne, *op. cit.*, p. 167.
42 See A. Gide, S. Freud, R. Fueloep-Miller, R. Lauth, E. Vivas, N. Berdyaev, R. Poggioli in the bibliography.
43 *The Diary of a Writer*, p. 759.
44 *Ibid.*, p. 760.
45 *Ibid.*, p. 753.
46 *Ibid.*, p. 761.
47 *Ibid.*, p. 150.

48   *Ibid.*, p. 762.

49   *Ibid.*

50   *Ibid.*, p. 234.

51   *Ibid.*, p. 237.

52   *Ibid.*, pp. 210 ff., 763 ff.

53   *Ibid.*, p. 770 f.

54   *Ibid.*, p. 772.

55   *Ibid.*, p. 775.

56   *Ibid.*, p. 777.

57   Fueloep-Miller, *op. cit.*, p. 83.

58   *Ibid.*

59   *Ibid.*, p. 84. See also C. M. Woodhouse and S. Freud in the bibliography.

60   *Crime and Punishment,* Modern Library edition, p. 528.

61   Fueloep-Miller, *op. cit.*, p. 89.

62   See Dostoevsky's Collected Works, Macmillan edition, 1950.

63   Fueloep-Miller, *op. cit.*, p. 91. See also various articles on specific problems in the field of psychology which Dostoevsky analyzed and anticipated in the bibliography.

CHAPTER FIVE

1   Vladimir Seduro, *Dostoevsky in Russian Literary Criticism 1846–1956* (New York, 1957), pp. 28–38.

2   F. W. J. Hemmings, *The Russian Novel in France, 1884–1914* (London, 1950), p. 228.

3   Helen Muchnic, *Dostoevsky's English Reputation (1884–1936)* (Northampton, Mass.), 1939, p. 128.

4   D. H. Lawrence, *Selected Literary Criticism,* ed. by Anthony Beal (New York, 1956), pp. 229–241.

5   Muchnic, *op. cit.*, pp. 151–152.

6   *Ibid.*

7   Hemmings, *op. cit.*, p. 235.

8   C. M. Woodhouse, *Dostoievsky* (London, 1951), p. 107.

9   Fyodor Dostoevsky, *The Short Novels of Dostoevsky,* Introduction by Thomas Mann (New York, 1951), p. xix.

10   Seduro, *op. cit.*, pp. 3–21

11   *Ibid.*, p. 95.

12   *Ibid.*, pp. 202–232.

13   *Ibid.*, p. 84.

14   *Ibid.*

15 *Ibid.*, p. 87.

16 *Ibid.*, p. 281.

17 *Ibid.*, p. 285.

18 *Ibid.*, p. 304.

19 In England, interest in Dostoevsky culminates the interest in Russian culture itself. He was not widely read until 1912, because of the lack of translations. In fact, not until 1921 were all of his artistic works rendered into English by Constance Garnett. In Germany, the translation of Dostoevsky began in 1850 and, in both France and Germany, all his works were fully known by 1890.

20 The "ecstatic" tradition of Dostoevsky criticism began in Germany with H. Hesse's essay in 1922 and continued in S. Zweig (1930).

21 René Fueloep-Miller, *Fyodor Dostoevsky: Insight, Faith and Prophecy* (New York, 1950), Chs. VI and VII. See also the works of R. Lauth, Z. Maurina, A. Gide, E. Lubac, W. Hubben, and L. A. Zander in the bibliography.

22 L. A. Zander, *Dostoevsky*, tr. by N. Duddington (London, 1948), p. 15.

23 *Ibid.* "Geneva ideas" refers to the doctrines of socialism and communism with which Dostoevsky became acquainted at first hand. He attended the conference of the socialists while in Geneva in 1868.

24 Seduro, *op. cit.*, p. 207.

25 Eleseo Vivas, *Creation and Discovery* (New York, 1955), p. 50.

26 Fyodor Dostoevsky, *The Diary of a Writer*, tr. by Boris Brasol, (New York, 1950), I, 83.

27 The novel *The Possessed* illustrates this point.

28 Nietzsche declared that Dostoevsky was the one person from whom he had learned anything significant in psychology. He read *Crime and Punishment* in the sixties, but his own work with the "superman" theory, *Thus Spake Zarathustra*, was written in 1883. See also H. Lubac, R. Lauth, N. Zernov in the Bibliography.

29 Fyodor Dostoevsky, *Crime and Punishment* (New York, 1951), pp. 27–36, 42–47.

30 The point beyond the logical plane of being in logic itself is considered to be a fallacy; however, from the religious point of view, this "transition to another plane of being" is called mira-

cle, and is above all, desired. See Zander, *op. cit.*, pp. 15–30, for the description and analyses of the two miracles in Dostoevsky's novels. *Crime and Punishment* and *The Brothers Karamazov.*

31 Fyodor Dostoevsky, *Notes From Underground* (New York, 1951), pp. 53–54.

32 Robert L. Jackson, *Dostoevskij's Underground Man in Russian Literature* (The Hague, 1958), pp. 27–28. On March 26, 1864, Dostoevsky wrote to his brother Mihail: ". . . It really would have been better not to have printed the penultimate chapter (the main one where the very idea is expressed) [chapter x in Part I] than to have printed it as it is, that is, with sentences thrown together, contradicting each other. But what is to be done! The swinish censors let pass those places where I ridiculed everything and blasphemed *for show,* but where I deduce from all this the need for faith and Christ—this is forbidden. Just who are these censors, are they in conspiracy against the government or something?"

33 In his book *The Impact of Science on Society* (New York, 1953), pp. 91–92, Bertrand Russell stated: ". . . our age needs . . . compassion and a wish that mankind should be happy; . . . The root of the matter is a very simple and old-fashioned thing . . . the thing I mean— . . . is love, Christian love or compassion. If you feel this, you have a motive for existence, a guide in action, a reason for courage, an imperative necessity for intellectual honesty." By permission of Simon and Schuster, Inc.

34 Vassili V. Zenkovsky, *A History of Russian Philosophy,* tr. by George L. Kline (New York, 1953), I, 147.

35 *Ibid.*

36 *Ibid.*

37 *Ibid.*

38 *Ibid.* See also Paul Ramsey, *Basic Christian Ethics* (New York, 1950), pp. 276–277, on Christian naturalism.

39 Zenkovsky, *op. cit.,* pp. 147–148.

40 Zander, *op. cit.,* pp. 30–31. See also footnote 30.

41 *Ibid.,* pp. 15–30.

42 George A. Panichas, "The Spiritual Art of Dostoevsky," *St. Vladimir's Seminary Quarterly* (Fall, 1958), II, no. 4, p. 27.

43 Nicholas Berdyaev, *The Spirit of Dostoevsky,* tr. by Donald Attwater (New York, 1957), p. 31.
44 Zenkovsky, *op. cit.,* p. 415.
45 See Dostoevsky's statement of faith in Ch. II of this work: "His Life in Siberian Exile." See also N. Berdyaev, *op. cit.,* pp. 111–132.
46 Paul Tillich, *Systematic Theology* (Chicago, 1957), II, 26.
47 Ethel Colburn Mayne, *Letters of Fyodor Michailovitch Dostoevsky to His Family and Friends* (London, 1914), p. 197.
48 Fyodor Dostoevsky, *The Brothers Karamazov,* Modern Library Giant edition (New York, n. d.), p. 335.
49 Fyodor Dostoevsky, *The Diary of a Writer,* I, 33.
50 Vivas, *op. cit.,* p. 58.
51 *The Diary of a Writer,* II, 1003.
52 *Ibid.*
53 Berdyaev, *op. cit.,* pp. 36–37. Dostoevsky loved Europe very much, and he wrote: "Europe is as precious as Russia; every stone in her is cherished and dear. Europe was as much our fatherland as Russia. Oh, even more so. It is impossible to love Russia more than I do, but I never reproached myself because Venice, Rome, Paris, the treasures of their arts and sciences, their whole history are dearer to me than Russia. Oh, those old, alien stones, those wonders of God's ancient world, those fragments of holy wonders are dear to the Russian, and are even dearer to us than to the inhabitants of those lands themselves." *Winter Notes On Summer Impressions,* tr. by Richard Lee Renfield (New York, 1955), p. 29. Dostoevsky also wrote in one of his letters: "The beautiful is the ideal; but ideals, with us as in civilized Europe, have long been wavering. There is in the world only one figure of absolute beauty: Christ." Mayne, *op. cit.,* p. 142.
54 V. Ivanov, *Freedom and the Tragic Life,* tr. by N. Cameron (London, 1952), p. 110.
55 Zenkovsky, *op. cit.,* p. 432.
56 *The Brothers Karamazov,* p. 111.
57 Mayne, *op. cit.,* pp. 233–234.
58 *The Diary of a Writer,* I, 150–151.
59 Zander, *op. cit.,* pp. 12–13.
60 *The Brothers Karamazov,* p. 336. For a statement parallel to

Dostoevsky's Christological foundation, see Paul Tillich, *op. cit.*, II, 118–137.

61 Janko Lavrin, *Dostoevsky* (New York, 1947), p. 41.

62 *The Brothers Karamazov*, p. 239.

63 *Ibid.*, p. 253.

64 *Ibid.*, p. 254.

65 *The Diary of a Writer*, I, 9–17.

66 This is the premise in the novel *Crime and Punishment*.

67 See N. Berdyaev, *The Destiny of Man*, tr. by N. Duddington (London, 1948), "The Problem of Ethical Knowledge," pp. 1–22.

68 *Ibid.* See also Paul Ramsey, *Basic Christian Ethics* (New York, 1950), pp. 92–116.

69 This is Raskolnikov's assertion in *Crime and Punishment*.

70 Zander, *op. cit.*, p. 31.

71 *The Brothers Karamazov*, pp. 337–338.

72 Panichas, *op. cit.*, p. 25.

73 *Ibid.*

74 *The Brothers Karamazov*, pp. 585–591.

75 *Ibid.*, pp. 819–820.

76 *Ibid.*, p. 821.

77 Even the worst reprobate, old Karamazov, was clearly conscious of the fact that Alyosha alone did not condemn him.

78 *The Brothers Karamazov*, pp. 585–591.

79 *Ibid.*, pp. 821–822.

80 Vladimir Šajković, "Notes on Dostoevsky," unpublished materials.

81 *Ibid.* The "loftiest idea of human existence" is the idea of immortality. See *The Diary of a Writer*, I, 539.

82 Šajković, *op. cit.*

83 *The Brothers Karamazov*, p. 242.

84 Seduro, *op. cit.*, p. 211.

85 *Ibid.*, p. 214.

86 *Ibid.*

87 *Ibid.*, p. 219.

88 *Ibid.* The work of Bakhtin is today almost unknown outside Soviet Russia, and in the USSR he is ignored. He was, of course, criticized severely for "ignoring the class character of Dostoevsky's ideology." In fact, Bakhtin absolutely denied the influence of concrete social factors—family or class—on the

characters; Dostoevsky's characters are dialogues of man with himself, of man with man. *Ibid.*, pp. 227–229, 232.

89 *Notes From Underground*, Macmillan edition, p. 69.

90 *Ibid.*

91 *Ibid.*, p. 71.

92 The dimension of the irrational is metaphysical freedom, the realm of spirit.

93 *Notes From Underground*, p. 67.

94 Herman Dooyeweerd, *In the Twilight of Western Thought*, Studies in the Pretended Autonomy of Philosophical Thought, The Presbyterian and Reformed Publishing Company (Philadelphia, 1960), p. 186.

95 Mayne, *op. cit.*, pp. 6–7.

96 Šajković, *op. cit.*

97 *Ibid.*

98 Zenkovsky, *op. cit.*, p. 419.

99 Berdyaev, *op. cit.*, p. 67.

100 Fyodor Dostoevsky, *The House of the Dead*, Macmillan edition (New York, 1950), pp. 275–276.

101 Sajkovic, *op. cit.*

102 John Dewey, *Problems of Men*, Philosophical Library (New York, 1946), p. 300.

103 *Notes From Underground*, p. 68.

104 *Ibid.*, pp. 74–75.

105 *Ibid.*, pp. 68–69.

106 *Ibid.*, p. 62.

107 *Ibid.*, p. 78.

108 St. Augustine taught the existence of two freedoms. See Berdyaev, *op. cit.*, p. 688 ff.

109 Šajković, *op. cit.*

110 *Ibid.*

111 See *The Brothers Karamazov*, Modern Library Giant Edition, pp. 380–381, and *Crime and Punishment*, tr. by David Magarshack, Penguin Books edition, pp. 555–559. Also L. A. Zander, Dostoevsky, tr. by N. Duddington (London, 1948), pp. 15–35.

112 *The Brothers Karamazov*, p. 333.

113 Sajković, *op. cit.*

114 Berdyaev, *op. cit.*, p. 89.

115 The exact meaning of the Russian is translated: Guilt and Expiation.

116 *Crime and Punishment,* p. 231.

117 *Ibid.*

118 *Ibid.*

119 *Ibid.,* p. 233. Nietzsche's words echo Raskolnikov: "Mankind is much more of a means than an end . . . mankind is merely the experimental material. . . . The object is to attain that enormous *energy of greatness* which can model the man of the future by means of discipline and also by means of the annihilation of millions of the bungled and botched, and which can yet avoid *going to ruin* at the sight of the suffering created thereby, the like of which has never been seen before." Bertrand Russell, *The Will to Doubt* (New York, 1958), pp. 91–92.

120 *Ibid.,* pp. 392, 395. Dostoevsky always drives a concrete fact to its extreme. In this case, the old usuress was bleeding innocent people; her life was "worthless." Further, the deed is complicated by the sister of the old woman who walks in on the scene of the murder; Raskolnikov is forced to kill her, too. The deed itself is the "extreme" one of taking life. In *The Brothers Karamazov,* Ivan takes the "extreme" and unanswerable case of innocent children who suffer the sadistic cruelties from adults in presenting the problem of suffering to the moral consciousness. Every account of Ivan is a fact from the newspapers of the time, as Dostoevsky wrote in a letter to his editor. Kirillov in *The Possessed* also drives home the extreme consequence of the "illusion" of God; if God is *not,* then man is God. The final proof required is for man to overcome death. This means someone must take the "first step" and take his own life, in order to show mankind the "Truth." Kirillov acts and commits suicide to awaken mankind to the "Truth."

121 All the obvious socio-environmental reasons are present in Raskolnikov's case, but they are not the causes or motivations for the crime.

122 *The Diary of a Writer,* I, 13. See also Mayne, *op. cit.,* pp. 218–220.

123 I refer the reader to Chs. III and IV of this work.

124 See Boris Pasternak, *Dr. Zhivago,* tr. by Max Hayward and Manya Harari (New York, 1958). Pasternak's novel is a monument to the countless people who lived through the horrors and tragedies of the revolution, to the families—the old and

the young—whose lives were shattered beyond repair. The essence of Dostoevsky's compassion and understanding is present in the texture of the work. Pasternak is the new link in the chain of the great Russian classic thinkers.

125 *The Brothers Karamazov,* p. 677.

126 The description of evil today can be studied in T. S. Eliot's *Wasteland,* in Sartre's works, and in the novels of Franz Kafka. Man's consciousness has moved far from Dante's *Inferno* and the Pilgrim Fathers' "hell-fire and brimstone."

127 In anticipating the proposition that in order to purge oneself from evil one should commit crime (which someone might deduce from Dostoevsky), Berdyaev said: "Only an immature or enslaved mind would deduce from Dostoievsky's thesis that we must choose to follow the path of wickedness in order to enrich our consciousness and profit from a new experience. The theory that evil is only a moment in the evolution of good cannot be imputed to him; this evolutionary optimism . . . is entirely opposed to his spirit. He was no evolutionist; evil for him was evil, to be burned in the fires of hell, and that is where he cast it. He teaches plainly that it is not a thing to be juggled with, that it is madness to think that a man can deliberately enter on a course of wickedness to get what he can out of it and then threw himself into the arms of the good: such an argument cannot be taken seriously and indicates a worthless state of mind. Certainly the tragic experience of evil can profit a man and sharpen his understanding, certainly he cannot thereafter return to his former stage of development; but when a sinning man begins to think that evil is enriching him, that it is leading him to the good, that it is only a stage in his progress, from that moment he has failed completely: he goes all to pieces and every door to improvement and regeneration is closed to him. . . . To climb from evil to a high spiritual level one must denounce the evil in oneself and suffer terribly, and these sufferings Dostoievsky depicted." Berdyaev, *op. cit.,* pp. 93–94.

128 *Ibid.,* p. 93. Raskolnikov's conscience is an illustration. Zossima has the following to say about "hell and hell fire:" "What is hell? I maintain that it is the suffering of being unable to love. . . . They talk of hell fire in the material sense. I don't go into that mystery and I shun it. But I think if there were

fire in the material sense, they would be glad of it, for, I imagine, that in material agony, their still greater spiritual agony would be forgotten for a moment. Moreover, that spiritual agony cannot be taken from them, for that suffering is not external but within them. . . ." p. 338.

129 *The Diary of a Writer*, I, 15–16.

130 Berdyaev, *op. cit.*, p. 108.

131 *Ibid.*, p. 109.

132 Henri Troyat, *Firebrand: The Life of Dostoevsky*, tr. from the French by Norbett Gutemann (New York, 1946), p. 135.

133 *Notes From Underground*, p. 71.

134 *The Brothers Karamazov*, p. 239.

135 *Ibid.*

136 *Crime and Punishment*, pp. 392–395.

137 *The Diary of a Writer*, II, 622.

138 *Ibid.*

139 *The Idiot*, tr. by David Magarshack, Baltimore, 1955, p. 433.

140 Dmitri in *The Brothers Karamazov* exclaims that "we are all responsible to all," even though he would be deep in a mine in a Siberian prison, he would cry out, and even there "sing from the bowels of the earth a glorious hymn to God, with Whom is joy." p. 720.

141 *The Idiot*, pp. 595–596.

142 *The Brothers Karamazov*, p. 382.

143 Panichas, *op. cit.*, p. 20.

144 *Ibid.*, p. 32.

CHAPTER SIX

1 Fyodor M. Dostoevsky, *The Diary of a Writer (New York, 1949)*, II, 572–573.

2 *Ibid.*, I, 490.

3 *Ibid.*, II, 1001.

4 *Ibid.*, p. 1002.

5 *Ibid.*, I, 150–154.

6 George C. Strem, "The Moral World of Dostoevsky," *The Russian Review*, vol. 16, no. 3 (July, 1957), p. 26.

7 J. Donald Butler, "Building a Philosophy of Education," *Foundations of Education*, ed. by Frederick Gruber, The Martin Brumbaugh Lectures, First Series, University of Pennsylvania Press (Philadelphia, 1957), p. 83.

8 Frederick Eby, *The Development of Modern Education in Theory, Organization, and Practice,* by permission of Prentice-Hall, Inc. (Englewood Cliffs, New Jersey, 1952), pp. 629–630.

9 Yervant H. Krikorian, ed., *Naturalism and the Human Spirit,* Columbia University Press (New York, 1949), pp. 242–243.

10 *Ibid.*

11 *Ibid.,* pp. 357–358.

12 Paul Ramsey, *Basic Christian Ethics,* Charles Scribner's Sons (New York, 1950), p. 269. One branch of naturalism today goes so far as to define science as "invention" rather than discovery: "science is a symbolic system by which our experiences can be correlated in a practical way. . . ." The argument ends in a solipsism. See "A Colloquy on the Unity of Learning," *Daedalus* (Fall, 1958), 87, no. 4, pp. 158–159.

13 Strem, *op. cit.,* p. 15.

14 Ethel Colburn Mayne, *Letters of Fyodor Michailovitch Dostoevsky to His Family and Friends* (London, 1914), p. 236.

15 Butler, *op. cit.,* p. 92.

16 *Ibid.,* p. 93.

17 See article of K. C. Hill, "Crime and Punishment as Philosophy," *General Education* (1953), 7:122–132.

18 Herman Dooyeweerd, *op. cit.;* after completing this present work, the four volume edition of Dooyeweerd's *A New Critique of Theoretical Thought,* tr. into English by David H. Freeman and H. De Jongste, Uitgeverij H. J. Paris-Amsterdam and The Presbyterian and Reformed Publishing Company (Philadelphia, 1953–58), has come into my possession. This scholarly work is of utmost importance for modern philosophy; it sustains the direction which I have tried to point out in this work on Dostoevsky.

APPENDIX

Selections from Dostoevsky's Writings
A Bibliographical Handbook

THE TEACHER of English in junior and senior high schools has a multiple task with students: to help them further the mastery of the fundamental skills of language (grammatical structure and syntax in writing, reading and oral expression); to transmit direct knowledge in both language and literature; to awaken the understanding and appreciation of the richness of one's own language and the literatures of many people as well as one's own. A fourth task is more often a by-product, that is, the ideals, attitudes, and realities of life which personally touch the heart and mind and challenge the student in the reading of literature. Yet it is this fourth factor in teaching which is the most momentous. In the meeting of characters and situations of the novelists and dramatists, from the imaginations of the poets, in the thought of the essayists, students find life values. Their own values and prejudices may be challenged, conscious thought-feeling may be awakened, and strivings for one's life vocation may be evoked.

For the past twelve years, many of the following selections from the writings of F. M. Dostoevsky have been introduced to students from the seventh to the twelfth grades, in public and in private schools, by colleagues and myself. The inspiration many students gained from the reading and the discussion of selected works from Dostoevsky is incalculable. Dostoevsky has stirred many students *to begin* the difficult task of clarifying their thoughts; he has reinforced their idealism, and has helped them to better face hard realities of life without assuming an attitude of cynicism in our troubled world today. I do not know of a junior or a senior, among the hundreds of students who have passed through my classes, who did not hold *Crime and Punishment* to be the "greatest" novel of his life.

In the teaching of and in understanding of our national ideals and citizenship, universal brotherhood, the problem of freedom, happiness, and so on in our social studies classes, selections from Dostoevsky offer rich and profound challenges. In senior classes, selections from Dostoevsky, together with selections from Plato, J. S. Mill, Milton, E. Burke, T. Jefferson, B. Franklin, *et al.*, have been read, and have opened fruitful comparative discussions on the above-mentioned issues. Students have been greatly inspired, and not in answers so much as in the provoking of their own creative, original thought.

The following section has been included as an aid to both teachers and students, for the purpose of further introducing special selections from the works of Dostoevsky. It is in the form of a bibliographical handbook; his works are available in current publications.

SEVENTH & EIGHTH GRADES

Literature classes:

"The Heavenly Christmas Tree" (also called "A Little Boy at Christ's Christmas Tree," a short story, Diary of a Writer, Vol. I, 168–172, 4½ pp.).

"The Peasant Marey," Diary of a Writer, Vol. I, 207–210, 4 pp.

"A Meeting With the Schoolboys" (complete scene from the novel *The Brothers Karamazov*, Modern Library Giant edition, Random House, New York, 182–186, 4 pp.).

EIGHTH GRADE

Literature classes:

Book X "The Boys" (from the novel *The Brothers Karamazov*, 545–591, 46 pp.).

Epilogue, III, "Ilusha's Funeral. The Speech at the Stone" (from same novel as above, 813–822, 9 pp.).

NINTH & TENTH GRADES

Literature classes:

"The Heavenly Christmas Tree" (see above).

"White Nights" (or A Sentimental Story from the Diary of a Dreamer, a short story, Macmillan, 1950 edition of *Works*, 1–50, 50 pp.).

Selections from the Letters of Dostoevsky (These are included in this section as they are out of print in English editions.)

Selections from the novel The Brothers Karamazov:

1. The peasant women, Madame Holahov, Lise and Father Zossima (45–58, 13 pp.).
2. "A Meeting with the Schoolboys" (182–186, 4 pp.).
3. Book X, "The Boys" (545–591, 46 pp.).
4. Epilogue, III, "Ilusha's Funeral. The Speech at the Stone" (813–822, 9 pp.)

History and literature classes:

"The Legend of the Grand Inquisitor" from the novel *The Brothers Karamazov* (255–274, 19 pp.).

On freedom, true democracy

Selections from the August, 1880, Pushkin issue of *A Diary of a Writer*, Vol. II.

On happiness: "But what kind of happiness would it be if it were based upon somebody's unhappiness?" (973–974)

On a nation's ideals and on citizenship (1000–1002)

ELEVENTH & TWELFTH GRADES

Literature classes:

Short Stories (*Diary of a Writer* or
Macmillan 1950 edition
of complete works.)

"The Heavenly Christmas Tree"

"The Little Hero"

"White Nights" (a romance)

"A Faint Heart" (a young man dies from happiness)

"An Unpleasant Predicament" (a young general pays a visit
to the wedding feast of his
subordinate clerk)

"The Honest Thief" (also read N. Gogol's "The Cloak" for
comparative study)

"The Dream of a Ridiculous Man" (utopia)

Selections from the Letters of Dostoevsky (These are included
in this section.)

Selections from the novel The Brothers Karamazov:

Same as ninth & tenth grades with the following additions:

"The Brothers Make Friends" (237–255, 18 pp.)

Father Zossima's teachings (327–342, 15 pp.)

On Dreams:

"The Devil. Ivan's Nightmare" (from the novel *The
Brothers* Karamazov,
673–690, 21 pp.)

Raskolnikov's dreams from *Crime & Punishment.*

Novels

Crime and Punishment (the superman idea)*

A Raw Youth (autobiography of a nineteen-year-old student)

*Seniors who have read Shakespeare's *Hamlet* could work on papers and discussions on the two heroes Raskolnikov and Hamlet:
two "modern" young men.

ELEVENTH & TWELFTH GRADES

History classes:

Selections from the August, 1880, Pushkin issue of *A Diary of a Writer* (*see* ninth & tenth grades).

Comparative study of Part I *Notes From Underground* with the story "The Dream of a Ridiculous Man" (problems of the meaning of life, freedom, reason, 2 plus 2 equals 4).

"The Legend of the Grand Inquisitor" (*see* ninth & tenth grades).

From *Diary of a Writer:*

> On juveniles: Vol. I, 172–182, 10 pp.
>
> Vol. I, 330–339, 9 pp.

SELECTIONS FROM THE LETTERS OF
F. M. DOSTOEVSKY

LETTERS TO HIS BROTHER MICHAEL

Petersburg
August 9, 1838

(The letter begins with explanations of why Dostoevsky has not written to his brother for so long: he has not had a kopek.)

It is true that I am idle—very idle. But what will become of me, if everlasting idleness is to be my only attitude towards life? I don't know if my gloomy mood will ever leave me. And to think that such a state of mind is allotted to man alone— the atmosphere of his soul seems compounded of a mixture of the heavenly and the earthly. What an unnatural product, then, is he, since the law of spiritual nature is in him violated. . . . This earth seems to me a purgatory for divine spirits who have been assailed by sinful thoughts. I feel that our world has become one immense Negative, and that everything noble, beautiful, and divine, has turned itself into a satire. If in this picture there occurs an individual who neither in idea nor effect harmonizes with the whole—who is, in a word, an entirely unrelated figure—what must happen to the picture? It is destroyed, and can no longer endure.

Yet how terrible it is to perceive only the coarse veil under which the All doth languish! To know that one single effort of the will would suffice to demolish that veil and become one with eternity—to know all this, and still live on like the last and least of creatures. . . . How terrible! How petty is man! Hamlet! Hamlet! When I think of his moving wild speech, in which resounds the groaning of the whole numbed universe, there breaks from *my* soul not one reproach, not one sigh. . . . That soul is then so utterly oppressed by woe that it fears to grasp the woe entire, lest so it lacerate itself. Pascal once said: He who protests against philosophy is himself a philosopher. A poor sort of system!

[Dostoevsky goes on to enlarge on his brother's and his own financial difficulties.]

However, it is time to speak of other things. You plume yourself on the number of books you have read. . . . But don't please imagine that I envy you that. At Peterhoff I read at least as many as you have. The whole of Hoffmann in Russian and German (that is, "Kater Murr," which hasn't yet been translated), and nearly all Balzac. (Balzac is great! His characters are the creations of an all-embracing intelligence. Not the spirit of the age, but whole millenniums, with all their strivings, have worked towards such development and liberation in the soul of man.) Besides all these, I read Goethe's "Faust" and his shorter poems, Polevois' History, "Ugolino" and "Undine" (I'll write at length about "Ugolino" some other time), and, finally, Victor Hugo, except "Cromwell" and "Hernani." Farewell. Write to me, please, as often as you possibly can, for your letters are a joy and solace. Answer *this* at once. I shall expect your reply in twelve days at the very latest. Do write, that I may not utterly languish.

Thy brother,

F. Dostoevsky

Petersburg
October 31, 1838

How long since I've written to you, dear brother! That hateful examination—it prevented me from writing to you and Papa, and from looking up I. N. Schidlovsky. And what came of it all? I have not yet been promoted. O horror! to live another whole year in this misery! I should not have been so furious did I not know that I am the victim of the sheerest baseness. The failure would not have worried me so much, if our poor father's tears had not burned into my soul. I had not hitherto known the sensation of wounded vanity. If such a feeling had got hold of me, I might well have blushed for myself. . . . But now you must know that I should like to crush the whole world at one blow. . . . I lost so much time before the examination, and was ill and miserable besides; but *underwent* it in the fullest and most literal sense of the word, and yet have failed. . . . It is the decree of the Professor of Algebra, to whom, in the course of the year, I had been somewhat cheeky, and who was base enough to remind me of it today, while ostensibly explaining to me the reason for my failure. Out of ten full marks I got an average of nine and a half, and yet I'm left. . . . But hang it all, if I must suffer, I will. . . . I'll waste no more paper on this topic, for I so seldom have an opportunity to talk with you.

My friend, you philosophize like a poet. And just because the soul cannot be for ever in a state of exaltation, your philosophy is not true and not just. To *know* more, one must *feel less*, and *vice versa*. Your judgment is feather-headed—it is a delirium of the heart. What do you mean precisely by the word *know*? Nature, the soul, love, and God, one recognizes through the heart, and not through the reason. Were we spirits, we could dwell in that region of ideas over which our souls hover, seeking the solution. But we are earth-born beings, and can only guess at the Idea—not grasp it by all sides at once. The guide for our intelligences through the temporary illusion into the innermost centre of the soul is called *Reason*. Now, Reason is a material capacity, while the soul or spirit lives on the thoughts which are whispered by the heart. Thought is born in the soul. Reason is a tool, a machine, which is driven by the spiritual fire. When human reason (which would demand a chapter for itself) penetrates into the domain of knowledge, it works independently of the *feeling*, and consequently of the *heart*. But when our aim is the understanding of love or of nature, we march towards the very citadel of the heart. I don't want to vex you, but I do want to say that I don't share your views on poetry or philosophy. Philosophy cannot be regarded as a mere equation where nature is the unknown quantity! Remark that the poet, in the moment of inspiration, comprehends God, and consequently does the philosopher's work. Consequently poetic inspiration is nothing less than philosophical inspiration. Consequently philosophy is nothing but poetry, a higher degree of poetry. It is odd that you reason quite in the sense of our contemporary philosophy. What a lot of crazy systems have been born of late in the cleverest and most ardent brains! To get a right result from this motley troop one would have to subject them all to a mathematical formula. And yet they are the "laws" of our contemporary philosophy! I have jabbered enough. And if I look upon your flabby system as impossible, I think it quite likely that my objections are no less flabby, so I won't bother you with any more of them.

Brother, it is so sad to live without hope! When I look forward I shudder at the future. I move in a cold arctic atmosphere, wherein no sunlight ever pierces. For a long time I have not had a single outbreak of inspiration. . . . Hence I feel as the Prisoner of Chillon felt after his brother's death. The Paradise-bird of poetry will never, never visit me again —never again warm my frozen soul. You say that I am reserved; but all my former dreams have long since forsaken me, and from those glorious arabesques that I once could fashion all the gilding has disappeared. The thoughts that used to kindle my soul and heart have lost their glow and ardency; or else my heart is numbed, or else. . . . I am afraid to go on with that sentence. I won't admit that all the past was a dream, a bright golden dream.

. . . Now listen. I think that the poet's inspiration is increased by success. Byron was an egoist; *his* longing for fame was petty. But the mere thought that through one's inspiration there will one day lift itself from the dust to heaven's heights some noble, beautiful human soul; the thought that those lines over which one has wept are consecrated as by a heavenly rite through one's inspiration, and that over them the coming generations will weep in echo . . . that thought, I am convinced, has come to many a poet in the very moment of his highest creative rapture. But the shouting of the mob is empty and vain. There occur to me those lines of Pushkin where he describes the mob and the poet:

So let the foolish crowd, thy work despising, scream,
And spit upon the shrine where burns thy fire supreme,
Let them in childish arrogance thy tripod set a-
                    tremble. . . .

Wonderful, isn't it? Farewell,

Your friend and brother,
F. Dostoevsky

Postscript:

By the way, do tell me what is the leading idea in Chateaubriand's work "Genie du Christianisme." I read lately in *Ssyn Otetschestva* an attack by the critic Nisard on Victor Hugo. How little the French esteem him! How low does Nisard rate his dramas and romances! They are unfair to him; and Nisard (though he is so intelligent) talks nonsense. Tell me, too, the leading motive of your drama; I am sure it is fine.

I pity our poor father! He has such a remarkable character. What trouble he has had. It is so bitter that I can do nothing to console him! But, do you know, Papa is wholly a stranger in the world. He has lived in it now for fifty years, and yet he has the same opinions of mankind that he had thirty years ago. What sublime innocence! Yet the world has disappointed him, and I believe that that is the destiny of us all. Farewell.

Petersburg
January 1, 1840

I thank you from my heart, good brother, for your dear letter. I am certainly quite a different sort of person from you; you could never imagine how delightfully my heart thrills when they bring me a letter from you, and I have invented a new sort of enjoyment: I put myself on the rack. I take your letter in my hand, turn it about for some minutes, feel it to see whether it's long, and when I've satiated myself with the sealed enevelope, I put it in my pocket. . . .

I believe that in human life are infinite pain and infinite joy. In the poet's life spring thorns and roses. The lyric is like the poet's shadow, always with him, for he is an articulate creature. . . .

[Dostoevsky speaks of reading with a friend Homer, Shakespeare, Schiller and Hoffman. Later he writes about Pushkin, Schiller and others:]

Pushkin and Schiller . . . have no smallest point of resemblance. Now between Pushkin and Byron one *might* speak of a likeness. But as to Homer and Victor Hugo, I positively believe that you have chosen to misunderstand me! This is what I meant: Homer (a legendary figure, who was perhaps sent to us by God, as Christ was) can only be placed with Christ; by no means with Victor Hugo. Do try, brother, to enter truly into the Iliad; read it attentively (now confess that you never have read it) . Homer, in the Iliad, gave to the ancient world the same organization in spiritual and earthly matters as the modern world owes to Christ. Do you understand me now? Victor Hugo is a singer, clear as an angel, and his poetry is chaste and Christian through and through; no one like him in that respect—neither Schiller (if Schiller is a Christian poet at all), nor the lyric Shakespeare, nor Byron, nor Pushkin. I have read his Sonnets in French. Homer alone has the same unshakeable belief in his vocation for poetry and in the god of poetry whom he serves—in that sole respect his poetry is like Victor Hugo's, but *not* in the ideas with which Nature gifted him, and which he succeeded in expressing—I never meant the ideas at all, never. I even think that Dershavin stands higher as a lyricist than either of those two.

Postscript:

I must give you one more scolding. When you talk about form in poetry, you seem to me quite crazy. I mean it seriously. . . . But do tell me how, when you were talking about forms, you could advance the proposition that neither Racine nor Corneille could please us, because their forms were bad? You miserable wretch! And then you add with such effrontery: "Do you think, then, that they were both bad poets?" Racine no poet—Racine the ardent, the passionate, the idealist Racine, no poet! Do you dare to ask that? Have you read his "Andromaque"—eh? Have you read his "Iphigenie"? Will you by any chance maintain that it is not splendid? And isn't Racine's Achilles of the same race as Homer's? . . .

[About Corneille Dostoevsky writes:]

. . . with his titanic figures and his romantic spirit, nearly approaches Shakespeare, and what does the romantic stand for, if it doesn't reach its highest development in the "Cid"?

From March 24, 1845
Letter

I read a great deal, and it has a curious effect on me. When I re-read anything that I knew years ago, I feel fresh powers in myself. I can pierce to the heart of the book, grasp it entire, and from it draw new confidence in myself. . . .

Brother, in literary matters I am not the same person that I was a couple of years ago. Then it was all childishness and folly. These two years of hard study have taken much from me, and brought much to me.

Letter of 1847 (excerpt)

I must once more beg you to forgive me for not having kept my word, and written by the next post.

[Dostoevsky is aware and concerned with his brother's health and his burdens:]

But don't lose courage, brother. Better days will come. And

know this, the richer we are in mind and spirit, the fairer will our life appear. It is indeed true that the dissonance and lack of equilibrium between ourselves and society is a terrible thing. External and internal things should be in equilibrium. For, lacking external experiences, those of the inward life will gain the upper hand, and that is most dangerous. The nerves and the fancy then take up too much room, as it were, in our consciousness. Every external happening seems colossal, and frightens us. We begin to fear life. It is at any rate a blessing that Nature has gifted you with powers of affection and strength of character. . . .

[About his own character, Dostoevsky writes in the Post-script:]

. . . but even when my heart is warm with love, people often can't get so much as one friendly word out of me. At such times I have lost control of my nerves. I appear ludi-crous, repellent, and have to suffer inexpressibly from the mis-understanding of my fellow-creatures. People call me arid and heartless. . . . I can show myself to be a man of feeling and humour only when external circumstances lift me high above the external daily round. When that is not my state, I am always repellent.

From the Fortress
July 18, 1849

Dear Brother,

I was inexpressibly glad of your letter, which I got on July 11. At last you are free, and I can vividly imagine how happy you were when you saw your family again. How impatiently they must have awaited you! I seem to see that your life is beginning to shape itself differently. With what are you now occupied, and, above all, what are your means of support? Have you work, and of what sort? Summer is indeed a burden in the town. You tell me only that you have taken a new house; and probably it is much smaller. It is a pity you couldn't spend the whole summer in the country. I thank you for the things you sent; they have relieved and diverted me.

You write, my dear fellow, that I must not lose heart. Indeed, I am not losing heart at all; to be sure, life here is very monotonous and dreary, but what else could it be? And after all it isn't invariably so tedious. The time goes by most irregularly, so to speak—now too quickly, now too slowly. Sometimes I have the feeling that I've grown accustomed to this sort of life, and that nothing matters very much. Of course, I try to keep all alluring thoughts out of my head, but can't always succeed; my early days, with their fresh impressions, storm in on my soul, and I live all the past over again. That is in the natural order of things. The days are now for the most part bright, and I am somewhat more cheerful. The rainy days, though, are unbearable, and on them the casemate looks terribly grim. I have occupation, however, I do not let the time go by for naught; I have made out the plots of three tales and two novels; and am writing a novel now, but avoid over-working. Such labour, when I do it with great enjoyment (I have never worked so much *con amore* as now), has always agitated me and affected my nerves. While I was working in freedom I was always obliged to diversify my labours with amusements; but here the excitement consequent on the work has to evaporate unaided. My health is good, (on the whole) . . . When our case will be finished I can't say at all, for I have lost all sense of time, and merely use a calendar upon which I stroke out, quite passively, each day as it passes: "That's over!" I haven't read much since I've been here: two descriptions of travel in the Holy Land, and the works of Demetrius von Rostov. The latter interested me very much; but that kind of reading is only a drop in the ocean; any other sorts of books would, I imagine, quite extraordinarily delight me, and they might be very useful, for thus I could diversify my own thoughts with those of others, or at all events capture a different mood. . . . Don't be too anxious on my account. I have but one wish—to be in good health; the tedium is a passing matter, and cheerfulness depends in the last resort upon myself. Human beings have an incredible amount

of endurance and will to live; I should never have expected
to find so much in myself; now I know it from experience.
Farewell! . . .

Excerpts from
The Fortress
August 27, 1849

I rejoice that I may answer you, dear brother, and thank
you for sending the books. I rejoice also that you are well, and
that the imprisonment had no evil effects upon your constitution. . . .

I have nothing definite to tell you about myself. As yet I
know nothing whatever about our case. My *personal* life is as
monotonous as ever; but they have given me permission to
walk in the garden, where there are almost seventeen trees!
This is a great happiness for me. Moreover, I am given a
candle in the evenings—that's my second piece of luck. . . .
Will you send me some historical works? That would be
splendid. But the best of all would be the Bible (both
Testaments). I need one. Should it prove possible send it in a
French translation. But if you could add as well a Slav edition, it would be the height of bliss.

Excerpts from last letter
The Fortress
December 22, 1849

Brother, my precious friend! all is settled! I am sentenced to
four years' hard labour in the fortress (I believe, of Oren-
burg) and after that to serve as a private. To-day, the 22nd
of December, we were taken to the Semionov Drill Ground.
There the sentence of death was read to all of us, we were
told to kiss the Cross, our swords were broken over our
heads. . . . Then three were tied to the pillar for execution.
I was the sixth. Three at a time were called out; consequently,
I was in the second batch and no more than a minute was
left me to live. I remembered you, brother, and all yours; during the last minute you, you alone, were in my mind. Only
then I realised how I love you, dear brother mine! I also

managed to embrace Plescheyev and Durov who stood close
to me and to say good-bye to them. Finally the retreat was
sounded, and those tied to the pillar were led back, and it was
announced to us that His Imperial Majesty granted us our
lives. Then followed the present sentences. . . .

Brother! I have not become downhearted or low-spirited.
Life is everywhere life, life in ourselves, not in what is outside us. There will be people near me, and to be a *man*
among people and remain a man for ever, not to be downhearted nor to fall in whatever misfortunes may befall me—
this is life; this is the task of life. I have realised this. This
idea has entered into my flesh and into my blood. Yes, it's
true! The head which was creating, living with the highest
life of art, which had realised and grown used to the highest
needs of the spirit, that head has already been cut off from
my shoulders. There remain the memory and the images
created but not yet incarnated by me. They will lacerate me,
it is true! But there remains in me my heart and the same
flesh and blood which can also love and suffer, and desire,
and remember, and this, after all, is life. *On voit le soleil!*
Now, good-bye, brother! Don't grieve for me! . . . Think of
the future of your children. . . . Live positively. There has
never yet been working in me such a healthy abundance of
spiritual life as now. . . .

Can it be that I shall never take a pen into my hands? I
think that after the four years there may be a possibility. I
shall send you everything that I may write, if I write anything, my God! How many imaginations, lived through by
me, created by me anew, will perish, will be extinguished in
my brain or will be spilt as poison in my blood! Yes, if I am
not allowed to write, I shall perish. Better fifteen years of
prison with a pen in my hands!

. . . When I look back at the past and think how much
time has been wasted in vain, how much time was lost in de-
lusions, in errors, in idleness, in ignorance of how to live, how
I did not value time, how often I sinned against my heart

and spirit,—my heart bleeds. Life is a gift, life is happiness, each minute might have been an age of happiness. *Si jeunesse savait!* Now, changing my life, I am being reborn into a new form. Brother! I swear to you that I shall not lose hope, and shall preserve my spirit and heart in purity. I shall be reborn to a better thing. That is my whole hope, my whole comfort! . . .

TOPIC EXCERPTS FROM DOSTOEVSKY'S LETTERS

MEN ARE—MEN

Omsk, February 22, 1854

. . . For that matter, men everywhere are just—men. Even among the robber-murderers in the prison, I came to know some men in those four years. Believe me, there were among them deep, strong, and beautiful natures, and it often gave me great joy to find gold under a rough exterior. And not in a single case, or even two, but in several cases. Some inspired respect; others were downright fine. I taught the Russian language and reading to a young Circassian—he had been transported to Siberia for robbery with murder. How grateful he was to me! Another convict wept when I said good-bye to him. Certainly I had often given him money, but it was so little, and his gratitude so boundless. My character, though, was deteriorating; in my relations with others I was ill-tempered and impatient. They accounted for it by my mental condition, and bore all without grumbling. Apropos: what a number of national types and characters I became familiar with in the prison! I lived *into* their lives, and so I believe I know them really well. Many tramps' and thieves' careers were laid bare to me, and, above all, the whole wretched existence of the common people. Decidedly I have not spent my time there in vain. I have learnt to know the Russian people as only a few know them. I am a little vain of it. I hope that such vanity is pardonable.

ON HIS FAITH

Omsk, Beginning of March, 1854

. . . I don't know why, but I guess from your letter that you returned home in bad spirits. I understand it; I have sometimes thought that if ever I return home, I shall get more grief than joy from my impressions there. I have not lived your life, and much in it is unknown to me, and indeed, no one can really know exactly his fellow-mortal's life; still, human feeling is common to us all, and it seems to me that everyone who has been banished must live all his past grief over again in consciousness and memory, on his return home. It is like a balance, by which one can test the true gravity of what one has endured, gone through, and lost. God grant you a long life! I have heard from many people that you are very religious. But not because you are religious, but because I myself have learned it and gone through it, I want to say to you that in such moments, one does, "like dry grass," thirst after faith, and that one finds it in the end, solely and simply because one sees the truth more clearly when one is unhappy. I want to say to you, about myself, that I am a child of this age, a child of unfaith and skepticism, and probably (indeed I know it) shall remain so to the end of my life. How dreadfully has it tormented me (and torments me even now)—this longing for faith, which is all the stronger for the proofs I have against it. And yet God gives me sometimes moments of perfect peace; in such moments I love and believe that I am loved; in such moments I have formulated my creed, wherein all is clear and holy to me. This creed is extremely simple; here it is: I believe that there is nothing lovelier, deeper, more sympathetic, more rational, more manly, and more perfect than the Saviour; I say to myself with jealous love that not only is there no one else like Him, but that there could be no one. I would even say more: if anyone could prove to me that Christ is outside the truth, and if the truth really did exclude Christ, I should prefer to stay with Christ and not with truth.

HAPPINESS

October 18, 1855

I believe that happiness lies in a clear conception of life and in goodness of heart, not in external circumstances. Is it not so?

One's views alter; one's heart remains the same.

WORK

May 31, 1858

. . . Believe me, in all things labour is necessary—gigantic labour. Believe me that a graceful, fleet poem of Pushkin's consisting of but a few lines, *is* so graceful and so fleet simply because the poet has worked long at it, and altered much.

AMBITION

May 3, 1860

. . . Ambition is a good thing, but I think that one may take it as one's aim only in things which one has set one's-self to achieve, has made the reason for one's existence. In anything else it's nonsense. The only essential is to live with ease; and moreover one must sympathize with one's fellow-creatures, and strive to win their sympathy in return. And if, indeed, one had no other determined aim, this would by itself more than suffice.

MEDIOCRITY

September 29, 1867

Most of all I dread mediocrity: a work should either be very good or very bad, but, for its life, not mediocre. Mediocrity that takes up thirty printed sheets is something quite unpardonable.

ON EDUCATION

October 10, 1867

. . . I also think you very intelligent. Only one thing is against you: your lack of education. But if you really have no desire to learn something, at least hear my advice: you must, in any case, be earnest about your moral development, so far as that is capable of going without education (but, for education, one shall strive unto one's life's end).

RESPONSIBILITY

June 11, 1870

. . . the sons of men have *not* the right to turn away from anything that happens on the earth and ignore it; no, on the highest moral grounds they have not.

THE TRUE GOOD

March 27, 1878

Every human being, who can grasp the *truth* at all, feels in his conscience what is good and what is evil. . . . Believe me: it is uncommonly important and useful to set a good example even in a narrow sphere of activity, for in that way one influences dozens and hundreds of people.

APHORISMS

August 17, 1870 and
December 19, 1880

Without pain, one comprehends not joy. Ideals are purified by suffering, as gold is by fire.

The first sign of true fellowship with the people is veneration and love for that which the great mass of people loves and venerates—that is to say, for God and its faith.

THE NOBLE MAN

January 1, 1868

. . . Three weeks ago I attacked another novel, and am now working day and night. The idea of the book is the old one which I always have so greatly liked; but it is so difficult that hitherto I never have had the courage to carry it out; and if I'm setting to work at it now, it's only because I'm in a desperate plight. The basic idea is the representation of a truly perfect and noble man. And this is more difficult than anything else in the world, particularly nowadays. All writers, not ours alone but foreigners also, who have sought to represent Absolute Beauty, were unequal to the task, for it is an infinitely difficult one. The beautiful is the ideal: but ideals with us, as in civilized Europe, have long been wavering. There is in the world only one figure of absolute beauty: Christ. That infinitely lovely figure is, as a matter of course, an infinite marvel (the whole Gospel of St. John is full of this thought: John sees the wonder of the Incarnation, the visible apparition of the Beautiful). I have gone too far in my explanation. I will only say further that of all the noble figures in Christian literature, I reckon Don Quixote as the most perfect. But Don Quixote is noble only by being at the same time comic. And Dickens's Pickwickians (they were certainly much weaker than Don Quixote, but still it's a powerful work) are comic, and this it is which gives them their great value. The reader feels sympathy and compassion with the Beautiful, derided and unconscious of its own worth. The secret of humour consists precisely in this art of wakening the reader's sympathy.

TOPIC SELECTIONS FROM *Diary of a Writer*

MAN AND SOCIETY

The best man is he who has not bowed before material temptation; who is incessantly seeking works for God's cause;

who loves truth and, whenever the occasion calls for it, rises to serve it, forsaking his home and his family and sacrificing his life.

(Vol. I, p. 490)

There are people who command everybody's respect, even the respect of those who disagree with their ideas.

(Vol. I, p. 272)

One can very much respect a man, even though radically disagreeing with his ideas.

(Vol. I, p. 29)

He who has too much compassion for the offender, probably has no pity for the offended.

(Vol. I, p. 326)

It seems to me that, generally speaking, it is as difficult for an advocate to avoid falsehood and to preserve honesty and conscience as for any man to attain a paradisiacal state.

(Vol. I, p. 214)

To love the universal man necessarily means to despise, and, at times, to hate the real man standing at your side.

(Vol. I, p. 33)

month calls himself a fool—in our day this is an unheard-of faculty! Indeed: by locking up the other fellow in a madhouse one can't prove one's own intelligence.

("Bobok," Vol. I, p. 44)

He, I take it, is the most intelligent who at least once a
I think this way: it is possible to rationalize and to perceive a thing correctly and at once, but to become a man at once is impossible: one has to mould oneself into a man. Here discipline is required.

(Vol. II, p. 604)

It is a fact that half of one's affliction vanishes if only someone can be found to share the guilt of it, and it is all the more disappointing if absolutely no one can be found.

(Vol. I, p. 119)

The ability to be a citizen is exactly the ability to lift one-self to the level of the common opinion of the country.

(Vol. I, p. 11)

The civic forms of a people assume the character in which their religion is expressed. Therefore the civic ideals are always directly and organically tied to the moral ideals, and—what is most important—the former indisputably are derived only from the latter. Civic ideals never appear *of their own accord* because when they do appear they have as their only object the consummation of the moral aspirations of the given nationality, in the form and in so far as these moral aspirations have moulded themselves in that nationality.

On this ground "self-betterment in a religious sense" in the life of the peoples is the foundation of everything.

(Vol. II, p. 1001)

The belief that one wishes and can utter the last word to the world; that it can be revived through the abundance of one's vital force; faith in the sacredness of one's ideals, in the strength of one's love, of one's thirst for serving mankind—nay, such a faith is a guaranty of the loftiest life of the nations, and it is only through this faith that they are in a position to render to humanity the full measure of that service which at the time of their inception, they have been destined to render by nature herself, and to bequeath to future mankind. Only a nation fortified with such faith is entitled to sublime life.

(Vol. II, p. 577)

If society should stop pitying the weak and persecuted, it would be painfully afflicted itself; it would grow hard and wither; it would become lewd and sterile. . . .

(Vol. I, p. 236)

SCIENCE

Science is a universal thing: it was invented not by some one people in Europe but by all peoples, beginning with the ancient world; thus science is a successful proposition.

(Vol. I, p. 282)

There is no such old theme about which something new could not be said.

(Vol. I, p. 398)

ART

The aim of art is not to portray these or those incidents in the ways of life but their general idea, sharp-sightedly divined and correctly removed from the whole multiplicity of analogous living phenomena.

(Vol. I, p. 90)

Not only to create and write artistic works, but also to discern a fact, something of an artist is required.

(Vol. I, p. 469)

Poesy is, so to speak, the inner fire of every talent.

(Vol. I, p. 216)

"Reality should be represented as it is" they [the artists] say, whereas there is no such reality, never has been because, to man, the substance of things is inaccessible, while he apperceives nature as it reflects itself in his idea after having passed through his senses. This is why one should give more leeway to the idea without fearing the ideal.

(Vol. I, p. 83)

What is genre, in substance? Genre is an art of portraying contemporaneous, current reality which the artist has personally felt and seen with his own eyes, as distinguished, for instance, from historical reality which cannot be beheld with one's own eyes, and which is being portrayed not in a fluent but completed state.

(Vol. I, p. 83)

Literary talent, for example, is the ability to say or express well that which a nullity will say and express badly. . . . As far as I am able to observe men of talent, both living and dead, it does seem to me that in the rarest cases only is a man capable of mastering his gift; and that, contrarywise, talent almost always enslaves its owner—grabbing him, so to speak, by his neck . . . carrying him far away from the right road. . . .

(Vol. I, p. 215)

RELIGION AND PHILOSOPHY

Truth, even as the sun, cannot be hidden.

(Vol. II, p. 608)

Without ideals, that is, without even vaguely specified longings for the better, no good reality can ever ensue.

(Vol. I, p. 239)

Happiness is not in happiness but in its pursuit.

(Vol. I, p. 193)

Faith and mathematical proofs are two incompatible things.

(Vol. I, p. 270)

Idealists often forget that idealism is in no sense a shameful thing. In both the idealist and the realist, if only they be honest and magnanimous, the substance is identical—love of mankind—and their object is identical—man; it is only the *forms* of the representation of the object that are different.

(Vol. I, p. 387)

We have totally forgotten the axiom that truth is the most poetic thing in the world, especially in its pure state. More than that: it is even more fantastic than the ordinary human mind is capable of fabricating and conceiving.

(Vol. I, p. 135)

Making man responsible, Christianity *eo ipso* also recognizes his freedom.

However, making man dependent on any error in the social organization, the environmental doctrine reduces man to absolute impersonality, to a total emancipation from all personal moral duty, from all independence; reduces him to a state of the most miserable slavery that can be conceived.

(Vol. I, p. 13)

The human mind, once having rejected Christ, may attain extraordinary results.

(Vol. I, p. 151)

ON ACTIVE LOVE

As a matter of fact, it is not necessary to conceive the giving away of property as a *binding* condition, since in the matter of love *constraint* resembles a uniform, fidelity to the letter. The conviction that one has complied with the letter leads to haughtiness, formalism, and indolence. One has to do only that which one's heart dictates: if it orders a man to give away his fortune—let him give it away; if it orders him to go and work for all men—let him go and work. But even here, don't follow the example of certain dreamers, who straightway get hold of a wheelbarrow and say: "I am not a nobleman—I want to work as a peasant." The wheelbarrow, too, is a uniform.

Neither the giving away of property, nor the wearing of a peasant coat are obligatory: all this is mere letter and formality: *only your resolution to do everything for the sake of active love,* everything within the limits of your possibility. Everything which you sincerely consider possible for yourself—is obligatory and important.

(Vol. II, p. 622)

SOURCE BOOKS FOR LETTERS:

Mayne, Ethel Colburn, tr., *Letters of Fyodor Michailovitch Dostoevsky* to his Family and Friends, Chatto & Windus, London, 1914.

Koteliansky, S. S., and J. Middleton Murry, trs., *Dostoevsky: Letters and Reminiscences*, Alfred A. Knopf, New York, 1923. The December 22, 1849 letter only.

Brasol, Boris, tr., *The Diary of a Writer*, Charles Scribner's Sons, New York, 1949, 2 vols.

Chronological Table of the
Works of F. M. Dostoevsky

1846 *Poor Folk*
     The Double
     "Mr. Proharchin"
1847 "Novel in Nine Letters"
     "The Landlady"
1848 "Another Man's Wife" (also called "The Jealous Husband")
     "A Faint Heart"
     "Mr. Polzunkov"
     "Out of the Service"
     "The Honest Thief"
     "The Christmas Tree and a Wedding"
     "White Nights"
1849 *Nyetochka Nezvanovna* (unfinished novel)
     "The Little Hero" (written in the Fortress; published in 1857)
1855 Poem
1859 "The Uncle's Dream"
     "The Village of Stepanchikovo" (or "The Friend of the Family")
1860 Collection of Works, 2 vols., First edition
1861 Series of articles on Russian literature (*Vremya*)
1862 *The Insulted and Injured*
     House of the Dead
     "An Unpleasant Predicament" (also called "A Silly Anecdote")
1863 *Winter Notes on Summer Impressions*
1864 *Notes From Underground*
1865 "The Crocodile"
1866 *Crime and Punishment*
1867 *The Gambler*

1868   *The Idiot*
1870   *The Eternal Husband*
1871–72   *The Possessed*
1873   *The Diary of a Writer* (in *Grazhdanin*)
    series of articles and "Bobok"
                  "Vlas"
1873–74   Political articles in *Grazhdanin*
1875   *The Raw Youth*
1876   *Diary of a Writer* (own publication)
    "The Peasant Marei"
    "The Heavenly Christmas Tree"
    "A Gentle Spirit"
    Other articles
1877   *Diary:* many articles and
    "The Dream of a Ridiculous Man"
1879–80   *The Brothers Karamazov*
1880   Pushkin Address (August issue: *Diary*)
1881   January issue of *Diary*

Acknowledgments

THE AUTHOR wishes to thank the following authors, translators, and publishers for their kind permission to quote from their works listed below, which may not be reproduced in any form without the consent of the copyright owners:

George Allen and Unwin, Ltd., London, *Dostoevsky*, Edward Hallett Carr, 1949, 2nd ed.

Association Press, New York, *The Spirit of Dostoevsky*, Nicholas Berdyaev, translated by Donald Attwater, © 1934.

Geoffrey Bles, Ltd., London, *The Origin of Russian Communism*, Nicholas Berydaev, translated by R. M. French, 1948.

Carnegie Press, Pittsburgh, *Russia's Educational Heritage*, William H. E. Johnson, 1950.

The University of Chicago Press, Chicago, *Systematic Theology*, Vol. II, Paul Tillich, copyright 1957 by the University of Chicago.

Columbia University Press, New York, *A History of Russian Philosophy*, Vassili V. Zenkovsky, translated by George L. Kline, 2 vols., 1953; *Dostoyevski in Russian Literary Criticism*, Vladimir Seduro, 1957; *Naturalism and the Human Spirit*, Yervant H. Krikorian, ed., 1949.

Criterion Books, Inc., New York, *Winter Notes on Summer Impressions*, Feodor M. Dostoevsky, translated by Richard Lee Renfield, foreword by Saul Bellow, © 1955.

Dial Press, New York, *The Short Novels of Dostoevsky*, Fyodor Dostoevsky, Introduction by Thomas Mann, 1951.

Alfred A. Knopf, Inc., New York, *Modern Russian History*, Alexander Kornilov, translated by Alex S. Kaun, 2 vols., © 1917, 1924, 1943, 1952.

The Macmillan Company, New York, *Dostoevsky,* Edward Hallett Carr, 1949, 2nd ed.; *Dostoevsky, A Study,* Janko Lavrin, 1947; *The Russian Idea,* Nicholas Berdyaev, 1948; *Four Prophets of Our Destiny,* William Hubben, 1952; *Notes From Underground,* Fyodor M. Dostoevsky, translated by Constance Garnett, 1951 ed.

Meridian Books, New York, *The Spirit of Dostoevsky,* Nicholas Berdyaev, translated by Donald Attwater, 1957.

University of Michigan Press, Ann Arbor, *The Origin of Russian Communism,* Nicholas Berdyaev, translated by R. M. French, 1960.

Modern Library (Random House), New York, *The House of the Dead, Crime and Punishment, The Brothers Karamazov,* F. M. Dostoevsky.

Mouton and Co., N. V., The Hague, *Dostoevskij's Underground Man in Literature,* Robert L. Jackson, 1958.

The Noonday Press, New York, *Creation and Discovery,* Eleseo Vivas, 1955.

New York *Herald Tribune,* "The Other Russia," Albert Camus, December 19, 1957.

Oxford University Press, Inc., New York, *Dostoevski: The Making of a Novelist,* Ernest J. Simmons, 1940.

Penguin Books, Inc., Baltimore, Md., and Middlesex, England, *The Idiot,* F. M. Dostoevsky, translated by David Magarshack, 1955.

The University of Pennsylvania Press, Philadelphia, *Foundations of Education,* Frederick Gruber, ed., First Series, 1957.

Philosophical Library, New York, *The Will to Doubt,* Bertrand Russell, 1958; *Problems of Men,* John Dewey, 1946.

Prentice-Hall, Inc., Englewood Cliffs, N. J., *The Development of Modern Education in Theory, Organization, and Practice,* Frederick Eby, © 1952, 2nd ed.

S. C. M. Press, Ltd., London, *Dostoevsky,* L. A. Zander, translated by Natalie Duddington, 1948.

Charles Scribner's Sons, New York, *Basic Christian Ethics,* Paul Ramsey, 1950; *Fyodor Dostoevsky,* René Fueloep-Miller, 1950; *The Diary of a Writer*, F. M. Dostoevsky, translated by Boris Brasol, 1949.

Simon and Schuster, Inc., New York, *The Impact of Science on Society*, Bertrand Russell, © 1953.

Y. M. C. A. Press, Paris, *The Spirit of Dostoevsky*, Nicholas Berdyaev, translated by Donald Attwater, © 1934.

Bibliography

PRIMARY SOURCES

THE WRITINGS OF DOSTOEVSKY

Arban, Dominique, *Correspondence de Dostoievski*, Calmann-Levy, Paris, 1949.

Briefe: Fiodor M. Dostojewskij: Alssohwanke Der Baden Unter Mir 1837–1881, Wiesbaden, n. d.

Dolinin, A. S., ed., *F. M. Dostoewskii—materialy i issledovanija* (articles and researches), Isdatel'stvo Akademii Nauk SSSR, Leningrad, 1935.

———*F. M. Dostoewskii—statji i materialy* (articles and materials). Isdatel'stvo Akademii Nauk SSSR, St. Petersburg, 1924–25.

Dostoevsky, Fyodor M., *The Brothers Karamazov,* Modern Library Giant Edition, New York, n.d.

———*The Diary of a Writer,* 2 vols., tr. by Boris Brasol, Charles Scribner's Sons, New York, 1949.

———*The Idiot,* tr. by David Magarshack, Penguin Books, Baltimore, 1955.

———*The Possessed,* Modern Library edition, New York, 1950.

———*Winter Notes on Summer Impressions,* tr. by Richard Lee Renfield, Introd. by Saul Bellow, Criterion Books, Inc., New York, 1955.

———*Works,* 12 vols., tr. by Constance Garnett, The Macmillan Company, New York, 1951.

———*Works,* 16 vols., in Russian YMCA Press, Paris, 1945.

Hill, Elizabeth and D. Mudie, *Letters of Dostoevsky to His*

Wife, Introd. by D. S. Mirsky, R. R. Smith, Inc., New York, 1930.

Koteliansky, S. S., tr. and ed., "New Letters of Dostoevsky," *Virginia Quarterly Review,* July–October, 1926, 2:275–284; 546–556.

Koteliansky, S. S., and John M. Murry, *Dostoevsky: Letters and Reminiscences by His Wife,* Alfred A. Knopf, New York, 1923.

Mayne, Ethel Colburne, *Letters of Fyodor Michailovitch Dostoevsky to His Family and Friends,* Chatto & Windus, London, 1914.

SECONDARY SOURCES

BIOGRAPHIES

Abraham, Gerald, *Dostoevsky,* Duckworth, London, 1936.

Carr, Edward Hallett, *Dostoevsky 1821–1881: A New Biography,* George Allen and Unwin, Ltd., London, 2nd edition, 1949.

Dostoevsky, Aimeé, *Fyodor Dostoevsky, A Study,* W. Heineman, London, 1921.

Koteliansky, S. S., tr., *Dostoevsky Portrayed by His Wife,* George Routledge and Sons, Ltd., London, 1926.

Lloyd, J. A. T., *A Great Russian Realist: Feodor Dostoieffsky,* John Lane Company, New York, 1922. Revised edition: Charles Scribner's Sons, New York, 1947.

Meier-Graefe, Julius, *Dostoevsky: The Man and His Work,* tr. by Herbert H. Marks, Harcourt-Brace and Company, New York, 1928.

Mochulskii, Konstantine, *Dostoevsky: Zhizn' i tvorchistvo* (Life and Work), YMCA Press, Paris, 1947.

Payne, Robert, *Dostoevsky: A Human Portrait,* Alfred A. Knopf, New York, 1961.

Persky, Serge, *La Vie et l'oeuvre de Dostoievsky,* Payot, Paris, 1918.

Slonim, Marc, *Three Loves of Dostoevsky*, Rinehart, New York, 1955.
Solovieff, Eugene, *Dostoevsky, His Life and Literary Activity*, tr. by C. J. Hogarth, George Allen and Unwin, Ltd., London, 1916.
Strakhov, N. N., *Biografiya, pisma i zametki iz zapisnoi knizhki F. M. Dostoevskogo* (Official biography with letters and notes from his notebooks), St. Petersburg, 1883.
Troyat, Henri, *Firebrand: The Life of Dostoevsky*, tr. by Norbett Gutemann, Roy Publishers, New York, 1946.
Woodhouse, C. M., *Dostoevsky*, Arthur Barker, Ltd., London, 1951.

CRITICAL WORKS

Beach, Joseph M., *The Twentieth Century Novel*, The Century Company, New York, 1932.
Berdyaev, Nicholas, *The Spirit of Dostoevsky*, tr. by Donald Attwater, YMCA Press, Paris, New York, 1934. New edition: Meridian Books, New York, 1957.
Brewster, D. and A. Burrell, *Dead Reckonings in Fiction*, Columbia University Press, New York, 1934.
Buber, Martin, *Israel and the World*, Schockton Books, New York, 1948.
Camus, Albert, *The Myth of Sisyphus and Other Essays*, tr. by Justin O'Brien, Alfred A. Knopf, New York, 1955.
———*The Rebel*, Foreword by Sir Herbert Read, tr. by Anthony Bower, Alfred A. Knopf, New York, 1954.
Capetanakis, D., *Shores of Darkness*, Devin-Adair, London, 1949.
Clutton-Brock, A., *Essays on Books*, E. P. Dutton Company, Inc., New York, 1920.
Collins, J., *Doctor Looks at Literature*, Doran, New York, 1923.
Curle, Richard, *Characters of Dostoevsky*, Wm. Heineman, London, 1950.
Dempf, Alois, *Die Drei Laster*, Karl Alber, Munich, 1946.

Eng, J. Van Der, *Dostoevskij romancier,* Mouton and Company, 's-Gravenhage, The Hague, 1957.

Faure, Elie, *Les constructeurs,* Plon, Paris, 1950.

Fayer, Mischa H., *Gide, Freedom and Dostoevsky,* Lane Press, Burlington, Vermont, 1946.

Fueloep-Miller, René, *Fyodor Dostoevsky: Insight, Faith and Prophecy,* tr. by R. and C. Winston, Charles Scribner's Sons, New York, 1950.

Freud, Sigmund, "A Psychoanalytic Study," *Stavrogin's Confession,* tr. by V. Woolf and S. S. Koteliansky, New York, 1947.

Gide, André, *Dostoievsky: Articles et causeries,* Plon, Paris, 1923.

Guardini, Romano, *Religiose Gestalten in Dostojewskijs Werk,* Hegner-Bucherei, Munich, 1947.

Hackett, F., *Horizons,* B. W. Huebsch, New York, 1918.

Hemmings, F. W. J., *The Russian Novel in France: 1884–1914,* Oxford University Press, London, 1950.

Hesse, Hermann, *In Sight of Chaos,* tr. by Stephen Hudson, Verlag Seldwyla, Zurich, 1923.

Hoffman, E. J., *Freudianism and the Literary Mind,* Louisiana State University Press, Baton Rouge, Louisiana, 1945.

Howe, Irving, *Politics and the Novel,* Meridian Books, New York, 1957.

Hubben, William, *Four Prophets of Our Destiny,* Macmillan Company, New York, 1952.

——*The Grand Inquisitor on the Nature of Man,* Liberal Arts Press, New York, 1948.

Huneker, James G., *Ivory, Apes and Peacocks,* Charles Scribner's Sons, New York, 1926.

Ivanov, Vyacheslav, *Freedom and the Tragic Life,* tr. by N. Cameron Harvill Press, London, 1952.

Jackson, Robert Louis, *Dostoevskij's Underground Man in Russian Literature,* Mouton and Company, The Hague, 1958.

Jarrett-Kerr, M., *Studies in Literature and Belief,* Harper Brothers, New York, 1955.

Kampman, Theoderich von, *Dostojewski in Deutschland*, Helios-Verlag, Munster i Westfalen, 1931.

Kaus, Otto, *Dostoievski et son destin*, tr. by George Cazenave, Rieder, Paris, 1931.

Kazin, Alfred, "Introductions" to *The Raw Youth*, Dial Press, New York, 1947, and to *Crime and Punishment*, World Publishing Company, New York, 1947.

Kohn, Hans, *Prophets and Peoples*, Macmillan Company, New York, 1947.

Lauth, Reinhard, *Die Philosophie Dostojewskis*, R. Piper and Company, Munich, 1950.

———*Was Vermag Der Mensch?*, R. Piper and Company, Munich, 1949.

Lavrin, Janko, *Dostoevsky, A Study*, Macmillan Company, New York, 1947.

———*An Introduction to the Russian Novel*, McGraw-Hill Book Company, New York, 1947.

Lawrence, D. H., *Selected Literary Criticism*, ed. by Anthony Beal, Viking Press, New York, 1956.

Lednicki, W., *Russia, Poland and the West*, Roy Publishers, New York, 1953.

Lossky, N., *Dostoevski i evo hristiyanskoe miroponimanie*, Chekhov Publishing House, New York, 1953.

Lubac, Henri de, S. J., *The Drama of Atheist Humanism*, tr. by Edith M. Riley, Sheed and Ward, New York, 1950.

Maceina, Antanas, *Der Grossinquisitor*, F. H. Kerle, Heidelberg, 1952.

Magarshack, David, "Introductions" to *The Devils* and *Crime and Punishment*, Penguin Books, Ltd., London, 1951, 1953.

Mann, Thomas, "Introduction" to *The Short Novels of Dostoevsky*, Dial Press, New York, 1951.

Matlaw, Ralph E., *The Brothers Karamazov Novelistic Technique*, Mouton and Company, 's-Gravenhage, The Hague, 1957.

Maugham, S., *The Art of Fiction*, Doubleday and Company, Inc., Garden City, New York, 1955.

Maurina, Zenta, *A Prophet of the Soul: Fyodor Dostoievsky*, tr. by C. P. Finlayson, James Clarke and Company, Ltd., London, n. d. (*ca.* 1935).

Merejkovsky, D. S., *Tolystoy as Man and Artist with an Essay on Dostoevsky*, Putnam, New York, 1902.

Muchnic, Helen, *Dostoevsky's English Reputation (1881-1936)*, Smith College Studies in Modern Languages, Northampton, Mass., Vol. XX, 1939.

——*Introduction to Russian Literature*, Doubleday and Company, Inc., Garden City, New York, 1947.

Mueller, G. E., *Philosophy of Literature*, Philosophical Library, New York, 1948.

Murry, J. Middleton, *Fyodor Dostoevsky: A Critical Study*, Secker, London, 1916.

Passage, Charles E., *Dostoevski, The Adapter*, University of North Carolina Press, Chapel Hill, 1954.

Pfleger, K., *Wrestlers with Christ*, Sheed and Ward, New York, 1938.

Phillips, E., ed., *Art and Psychoanalysis*, Criterion Press, New York, 1957.

Poggioli, R., *The Phoenix and the Spider*, Harvard University Press, Cambridge, Mass., 1957.

Powys, John C., *Dostoievsky*, John Lane, London, 1946.

Praz, Mario, *The Romantic Agony*, tr. by Angus Davidson, Meridian Book Company, New York, 1956.

Pritchett, V. S., *The Living Novel*, Reynal Hitchcock, New York, 1947.

Rahv, P., *Image and Idea*, New Directions Press, New York, 1949.

Roe, Ivan, *The Breath of Corruption*, Hutchinson and Company, Ltd., London, n. d.

Roubeczek, P., *Misinterpretation of Man*, Charles Scribner's Sons, New York, 1947.

Scott, Nathan A., Jr., *The Tragic Vision and the Christian Faith*, Association Press, New York, 1957.

Seduro, Vladimir, *Dostoevsky in Russian Literary Criticism, 1846-1956*, Columbia University Press, New York, 1957.

Sewall, Richard B., *Tragic Themes in Western Literature*, ed.

by C. Brooks, Yale University Press, New Haven, Conn., 1955.

Shestov, L., *In Job's Balances*, tr. by C. Coventry and C. A. Macartney, J. M. Dent and Sons, Ltd., London, 1932.

Simmons, Ernest J., *Dostoevski: The Making of a Novelist*, Oxford University Press, New York, 1940.

———*U S S R*, Cornell University Press, Ithaca, New York, 1947.

Slonim, Marc, *The Epic of Russian Literature*, Oxford University Press, New York, 1950.

Spector, I., *Golden Age of Russian Literature*, Caldwell, Ltd., Caldwell, Idaho, 1945.

Spengler, O., *The Decline of the West*, Vol. I, tr. by Charles F. Atkinson, Alfred A. Knopf, New York, 1944.

Stocker, Arnold, *Ame russe*, Annemasse, Geneve, 1945.

Strachey, G. L., *Characters and Commentaries*, Harcourt, Brace and Company, New York, 1933.

———*Literary Essays*, Chatto and Windus, London, 1948.

Van Doren, Mark, "Introduction" to *The Brothers Karamazov*, Literary Guild Edition, New York, 1932.

Vatai, Laslo, *Man and His Tragic Life*, tr. by L. Kecskemethy, Philosophical Library, New York, 1954.

Vivas, Eleseo, *Creation and Discovery*, Noonday Press, New York, 1955.

Warner, R., *Cult of Power*, John Lane, London, 1946.

Willcocks, M. P., *Between the Old World and the New*, Frederick A. Stokes Company, New York, n. d.

Wilson, Edmund, *The Shores of Light*, Farrar, Straus and Young, New York, 1952.

Yarmolinsky, A., *Dostoevsky*, Columbia University Press, New York, 1921, revised edition, 1957.

Zander, L. A., *Dostoevsky*, tr. by N. Duddington, S. C. M. Press, Ltd., London, 1948.

Zernov, Nicholas, *Three Russian Prophets: Khomiakov, Dostoevsky, Soloviev*, S. C. M. Press, Ltd., London, 1944.

Zweig, Stefan, *Three Masters*, tr. by Eden and Cedar Paul, Viking Press, New York, 1930.

CRITICAL ARTICLES

Adams, A. E., "Pobedonostsev's Thought Control," *Russian Review*, Oct., 1952, 11:241–6.

Alonzo, Pedro-Soler, "Selecciones, con un estudio Dostoevski," *Biblioteca enciclopedica popular*, Secretaria de Educación Publica, Mexico City, Mexico, 1947, 142 f.

Astrov, V., "Dostoevsky or E. A. Poe," *American Literature*, March, 1942, 14:70–4.

———"Hawthorne and Dostoevsky as Explorers of Human Conscience," *New England Quarterly*, June, 1942, 15:296–319.

Bierbaum, O. J., "Dostoevsky and Nietzsche," *Hibbert Journal*, July, 1911, 9:823–37.

Burchell, S. C., "Dostoieffsky and the Sense of Guilt," *Psychoanalytic Review*, 1930, 17:195–207.

Carr, E. H., "The Philosophy of Dostoevsky," *Spectator*, 1934, 153:684.

Charques, R. D., "Dostoevsky and the Slavic Idea," *Fortnightly*, April, 1951, 175:372–3.

Clive, G., "Teleological Suspense of the Ethical in Nineteenth Century Literature," *Journal of Religion*, April, 1954, 34:74–87.

Collins, J., "Tragedist, Prophet and Psychologist," *North American*, Jan., 1922, 215:66–83.

Dneprov, V., "The Esthetics of the Unconscious," *The Soviet Review*, Dec. 1961, 2, 12, 3–23.

Dodd, E. M., "Preaching Values in Dostoevsky's Writings," *London Quarterly Review*, July, 1944, 169:241–44.

Fagin, N. B., "Dostoevsky's Underground Man Takes Over," *Antioch Review*, March, 1953, 13:23–32.

Fiske, J. C., "Dostoevsky and Soviet Critics, 1947–48," *American Slavic and East European Review*, Feb., 1950, 9:42–56.

Florovsky, A., "Dostoevsky and the Slavonic Question," *Slavonic Review*, Dec., 1930, 9:411–23.

Fueloep-Miller, René, "Dostoevsky's Literary Reputation," *Russian Review*, Jan., 1951, 10:46–54.

———"Lost Dostoevsky Manuscripts," *Russian Review*, Oct., 1951, 10:268–82.

———"The Posthumous Life of Dostoevsky," *Russian Review*, Oct., 1946, 15:259–65.

Gersh, G., "Russian Imperialism: Dostoevsky," *Social Education Journal*, May, 1956, 20:201–2.

Gibian, George, "C. G. Carus *Psyche* and Dostoevsky," *American Slavic and East European Review*, Oct., 1955, 14:371–82.

———"Dostoevskij's. Use of Russian Folklore," *Journal of American Folklore*, 1956, 69:239–53.

———"Traditional Symbolism in Crime and Punishment," *PMLA*, Dec., 1955, 70:979–96.

Gross, John J., "Melville, Dostoevsky and the People," *Pacific Spectator*, Spring, 1956, 10:160–70.

Hacker, A., "Dostoevsky's Disciples: Man and Sheep in Political Theory," *Journal of Politics*, Nov., 1955, 17:590–613.

Hesse, H., "Downfall of Europe: The Brothers Karamazov," *English Review*, Aug., 1932, 35:108–20.

Hill, K. C., "Crime and Punishment as Philosophy," *General Education*, Jan., 1953, 7:122–32.

Howe, I., "Dostoevsky as a Journalist," *American Mercury*, Oct., 1949, 69:494–502.

Hunt, Joel, "Balzac and Dostoevskij: Ethics and Eschatology," *Slavic and East European Journal*, Winter, 1958, 16:307–24.

Jarrett, J. L., "Dostoevsky: Philosopher of Freedom, Love and Life," *Review of Religion*, Nov., 1956, 21:17–30.

Kaun, A., "Dostoevsky's Outlook," *American Review*, July–Dec., 1924, 2:263–67.

Kazin, A., "Dostoevsky the Columnist," *New Yorker*, June 25, 1949, 25:81–2.

Koenig, A. E., "Dostoevsky's Testament: The Diary of a Writer," *South Atlantic Quarterly*, Jan., 1954, 53:10–23.

Kohn, H., "Dostoevsky's Nationalism," *Journal of Historic Ideas*, Oct., 1945, 6:385–414.

Leshinsky, T., "Dostoevsky: Revolutionary or Reactionary?", *American Slavic Review*, Dec., 1945, 4:98–106.

Lohr, F., "Loneliness and Sanctity," *Catholic World*, Oct., 1952, 176:32–7.

Lvovsky, Z., "Dans le laboratoire de Dostoievsky," *Mercure France*, April 12, 1932, 235:319–32.

Manning, C. A., "Dostoevsky and Modern Russian Literature," *Sewanee Review*, Dec., 1932, 30:286–97.

—— "The Double of Dostoevsky," *Modern Language Notes*, Aug., 1944, 59:317–21.

—— "The Grand Inquisitor," *Anglican Theological Review*, 1933, 15:16–26.

—— "Hawthorne and Dostoevsky," *Slavonic Review*, Jan., 1936, 14:1–8.

Matlaw, R. E., "Structure and Integration in *Notes From Underground*," *PMLA*, March, 1958, 73:101–09.

Maugham, S., "The Brothers Karamazov," *Atlantic Monthly*, March, 1948, 181:89–94.

Maximoff, N., "Future of Russia: Marx, Tolstoi or Dostoevsky?", *Religion in Life*, Winter, 1954–55, 24:44–55.

Montgomery, R., "Dr. Adler on Dostoevsky," *New Age*, 1926, 40:54.

—— "Freud, Adler and Dostoevsky," *New Age*, 1929, 45:115–16.

Mortimer, R., "Dostoevsky and the Dream," *Modern Philology*, Nov., 1956, 54:106–16.

Noyes, R., "Dostoevski," *Nation*, April 8, 1915, 100:381–83.

Panichas, George A., "The Spiritual Art of Dostoevsky," *St. Vladimir's Seminary Quarterly*, Fall, 1958, 2:20–36.

Poggioli, Renato, "Dostoevski and Western Realism," *Kenyon Review*, 1952, 14:43–59.

Portnoff, G. E., "Cervantes and Dostoevsky," *Modern Language Forum*, May, 1934, 19:80–6.

Radar, M. M., "Dostoevsky and the Demiurge," *Sewanee Review*, July, 1931, 39:282–92.

Radziwill, C., "Dostoevsky: Writer and Man," *Commonweal*, Dec. 23, 1930, 12:322–24.

Rahv, P., "Legend of the Grand Inquisitor," *Partisan Review*, May, 1954, 21:249–71.

Ramsey, Paul, "God's Grace and Man's Guilt," *Journal of Religion*, Jan., 1951, 31:21–37.

―――― "No Morality without Immortality: Dostoevsky and the Meaning of Atheism," *Journal of Religion*, April, 1956, 36:90–108.

Rapaport, S., "Dostoevsky," *Contemporary*, June, 1932, 141:-765–70.

Richards, I. A., "God of Dostoevsky," *Forum*, Dec., 1927, 78:-88–97.

Roberts, P., "A Christian Theory of Dramatic Tragedy," *Journal of Religion*, Jan., 1951, 31:1–20.

Scharper, P., "Prophet with Honor," *Commonweal*, May 4, 1956, 64:125–6.

Singer, I., "The Aesthetics of 'Art for Art's Sake,'" *Journal of Aesthetics and Art Criticism*, Dec., 1953, 12:343–59.

Slonim, Marc, "Dostoevsky Under the Soviets," *Russian Review*, April, 1951, 10:118–30.

Smith, Samuel, "The Abnormal from Within," *Psychoanalytic Review*, Oct., 1935, 22.

Stammler, H., "Dostoevsky's Aesthetics and Schelling's Philosophy of Art," *Comparative Literature*, Fall, 1955, 7:313–23.

Strakosch, H. E., "Dostoevsky and the Man-god," *Dublin Review*, 1955, 229:142–53.

Strem, G. C., "The Moral World of Dostoevsky," *Russian Review*, July, 1957, 16:15–26.

Squires, P. C., "Dostoevsky's Doctrine of Criminal Responsibility," *Journal of Criminal Law*, March, 1937, 27:817–27.

―――― "Dostoevsky's Master Study of the Protest," *Science Monthly*, June, 1937, 44:555–57.

―――― "Raskolnikov: Criminalistic Protest," *Journal of Criminal Law*, Nov., 1937, 28:478–94.

Tate, A., "Dostoevsky's Hovering Fly, A Canarie on the Imagination and the Actual World," *Sewanee Review*, July, 1943, 51:353–69.

Teitelbaum, S. M., "Dostoevsky in France of 1880's," *American Slavic Review*, Nov., 1946, 5:99–108.

Thorn, W., "Dostoevsky as a Psychologist," *London Quarterly Review*, April, 1916, 125:177–88.

———— "Dostoevsky as a Religious Teacher," *Contemporary*, Aug., 1915, 108:220–28.

Vakeel, H. J., "Dostoevsky and Humor," *Contemporary*, Jan., 1950, 177:36–9.

Vivas, E., "Two Dimensions of Reality in *The Brothers Karamazov*," *Sewanee Review*, Jan., 1951, 59:23–49.

Weinreich, M. I., "Ideological Antecedents of The Brothers Karamazov," *Modern Language Notes*, June, 1949, 64:400–6.

Wernham, J. C. S., "Guardini, Berdyaev and The Legend of the Grand Inquisitor," *Hibbert Journal*, Jan., 1955, 53:157–64.

Wilcox, E. H., "Dostoevsky as Seen by His Daughter," *Fortnightly*, Feb., 1921, 115:229–39.

Williams, C., "The Ethics of Three Russian Novelists," *International Journal of Ethics*, 1925, 35:217–37.

Wilson, Edmund, "Meditations on Dostoevsky," *New Republic*, Oct. 24, 1928, 56:274–76.

Woodhouse, C. M., "Dostoevsky as a Prophet," *Bibliography of Nineteenth Century*, March, 1950, 147:174–83.

Wright, R., "Defining Dostoevsky," *Catholic World*, March, 1917, 104:820–25.

Yarmolinsky, A., "Aesthetics of Dostoevsky," *New Republic*, Sept. 27, 1922, 32:115–117.

———— "Dostoevsky: One of Us?", *New Republic*, Dec. 14, 1942, 107:797–98.

———— "Journalist as Prophet," *New Republic*, Dec. 4, 1949, 121:15–7.

RUSSIAN CIVILIZATION AND CULTURE

Baring, Maurice, *Landmarks in Russian Literature*, Macmillan Company, New York, 1910.

———— *The Mainsprings of Russia*, Thomas Nelson and Sons, London, 1914.

Beazley, Sir Charles R., Neville Forbes, and G. A. Birkett,

Russia from the Varangians to the Bolsheviks, Clarendon Press, Oxford, England, 1918.

Belinsky, Visarrion, *Selected Philosophical Works,* Foreign Language Publishing House, Moscow, 1948.

Berdyaev, Nicholas, *The Origin of Russian Communism,* tr. by R. M. French, Geoffrey Bles, London, 1948.

—————— *The Russian Idea,* Macmillan Company, New York, 1948.

Bowman, Herbert E., "Intelligentsia in Nineteenth Century Russia," *The Slavic and East European Journal,* Spring, 1957, 15:5–21.

—————— *Visarrion Belinski (1811–1848),* Harvard University Press, Cambridge, Mass., 1954.

Chernyshevsky, N. G., *Selected Philosophical Essays,* Foreign Language Publishing House, Moscow, 1953.

Crowson, Paul, *A History of the Russian People,* Longmans, Green and Company, New York, 1948.

Darlington, Thomas, *Education in Russia,* Wyman and Sons, Ltd., London, 1909.

Dobroliubov, N. A., *Selected Philosophical Essays,* Foreign Language Publishing House, Moscow, 1948.

Fedotov, G. P., ed., *A Treasury of Russian Spirituality,* Sheed and Ward, New York, 1948.

Gross, Felix, ed., *European Ideologies,* article by Elias Tartak, "Liberal Tradition in Russia: A. Hertzen and V. Soloveff," Philosophical Library, New York, 1948.

Howe, Sonia, *A Thousand Years of Russian History,* Williams and Norgate, London, 1915.

Johnson, William H. E., *Russia's Educational Heritage,* Carnegie Press, Pittsburgh, 1950.

Kirchner, Walther, *An Outline-History of Russia,* College Outline Series, Barnes and Noble, New York, 1950.

Kohl, J. G., *Russia and the Russians in 1842,* Philadelphia, 1843.

Kornilov, Alexander, 2 vols., *Modern Russian History,* tr. by Alex S. Kaun, Alfred A. Knopf, New York, 1952.

Lavrin, Janko, *Tolstoy*, Macmillan Company, New York, 1948.

Leary, Daniel B., *Education and Autocracy in Russia*, University of Buffalo Press, Buffalo, New York, 1919.

Lossky, N. O., *History of Russian Philosophy*, International Universities Press, Inc., New York, 1951.

Masaryk, Thomas G., 2 vols., *The Spirit of Russia*, tr. by Eden and Cedar Paul, Macmillan Company, New York, 1919. New edition, 1950.

Mazour, A. G., *The First Russian Revolution, 1825. The Decembrist Movement*. University of California Press, Berkeley, Calif., 1937.

Medvedkov, A. P., *Kratki istorija russki pedagogiki*, J. Bashmakov, St. Petersburg, 1913.

Miliukov, P. N., *Outlines of Russian Culture*, University of Pennsylvania Press, Philadelphia, 1942.

Pares, Sir Bernard, *History of Russia*, Alfred A. Knopf, New York, 1944.

Riasonovsky, N. N., "Some Comments on the Role of the Intelligentsia in the Reign of Nicholas I of Russia, 1825–1855," *The Slavic and East European Journal*, Fall, 1957, 15:163–76.

Schubart, Walter, *Russia and Western Man*, tr. by Amethe von Zeppelin, Frederick Ungar Publishing Company, New York, 1950.

Shore, Michael J., *Soviet Education*, Philosophical Library, New York, 1947.

Solovyev, Vladimir, *Lectures on Godmanhood*, Introd. and tr. by Peter P. Zouboff, Dennis Dobson, Ltd., London, 1948.

―――― *Russia and the Universal Church*, tr. by Herbert Rees, Geoffrey Bles, London, 1948.

―――― *A Solovyev Anthology*, arr. by S. L. Frank, tr. by N. Duddington, Charles Scribner's Sons, New York, 1950.

Tolstoy, Alexandra, *Tolstoy: A Life of My Father*, tr. by Elizabeth R. Hapgood, Harper and Brothers, New York, 1953.

Vernadsky, George, *A History of Russia*, Yale University Press, New Haven, Conn., 1944.

———— *Kievan Russia,* Yale University Press, New Haven, Conn., 1948.

Woody, Thomas, *New Minds: New Men?,* Macmillan Company, New York, 1932.

Zenkovsky, Vassili V., 2 vols., *A History of Russian Philosophy,* tr. by George L. Kline, Columbia University Press, New York, 1953.

INDEX

Index